PRAISE FOR *TICKET TO RIDE*

'Trains, dry wit, more trains, evocative descriptions, more trains, fascinating people and more trains – what is there not to like?'

Christian Wolmar

'Funny and illuminating from Crewe to Korea, Ticket to Ride *is a hugely entertaining account of the author's travels on the rails the world over – chance encounters fly like sparks'*

Sara Wheeler

'Like mini-odysseys, Chesshyre's railway journeys are by turns gentle and awesome, and full of surprises'

John Gimlette

'Tom's ticket certainly scores all the best rides: fast rides and slow ones, short trips and long ones. But most important are the names: why would any trainspotter (let alone a gricer) pass up the Reunification Express or, even better the Orient Express, *for a mere airplane?'*

Tony Wheeler

PRAISE FOR *TALES FROM THE FAST TRAINS*

'Compulsory reading'

Mark Smith, THE MAN IN SEAT 61

'Great fun, and an exhilarating read'

Sara Wheeler

'If you've "done" Paris and Bruges and are wondering, "Where next?", then this may be a quiet revelation'

Andrew Marr

EAST SUSSEX COUNTY COUNCIL
WITHDRAWN

'Splendid twenty-first-century railway adventure. At last this IS the age of the train'

NDEPENDENT

D0231163

'Chesshyre... is an interesting, knowledgeable, discerning tour guide and a most genial companion'

Alexander Frater, author of *Tales from the Torrid Zone*

'Transforms seemingly unsurprising familiar territory – whether the Eurostar terminal at St Pancras or the cities of Frankfurt and Antwerp – into the stage for insights and adventures'

Dea Birkett, author of *Serpent in Paradise*

PRAISE FOR *TO HULL AND BACK*

'Tom Chesshyre celebrates the UK... discovering pleasure in the unregarded wonders of the "unfashionable underbelly" of Britain. The moral, of course, is that heaven is where you find it'

THE MAIL ON SUNDAY

'You warm to Chesshyre, whose cultural references intelligently inform his postcards from locations less travelled'

THE TIMES

PRAISE FOR *HOW LOW CAN YOU GO?*

'Highly readable Bill Bryson-esque travel writing'

Clover Stroud, THE SUNDAY TELEGRAPH

'A hilarious record of a low-cost odyssey around the least salubrious corners of Europe'

Celia Brayfield, THE TIMES

PRAISE FOR *A TOURIST IN THE ARAB SPRING*

'This witty, perceptive book provides a fascinating read for lovers of thoughtful, imaginative and well-written travel literature'

Frank Barrett, THE MAIL ON SUNDAY

'A charming travel companion, entertaining and engaging'

TIMES LITERARY SUPPLEMENT

TICKET TO RIDE

AROUND THE WORLD ON 49 UNUSUAL TRAIN JOURNEYS

TOM CHESSHYRE

summersdale

TICKET TO RIDE

Summersdale Publishers Ltd
46 West Street
Chichester
West Sussex
PO19 1RP
UK

www.summersdale.com

Printed and bound by CPI Group (UK) Ltd, Croydon, CR0 4YY

ISBN: 978-1-84953-826-8

Substantial discounts on bulk quantities of Summersdale books are available to corporations, professional associations and other organisations. For details contact general enquiries: telephone: +44 (0) 1243 771107, fax: +44 (0) 1243 786300 or email: enquiries@summersdale.com.

For all train lovers

ABOUT THE AUTHOR

Tom Chesshyre's train travels include an 11,000-mile journey around Europe for his book on the European high-speed train revolution, and thousands of miles more across the UK for his weekly hotel column in *The Times*. He lives in London, and has visited almost 100 countries for his writing.

Tom is the author of *How Low Can You Go?: Round Europe for 1p Each Way (Plus Tax)*, *To Hull and Back: On Holiday in Unsung Britain*, *Tales from the Fast Trains: Europe at 186 mph*, *A Tourist in the Arab Spring* and *Gatecrashing Paradise: Misadventures in the Real Maldives*.

www.tomchesshyre.co.uk

CONTENTS

The time indicated on the timetable is not the time at which the train will leave; it is the time before which the train will definitely not leave

Sign at Agra station, India

Look at that: a 1953 EA! WOOO HOOO! Oh yeah, listen to that bell! Yeah, listen to that bell! Oh my God! WOOO-HOOO! She's so beautiful! All right!

Rail enthusiast in North Creek, New York

1 | CREWE STATION, ENGLAND: 'I'D GO ANYWHERE FOR A 37'

IT'S AN OVERCAST day at the end of platform five of Crewe railway station. An icy wind whips across the tracks, rattling a spiky metal fence. Every now and then, a train clatters past. The rails crackle and hiss, rumble and groan.

Time ticks slowly during a lull. A sleek cherry-red train adorned with the message *ARRIVE AWESOME* emerges beneath the leaden north-west English sky. It's the 17:05 Virgin service to Manchester. This event draws the attention of my companions. 'Pendolino', says one of the group. He's wearing a woolly hat, heavy-framed glasses and an ill-fitting black jacket. A flask of tea pokes out of his rucksack and a camera is looped round his neck. He does not raise his camera. 'Sardine can', he says dismissively.

'Dog box', says his friend, a giant figure in his early twenties (I'd guess) with ginger hair. He carries an old-fashioned shoulder bag and is peering through Buddy-Holly-style glasses. The way the giant says 'dog box' suggests this is not a term of endearment. 'A Pendolino, class 153,' he adds.

The first man says, 'Awful thing.'

The giant says, 'Ah, they drag.'

I am not sure what he means by this, but it does not sound complimentary either. The train moves onwards to Manchester. Silence resumes.

I ask the giant how tall he is, learning that he is 7 feet 4 inches and so good at basketball that he may join an American college team. 'When I get the ball, I just put it in the net: whoom!' he tells me. Not many trainspotters at the end of platform five at Crewe station over the years can have been able to claim that.

'The 422 was on the Nantwich line earlier,' says a tiny elderly man wearing two anoraks (yes, two) and a woolly hat. He glances up at the giant, who seems to be the group's leading train authority.

The giant corrects him: 'It was a 37422, with a 68001. A DRS.'

'Ahhhh,' says the tiny elderly man.

I ask the giant what DRS stands for. He looks at me with surprise. 'Direct Rail Services,' he says. This is the name of a freight operator.

'Three 37s are coming in a moment,' says the giant.

'I'd go anywhere for a 37,' says the man with the flask of tea.

The group edges towards the end of the platform, where a debate breaks out.

'It's set for platform three,' says a bald man in a denim jacket and a red shirt with a Virgin Trains logo. As might be expected, many rail company employees have an interest in trains.

'For ****'s sake!' says the giant.

He and the Virgin Trains man begin to sprint away, apparently heading for platform three.

The tiny elderly man wearing two anoraks, the man with the flask of tea and I watch them depart. They are uncertain whether the 37s will go to platform three. As I do not feel like racing around Crewe station on a chilly overcast day in the north-west of England, I decide to stick with their camp. Their opinion, however, changes as the 37s draw near. They look nervously at one another.

'Shall we?' asks the man with the tea.

'Yes! Yes!' Double-anorak nods.

They scurry off, clutching cameras that would otherwise swing wildly from their necks. I follow my new companions.

Regular passengers look on with bewilderment. We must make quite a spectacle. We arrive moments after the 37s have come to a halt. We have reached platform one, which is deemed to have the best view of the freight locomotives.

The giant says, 'Very fine examples of a 37.'

The Virgin Trains man says, 'Proper locos.'

The man wearing two anoraks, panting from his run, says, 'Locos. 1960s. English electric. Type three. Class 37. Over fifty years old.'

They snap away. The man with the flask of tea says he takes 200 shots a day, but will edit them to 60. Many of these will be posted online. We admire the three locomotives: solidly built with navy-blue bodies and bulbous mustard-yellow noses. DIRECT RAIL SERVICES is written on their sides. They are unlike any I can remember seeing on British railways – more like something you might expect to see crossing the American West – though I have never, admittedly, previously kept an eye out for class-37 freight locos at Crewe station.

I ask the group if they have spotted them before.

'Oh, many times. They're old friends,' says the Virgin Trains employee, not lifting his gaze from the locos.

I ask what they like most about trains.

'The smell of diesel. The sight of steam,' says the giant.

The man with two anoraks looks far away for a moment, as though recalling a long-lost love or a happy moment from his youth. Perhaps he is. After a while, he says, 'I just like travel and trains – always have done.'

The Virgin Trains employee cuts in: 'Why do we like trains? Why do we like them?' He pauses and lets the repeated question sink in. Of the four, he seems the most defensive about their passion for railways. He looks me squarely in the eyes. A horn blows across the tracks. Muffled announcements echo in the concourse. The engines of the 37 freight locomotives judder and grumble.

'Well,' he says. 'Well, I think you've just seen why.'

I suppose I have. What *is* it about trains? Trainspotters at Crewe station may be an extreme example of 'train love', but most people seem to have a soft spot for rail travel. Ask just about anyone what they think of travelling by train and a thoughtful expression tends to flicker across the features, often accompanied by a warm smile and a glint in the eye.

'There's a romance about trains,' is a common reply. 'I just like looking out of the window, seeing the world go by,' is another. 'I hate being stuck in a car or cooped up in a plane,' some will say. 'It's the motion: the clickety-clack,' say others. Or: 'You get to see places away from the mainstream, places you wouldn't otherwise visit.' Or: 'They're a greener way to go.' And, popular with those frustrated by the fast pace of modern life: 'I like to slow down; to stop rushing about; to take a break from it all.'

Underlying each response seems to be a gut feeling that trains offer a calmer, less stressful, more illuminating and somehow more *real* way of getting from A to B than other forms of travel.

Flying and driving just don't seem to elicit the same reaction. Why is that?

In his book *The Old Patagonian Express*, the great train-travel writer Paul Theroux describes a satisfactory flight as being one in which there is no accident, the food's OK and you arrive on time. You enter a dingy fuselage, he says, and count the minutes till you land.

That's as good as flying gets, according to Theroux, and I'm with him on that. A decent drive has a similar checklist: you did not have an accident; you did not get stuck in traffic; you did not break down; you avoided a speeding ticket; you arrived, more or less on schedule, without any dents in your bumpers. Yes, there are some famously beautiful drives and, let's face it, the experience is likely to be slightly different in a Maserati than in a battered Ford Mondeo, but most of the time driving involves little more than facing straight ahead, keeping an eye on the petrol gauge... and trying not to get sucked into road rage.

Perhaps it is the tedium of driving along characterless motorways or flying between identikit airports in identikit planes that has fuelled a recent bubble of interest in train travel. It certainly seems as though this rather quaint form of getting about that dates from the early nineteenth century – so old-fashioned next to super-jumbos, private jets, low-cost transatlantic flights, £30 hops on Wizz Air around Europe and the latest £200,000 sports cars drooled over by Jeremy Clarkson – is enjoying a quiet revival.

Facts and figures, plus many a nostalgic television programme starring Michael Portillo clasping a copy of Bradshaw's rail guide, seem to bear this out. While the precise number is tricky to establish, the current total length of railway tracks across the world is believed to be approximately 725,000 miles. This works out as the equivalent of an extraordinary 34 lines around the circumference of the globe. During a period when airlines have boomed with headline-grabbing prices catching the public's imagination, trains have been prospering too – the only difference being that word does not always get out as new tracks and services are *local*, so they tend to slip beneath the radar. A new railway in India or China might easily pass us by, while a cut-price fare from Gatwick to, say, Florida or Bangkok will be hard to miss: advertised across the media in papers, on TV and online.

Digging about a bit, however, it's clear that train travel is enjoying a resurgence not seen for many a year. Just take what's going on in Europe. In France, the Train à Grande Vitesse (TGV) network grows annually, with speeds increasing so much that some Parisians sick of the big smoke are considering moving to Bordeaux and commuting from there. In Spain, trains now zoom through most of the plains thanks to forward-thinking investment in tracks. As I write, this country has the most extensive set of high-speed lines in Europe, covering more than 1,900 miles. In Italy, millions of euros have been spent on long-distance routes between Milan and Naples and a line linking Milan and Zurich via a 38-mile tunnel through the Alps. The NEAT Gotthard Base Tunnel will be the world's longest train tunnel and will shave an hour off the current trip, reducing the journey time to 2 hours and 50 minutes. Swiss authorities have taken 20 years to complete the digging, during which 31 million tonnes of earth have been moved at a cost of £6.5 billion. Elsewhere, high-speed railways now connect Kraków and Gdynia via Warsaw and Gdańsk in Poland, where a network of lines is growing rapidly. In Britain, resistance to new tracks has been understandably fierce among those who do not want disruption near their homes, but work on High Speed 2, from London up to Birmingham and onwards in a Y-shape to Leeds and Manchester, is due to start, with extensions to Newcastle and Scotland under consideration.

Further afield, China has more high-speed train lines than the rest of the world combined: 19,000 kilometres and growing, most of which have been laid in the past dozen years. Proof, if it were needed, that where there's a will and an autocratic government with cash to blow, there's usually a way. Indian Railways has steadily widened its web of trains and carries an average of 23 million passengers a day, looked after by an army of 1.3 million employees. Many multibillion-rupee projects are planned, including bullet trains on a 1,375-mile stretch between Delhi and Chennai.

Just about everywhere you go across the globe – if you discount Africa (because of its many political troubles) and the polar caps (because they're mainly populated by penguins and polar bears) – it's an exciting time for trains. Sure, it may not always feel that way in major cities, where commuter services are usually so appalling – and don't I know it during the morning rush hour to Waterloo – but a rail revolution is under way.

This book hopes to explain why. The passion for trains runs strong, and not just in Crewe, as I am about to discover on a series of journeys from the depths of Siberia to little-visited parts of Kosovo, the forests of Finland, the badlands of America, the mountains of India, the paddy fields of China, the tea plantations of Sri Lanka and the dusty plains of Iran.

My aim is to capture the simple pleasures of trains; the gentle joy that comes from seeing the world as the wheels rattle and roll, and the miles tick by. The sounds, smells, sights, feel and the taste (in buffet cars) of train journeys – the reasons we seem to love trains so much.

It is not, however, all about my point of view. Far from it. It's about those of the people I meet along the way. One of the appeals of train travel is, of course, its sociability, especially if you are on a long ride. Trains offer a completely different social environment to planes – Theroux's nightmare of awful food and delays in which interaction with neighbours often boils down to asking if you can pass to go to the loo. And as for cars: what chance have you got of making pals on the M25, unless it's with a breakdown services employee?

Before I begin, though, let me return to Crewe.

I chose the station not just because of its renowned trainspotters, but also because of its place in the railway history of Britain – the country where passenger railways began back on 15 September 1830, when Robert Stephenson's *Rocket* pulled the first carriages on a proper line. The distance of this inaugural journey between Liverpool and Manchester was 35 miles, and on this first ride the *Rocket* touched 35 mph; so fast that some feared cows in passing fields would be frightened and cease producing milk, while others believed that passengers' eyes might be damaged.

In 1846 this historic line merged with two others to create the London and North Western Railway, considered by some to be the world's first major railway. It was a big moment, but the owners were in two minds about where to base the crucial 'works' to build locomotives and carriages. After toying with Edge Hill in Liverpool, Crewe was selected as it marked a convenient midpoint between Liverpool and Birmingham.

'Before that time there was nothing here: just fields,' says Mike Lenz, general manager at the Crewe Heritage Centre.

The pre-railway population of Crewe was about 70. The town and surrounding area are now home to 84,000 residents, plus a football team nicknamed the Railwaymen. If it wasn't for the railway, Crewe – as we know it – simply would not exist.

I meet Lenz at his office in a back room of the heritage centre, next to a display hall with a model railway. He's wearing a high-visibility jacket, leaning back in a swivel chair and looking slightly eccentric with his legs crossed and his eyes glancing through a tall glass window.

A train zooms by – a metre or so beyond the window. I almost jump backwards, it's so close.

'Great, isn't it,' says Lenz, his eyes fixed on the carriages as they thunder past.

The train disappears. And then I notice another sound. It's the grumble and grind of a different train, and it's coming from a monitor on his desk.

'Webcam,' says Lenz. 'Captures the sounds of the trains on our site.'

The heritage centre, which opened in 1987 and is run by a trust, is located within a V-shape of tracks right by Crewe station. Warehouses and yards are packed with old railway paraphernalia, shiny locos and carriages.

'Bombardier still has some works in Crewe,' says Lenz. He's referring to the Canadian aerospace and transport company. 'Locomotives were made until about 1990. Now it's just component repairs. They fix bogies.'

I ask what a bogie is.

Lenz looks at me in disbelief. 'A bogie is what the locomotive sits on.' I gather from this that he means the wheels and the chassis. The words 'trains' and 'steep learning curve' are suddenly springing to mind.

'All we have now is about 250 or 300, but there used to be 10,000 or more,' Lenz says, talking about staff numbers at Crewe Works. 'It's sad,' he says. As is another matter that seems to be weighing on his mind: 'Volunteers. Now we have guys in their forties and fifties, but it's getting the younger ones interested.'

By 'younger ones', Lenz means younger train volunteers who will enjoy rolling up their sleeves and getting their hands dirty polishing and repairing old locos and carriages.

'Are there just not enough trainspotters these days?' I ask.

He looks at me askance. Once again I appear to be demonstrating my train ignorance. 'I think that "rail enthusiasts" is now more appropriate,' he says, as another locomotive bombs by.

'What is the image of a rail enthusiast these days?' I ask.

'The image is changing,' Lenz replies, a little vaguely. He stares at me for a second or two. His look seems to be asking: *Are you taking the ****?* I'm not, though I can see he is unsure. There are so many jokes about the hobby – 'How many trainspotters does it take to change a light bulb? Three: one to change it, one to take down its serial number, and one to bring the anoraks and the flask of soup' – that I'm detecting a definite touchiness.

'In what way?'

'They're older. Back in the 1960s you had young children interested,' Lenz says, returning to what seems to be a favourite theme.

It was the era of steam trains, chugging to its end in the 1960s, when rail enthusiasm was instilled in so many, he explains. The phenomenon of 'trainspotting', which I dare to write (though not mention in the presence of Lenz), has its roots firmly in those days of steam. 'Spotters' are said to date originally from 1942, when a Southern Railway employee named Ian Allan published his seminal (in spotter circles) *ABC of Southern Locomotives*. This booklet was followed by many further *ABC* publications produced by Allan, considered by some to be the 'godfather of trainspotters', which allowed those with an interest to tick off steam locomotives they had sighted, or 'copped'.

Now, despite the absence of inspiring plumes of smoke along most railways, according to Lenz: 'We need those young people again. It's a tall order, but we do need them so they can come to us and learn how to operate and overhaul steam trains. If they don't come, they [the old working steam trains] are all going to disappear.'

We say goodbye and, as we do so, the monitor on Lenz's desk captures the sound of another Pendolino. His eyes glance down at the desk and I suddenly realise (or maybe I'm just imagining this) that he finds the sound of the wheels on the track somehow reassuring.

Following Lenz's advice, I take in the APT Prototype, BR Class 370 by the entrance to the heritage centre. And what a fine example of an APT Prototype, BR Class 370 it is: well polished and shiny, with carriages sporting natty checked seats.

Then I retire to the Crewe Arms Hotel, where Queen Victoria once stayed and where the manager shows me the bricked-up entrance to a tunnel between the hotel and the station that was dug so Queen Victoria could avoid the crowds.

'Oh yes, an awful lot of trainspotters stay here,' the manager says. 'The ones that take down train numbers.' Apparently, the hardcore rail enthusiasts usually request one of the rooms facing the station so they can indulge in a bit of extra spotting from the comfort of the hotel. 'It's almost all railway business round here.'

Many of the other guests are freight-line drivers, conductors or trainees from a nearby Virgin Trains training centre. So that everyone's in touch and on time, there's even a Crewe station departure board in the reception.

I have a drink in the bar, with old pictures of Crewe Works lining the walls, feeling that this is an appropriate place to begin these adventures. Most people round here – the manager, my fellow guests, the folk not far away at the end of the platforms – seem to love trains.

I'm in a train-hotel in train-land, and I'm about to set off into a train-world.

2 | KOSOVO AND MACEDONIA: 'YOU CAN SPOT A GRICER A MILE AWAY'

I'M NOT DONE with platform-dwelling 'rail enthusiasts' yet, though. Before I dig beneath the surface of the mainstream love of trains – and in order to understand the inner workings of train enthusiasm – I decide to become one for a few days.

That's right: I'm going to turn my hand at being a trainspotter for a week. A trainspotter on holiday, to be precise – in south-eastern Europe.

This involves signing up to a package tour to Kosovo and Macedonia organised especially for those who are fond of trains. The trip is arranged by Ffestiniog Travel, a company based in north Wales that offers 'rail holidays around the world'. One of its selling points is that the tours are designed for people 'who require their holiday to be as much about the railways as the destination'; in other words, for trainspotters, as well as those who simply get a kick out of travelling by rail.

The tour operator is a registered charity and something of a rail-enthusiast institution, established in 1974, with profits going towards the restoration of the Ffestiniog and Welsh Highland railways in north Wales. The Ffestiniog Railway is the oldest narrow-gauge railway company in the world, dating from 1836 and running for 13 miles from the harbour at Porthmadog to Blaenau Ffestiniog, using locomotives that are more than 150 years old. Meanwhile the Welsh Highland Railway, also narrow gauge, runs for 25 miles from Caernarfon to Beddgelert, the longest such heritage railway in Britain. Linked and covering a combined ascent of more than 700 feet into the foothills of dramatic mountains, the railways were originally built to transport slate from inland quarries to ships, using gravity to roll down to the coast with full loads and horses to drag empty wagons back up; until steam locomotives were introduced in the 1860s, that is.

The term 'narrow gauge' refers to the width of the tracks, which are precisely 1 foot 11½ inches apart on the Ffestiniog and Welsh Highland railways (I am reliably informed), whereas standard tracks in the UK, and 60 per cent of all train lines in the world, are separated by a gap of exactly 4 feet 8½ inches. This standard gauge was established by George Stephenson, the engineer behind the Manchester–Liverpool railway that opened in 1830 (and father of Robert, the designer of the *Rocket*). His picture used to be found on the back of the British £5 note. Standard gauge is also known as 'Stephenson gauge'.

Ffestiniog Travel began offering holidays after its base in Porthmadog became a ticketing office for British Rail in the 1970s, giving its directors the idea to put together breaks with train tickets included – and not just in Britain, but further afield in Europe too. British Rail had been in the process of de-staffing its smaller stations in the wake of cuts to rural services introduced by Dr Beeching, chairman of British Railways, in the 1960s. These notorious cutbacks, known as the Beeching Axe, resulted in the closure of 6,000 miles of tracks in Britain. The Ffestiniog directors' actions were therefore crucial to keeping a small part of the north Wales network going.

This is how I find myself on a station platform in the capital of Kosovo with about 30 serious and not so serious (and a few seriously serious) railway lovers. It's a sunlit afternoon in the former war zone in south-eastern Europe. All had been quiet at Pristina station until our arrival. All is not now. We have just arrived at the sleepy spot, but already most of our group have swarmed onto the tracks, brandishing cameras and snapping away merrily, even though there is not a train in sight. Other than us, the only two passengers awaiting the 16:30 to Peja are a pregnant woman and an elderly man wearing shades. Their jaws drop as our motley crew runs amok, taking pictures of the station, the tracks, signal boxes, signs and sidings. Among rail enthusiasts, as I have already discovered during my short acquaintance, it is not just the train that is of interest. It is anything and everything train-related.

Clambering about the tracks appears to be allowed. A burgundy-capped stationmaster is watching with an expression that somehow combines indifference and complete disbelief. It is a bizarre scene. The rail enthusiasts with their expensive cameras are not at all shy or reserved, as some had been a few minutes earlier on the bus. They are taking over the short platform and establishing themselves, gung-ho and full of gusto. Several have lined up at one end in readiness for our train, which is due shortly. They seem anxious to secure the perfect angle, and a few have bunched together at one spot.

Pristina station has the look of a gingerbread house, with peach-pink walls and arched doorways. Black-and-white pictures of old railways and stations are to be found in the ticket hall. I am standing by one of these, taking in proceedings, when I am joined by Johnnie, an IT consultant from Birmingham in his forties. He is tall and thin, with owlish eyes blinking beneath circular glasses and a 1970s-style moustache that curls round each side of his mouth. He wears faded jeans and prominently large pristine white trainers. Johnnie shows me the ticket he has just bought to Peja, about 60 kilometres west: a souvenir for the trip, as Ffestiniog Travel has chartered and paid for a private carriage. Then he points at the nearest, caption-less picture on the wall, recognising it.

'Penn Station before it was demolished and they built Madison Square Garden on it,' Johnnie says, referring to the station in New York which I will be visiting in a few weeks' time. It was torn down, he tells me, in 1963.

Rail enthusiasts are full of such handy titbits.

We gaze down the platform. The pregnant woman rises and comes over in readiness for the train. I ask her if she has seen any trainspotters before. She is from Peja and has some English.

'Nothing like this before. Not in my life,' she says.

There is a stirring on the platform. Everyone moves to the far end. The big event is coming soon. A faint trail of black smoke can be seen in the distance. The smoke draws closer and soon a big red train with yellow streaks growls into view, rattling up with a blast of its horn and a series of shrill whistles. Cameras click as though we're by the red carpet on Oscars night. There's electricity in the air. This is why Ffestiniog's customers have paid to come to Kosovo, for a journey that's continuing onwards to Macedonia and Albania to the south: trains they've never seen before.

At this happy moment, I am beside Steve, a 57-year-old retired accountant who once worked for the Shell oil and gas company. He's from Whitchurch in Shropshire and has already quietly confided in me that perhaps he retired too early. Rail enthusiasts are incredibly open about their lives, I am also discovering. Earlier, Steve had been among the more subdued of the group. Now, however, he is transformed: elated and beaming, full of life.

'A proper loco pulling dead carriages,' he says. 'This is what everyone was hoping for. They're delighted.'

I ask what he means by 'dead carriages'. It seems there's always some term or other I'm not au fait with.

'Usually there's an engine under the first carriage,' Steve says.

'Ah,' I reply, and nod knowingly, as though I really knew this all along.

Actually, I've just learnt something – and it's only the start. I'm about to discover a whole lot more.

'Rail enthusiasts get a bad press... but we're fair game for it'
Pristina to Peja, Kosovo

We board our dead carriage and sit on old red seats with a thin grey zigzag pattern as the train moves on to Peja. If you don't count a short burst from Mortlake to Vauxhall stations in south London, the Tube and my Virgin trains from London Euston to Crewe and back, this is the first proper ride of the adventure.

We clatter and sway past grim communist-era apartment blocks and tumbledown yards. Smoke from the engine sweeps past the window. There's something pleasing about the way it does this, almost as though we're on an old-fashioned steam train, rather than one that's simply pumping fumes into the sky.

Alan, our tour leader, advises us to look out for a train depot at a fork in the line. The depot comes into view, prompting another paparazzi-style volley of camera shots. The keenest photographers squeeze lenses out of little windows that open at the top of the main windows. There is no small competition to get the best position to do this. As we pass, all heads turn to regard the ramshackle structure. After this excitement, we continue on through green rolling hills with patchwork fields of crops and the occasional tractor.

We spent a day in Pristina before this ride, visiting an old steam engine (much photographed), the main square with its sad digital screen displaying the faces of those who died in the 1998–99 Kosovo War, an excellent little ethnological museum, and the capital's statue of Bill Clinton, who is highly regarded locally for sanctioning NATO action against the Serbs during the war. The statue is on Bill Clinton Boulevard. During this period of sightseeing, I got to know my new companions, and realised something almost from the start. There is a clear, though unofficial, pecking order among rail enthusiasts, a hierarchy based on railway knowledge: rail cred, if you like.

At the top of the tree is Colin Boocock, a silver-haired 'railway photographer and author' from Derby (he gives me his card), who is on this inaugural Kosovo–Albania trip with his wife Mary. There are a few couples on the break but most of the party consists of men travelling alone, as well as a couple of single women. Boocock seems to have semi-legendary status and is regarded as a fount of all train knowledge. A few years back he and Mary completed a round-the-world train trip. Before retiring to become a railway photographer and author, Boocock worked as a train maintenance engineer for British Rail and Railtrack, which ran the rail infrastructure in Britain from 1994 to 2002 after British Rail was privatised. He is such a train authority that there is an air of mystique surrounding him.

There are several other railway philosopher kings among our number, including those who wear their train knowledge lightly, such as Johnnie and Nick (who refers to himself as a 'self-employed train historian'), and two slightly secretive rail enthusiasts who take their trainspotting so seriously that they shun all cultural excursions, and conversation with others, in favour of taking an extra train or tram ride on the side, whenever possible. Among the best natured of the philosopher kings is Mike Steadman, a contributor to *Railway Herald* magazine who is travelling with his wife Wendy. Steadman is a 'semi-retired energy broker' from Hereford, with a bumbling, bombastic style and a bit of a belly, upon which a camera hanging from his neck always rests.

'Train photography is my forte. I've been published' are almost his first words to me. We are chugging along through Kosovan hills, passing the husks of burnt-out old stations that were destroyed during the civil war and are yet to be repaired. Some of the stations are still in service and used as points at which passengers are dropped off; a process that involves leaping from the train onto the dirt terrain by the tracks. The lack of building repair is down to the poor economy of Kosovo, which has been struggling in the wake of the destructive war that led to its declaration of independence from Serbia in 2008. This nationhood is still not recognised by Serbia, which lies just to the north of the tiny new country, the youngest in Europe (about the size of Devon).

I am not surprised to learn that Steadman has been to Crewe station 'many times'. He is quick to take on the role of trainspotter spokesman. 'We get a bad press, regularly,' he says, as we trundle along. 'But we're fair game for it. People can say what they want.'

He has a purist's approach to trainspotting: 'I don't want the *Orient Express* or the luxury Pullmans. I'm at the opposite end of the scale: rough and ready.'

Steadman says he has recently been on a train trip in Eritrea as well as Serbia, Montenegro, Croatia and Bosnia. 'Most of the time Wendy doesn't come. She says: "You go and I'll take control of the TV zapper." I don't collect train numbers like some people do. I just take photographs. I must have taken hundreds of thousands.' He checks his camera. 'In the past two days I've taken one thousand three hundred and eighty. I'm click-happy. I'll make no bones about it.'

Steadman pauses to take a few pictures of an old rusting train wagon, partially covered by weeds on the edge of the track. 'All those wagons there, they've had their axle boxes removed,' he says, adding that the metal from the axle boxes is taken for scrap.

The locomotive on our train is Norwegian, Steadman continues, and dates from 1961 (the legendary Boocock later tells us by way of clarification that, although it was in use in Norway, it was made in Sweden); the coaches are second-class Austrian carriages from a later period; a sign on the wall says: *NICHT RESERVIERT*. Such details are the meat and drink of rail enthusiasm, as I have so quickly discovered.

'In some foreign countries the locals cannot believe that people want to go down obscure branch lines or visit the depot,' Steadman says. 'I appreciate this is a niche market, but it exists.'

We pass through a tunnel and the carriage, which is unlit, goes pitch black. We exit and, totally contradicting what he said earlier, Steadman says that one of his favourite recent train journeys was in an opulent Pullman carriage travelling from Crewe to the Kyle of Lochalsh in Scotland. The Kyle of Lochalsh is another of my future destinations.

Steadman says, 'Five hundred pounds for a weekend. That's what it cost, and that's what I go to work for.'

Wendy, who has been silent up to now, but who has appeared more than content that her husband has someone who is willing to listen to him, says to me, 'You're not getting bored, are you? Once he gets going he's hard to stop.'

Steadman ignores this and turns to take a few snaps of another burnt-out station through the little top window. We are passing the village of Zllakuqan, which has a white church at its centre and high mountains rising beyond. These are the foothills of the Albanian Alps, also known as the 'Accursed Mountains', a nickname that seems well chosen judging by the jagged snow-capped peaks. The church, our local guide Ilir tells us, is Catholic. The religious make-up of Kosovo is both complicated and controversial. During the civil war more than a million mainly Muslim ethnic Albanians were forced to flee by the Serbian Orthodox army. Most were taken in packed railway carriages on a track leading to Macedonia in the south, which we are to travel along in a couple of days. The majority returned following the defeat of the Serbs, many of whom have in turn left the country for fear of reprisals (more than 200,000, it is believed, leaving about 40,000). Yet although Kosovo is now 95 per cent Muslim, a small number of the ethnic Albanian population is Catholic, making up about two per cent of the country. So Zllakuqan is both an oddity and a talking point. Were we not on the 16:30 from Pristina to Peja it is unlikely that any of us would have ever laid eyes on the village.

We pause near Zllakuqan to let an elderly man jump off. He is clutching a bucket. There is seemingly no station to speak of. He shuffles in the direction of a tractor in a field dotted with dark brown cows. In the carriage ahead, where locals are sitting, children are dangling their legs from the train's open door. It feels strange to be isolated from them in our own private carriage, but Alan explains that this was the best way of ensuring that the group had guaranteed seats.

Soft golden sunlight flickers on the surface of a meandering river as we move closer to the Accursed Mountains. We are in a quiet valley. More snow-capped peaks emerge to the north-west in the direction of Montenegro. We pass a few simple stone dwellings where local children give us the finger and shake their fists. The kids dangling their legs out of the train yell something at them and shake their fists and give them the finger back. This exchange of pleasantries is conducted with smiles on faces. It's just bravado; they don't really mean it (as far as I can tell). The smell of smoke from a bonfire wafts through the windows. The wheels of the train *rat-tat-tat* on the track.

In the run-up to Peja, I venture into the carriage with the locals. It's packed: standing room only. I ask two teenagers crammed by the door what they make of the tourist carriage attached to their usual train.

'I never saw a train lover before,' one of the girls says.

Her friend chuckles, and eyeballs me. So soon into my wanderings by rail, I seem to have achieved 'train lover' status in the eyes of two Kosovan teenagers at least.

An earnest man wearing a checked shirt overhears this and says, 'You are good for value: we need tourists.'

His neighbour says, 'Actually a lot of Kosovans love trains as they are very comfortable.'

'Do you take pictures and days off to see trains as a hobby?' I ask.

'Hmm,' he says. 'Hmm.'

The earnest man in the checked shirt says, 'Maybe that is a crazy… I don't know.'

I think he is being polite. Having survived the violent break-up of Yugoslavia and with a fledgling peace in place, perhaps it's more than understandable that travelling by train is simply a matter of getting from A to B, ideally in un-cramped conditions (though that's not the case today). There are more important concerns than taking pictures of locomotives in a country with an average annual income of about £3,600 and a northerly neighbour that says that Kosovo is a province that belongs to them. On a recent visit to Albania, Serbia's prime minister Aleksandar Vučić declared: 'Kosovo is part of Serbia and always will be.' Vučić was formerly a member of the Serbian Radical Party and during the civil war threatened that 100 Muslims would be killed for every single Serb in Bosnia, though he has since rebranded himself as a moderniser who wishes to attain membership of the European Union.

Our 1961 Swedish-built loco chugs along as I think about Kosovo's predicaments. The country clearly has a lot on its plate. We skirt a brewery and a five-a-side pitch where kids are playing and men are sitting on a fence drinking beer. Then we pull into Peja. It is 18:32. The driver blasts the horn and we disembark onto the tracks. There is no platform. Children are running about on the rails; a few had chased alongside the train as it arrived. Many pictures are taken of Peja station. It's in a natural amphitheatre, surrounded by the Accursed Mountains, and makes for a few good shots.

Taking a train is obviously not just about what you see and do on board. In these tales from the track, I intend to convey a flavour of some of the places visited along the way, their history and current affairs. It's not all about the trains. They do, after all, take you somewhere – often well off the beaten tourist trail. Yet given that my main aim is to understand our affection for train travel, I'm adopting a snapshot approach. I take the train, take the pulse and move on: no hanging about.

This first stop-off has plenty of interest. Peja is a tranquil city with a population of 60,000, a gurgling river, a market selling fake Hugo Boss jackets and Rolex watches, a handful of mosques, a statue of Mother Teresa (who hails from these parts), an inordinate number of cafes serving strong coffees for 50 cents (the currency is the euro), and a street named after Tony Blair.

Like Bill Clinton, Blair is revered for the part he played in allowing NATO strikes against the Serbs in the recent war. In the market, I meet a second-hand bookseller with a stall (next to another stall selling plastic guns for kids). He says, 'Oh yes, we like your Tony Blair. I hear that in your country you don't like him because he lie about the war in Iraq.' Others I encounter are of a similar point of view. It's intriguing to be somewhere where the former British prime minister – who has fallen from grace in so many people's eyes – is quite so revered.

Yet the reverence makes sense when you consider NATO's role in the country's recent history. Were it not for NATO, Peja would probably be referred to on our tour as Pec (the preferred Serbian name), Kosovo might not exist as a nation in its own right, and Slobodan Milošević, the former president of Serbia who died while on trial at the International Criminal Tribunal in The Hague, might have clung on to power and enforced the mass displacement of ethnic Albanians. The very architecture of Peja bears witness to the days of this key struggle to 'save' Kosovo. The city was badly damaged during the height of the conflict, resulting in the uninspiring modern buildings that pervade. There are, however, a few elegant remaining Ottoman-era *kullas* (houses with fortified towers).

Another local point of note is that Peja is home to the 'most beautiful women in Kosovo', according to my guidebook. And it's hard not to notice the striking local look: blonde hair (perhaps from a bottle), perfect poises, supermodel height, good fashion sense. No wonder one of the features of the market is its many wedding dresses laid out for inspection on a central square. There's a feeling of romance in the air. A lot of posing goes on, both among the women and the men, whose style tends towards tight T-shirts over bulging muscles, although there is nothing romantic about the queues of not-so-showy men on a street near the railway station, hoping to be picked up by construction bosses for casual work.

Our hotel is close to Tony Blair Street. Our train enthusiast group is staying in smart, compact rooms; there are no complaints. We dine at an American-style restaurant with a view of the Lumbardhi river. And in the morning we are taken by bus to a Serbian Orthodox monastery overseen by 25 nuns, and to the dome-topped Visoki Dečani Monastery with its fine onyx and purple-marble facade, also Serbian Orthodox, run by monks. Both date from the Middle Ages. The frescoes of saints are haunting: ghost-like apparitions in vivid reds, greens and blues that have somehow survived the centuries – and recent troubles.

One of the group nudges me and whispers in a Sid James voice, 'I know someone who used to be a monk. Trained, he did, but decided that he liked women too much. He married the woman next door and became an accountant.' He has a good cackle about this.

Trainspotters can have a dry sense of humour.

To understand the tensions between the remaining Serb population and the Islamic Albanian majority, you need only to experience the extreme security at these monasteries (there is no word for 'nunnery' in Kosovo; what others might call a nunnery is a 'monastery' that's home to nuns). At Visoki Dečani, Italian troops representing KFOR, the Kosovo Force operated by NATO to keep the peace, man a roadblock and a barbed-wire fence surrounds the UNESCO World Heritage Site. In 2004 an Albanian mob attacked the monastery, hurling Molotov cocktails at its ancient walls. Soldiers were brought in to prevent repeat violence.

'Ghastly plasticky shoulder bags from the 1980s. Anoraks.
Scruffy trainers'
Peja to Pristina, Kosovo

Peja is a diversion. We are soon returning eastwards to Pristina, before hitting the track south to Skopje, the capital of Macedonia.

On the train to Pristina, I make the acquaintance of Charlie Halliwell, a 63-year-old retired librarian from Islington in north London. She has been interested in railways for 30 years and has travelled the world, going as far as Australia to take *The Ghan*, a famous train that connects Adelaide in the south of the country to Darwin in the far north. She's been to 50 countries on train holidays, including India, Jordan, Syria and Canada. Charlie has short grey hair brushed to one side, an impish smile, glasses hanging from a cord round her neck and a scattergun style of conversation that makes keeping up difficult. She admits, early on, to being a 'high-energy person'. She has also, inadvertently, become an aficionado of rail enthusiasm through her own love of trains and train travel.

'Gricers!' she says, and looks at me to see if I recognise the word.

I don't.

'Gricers!' she continues. 'You can spot a gricer a mile away: ghastly plasticky shoulder bags from the 1980s. Anoraks. Scruffy trainers. They look a bit unloved. A fair number live alone. If they have a wife, they're a bit smarter. Generally, they look as though their minds are on other things.'

'Trains,' I suggest.

She ignores me; she's in full flow, speeding along like a locomotive without brakes as she proceeds to deliver a super-fast briefing on Rail Enthusiasts: An Insider's Guide from Someone Who Has Learnt to Put up with the More-Extreme-End-of-the-Spectrum Train Lovers (and Likes Them All Really).

'I don't care if I get yelled at if I get in the way of one of their pictures.' She's talking about when she's on the train poking her camera out of the window as the carriage curves round a bend. This is the classic moment for a shot of the carriages ahead or behind – and perfectly normal non-gricer rail-enthusiast behaviour. The people yelling at her would be the aforementioned gricers. 'No, I don't care. It would be nice if people would ask more nicely. I don't really mind being asked to move. I have no sensitivity.'

Charlie sighs and looks down the carriage as a couple of gricer types wobble along the aisle. Their cameras and camera bags seem almost to have become attached to their bodies, as though they never part company. Do they take them off at night? They are wearing faded sun hats similar to those favoured by cricketers, although the rims have flopped down. Their shirts are partially untucked and they have very sensible walking shoes that have never been – and will never under any circumstances be – considered fashionable. Their shorts are of the cargo variety, a couple of sizes too big and with plenty of pockets (perhaps for notebooks). They do not conform precisely to Charlie's just-given definition of 'gricer' but a definite air of 'gricer' accompanies them. Charlie gives me a *here are two classic examples* look, then smiles at them, and they smile back. Polite gricers.

Charlie tells me that she estimates that about five per cent of rail enthusiasts of the sort that might turn up at Crewe's platform five are women. I ask her why it's such a male-dominated hobby.

'It just is,' she says. 'All of my friends tend to be men who like trains. The sounds, the smells, as well as the swinging, the rocking, the movement, that's what it's about. Men regress to being little children. I'm a psychologist; I have a degree in psychology. I like to see the bigger picture. To withhold information, they say, is a crime. Knowledge is power.'

Charlie, I'm noticing, is not one to withhold information.

'What's the attraction of trains for you?' I manage to ask during a pause. 'How did you get into trains?'

'I think it was because my parents liked to move about. I was lucky. They had a Morris Minor and they liked going places, stopping along the way to take a look – to see trains or ships or whatever. Not sticking about in a boarding house in Bournemouth for a couple of weeks. For me it's all about movement.' She shifts tack, hardly taking a breath. 'Old transport: old trolleybuses, trams, ocean liners, steam trains. I like things old, technically basic, with good lines and well made, like how things used to be. Some of these ships these days, made in Belgian shipbuilding yards, they're just assembly kits. They don't look like ships. They're floating apartment blocks. They've lost their sheen.'

Charlie, who is a member of the Locomotive Club of Great Britain and who attends events held by the Railway and Canal Historical Society, categorises the different types of rail enthusiast that she knows of: 'First of all, there are "track bashers". They just like to cover every bit of track. They don't really care what's carrying them – the trains. Then, of course, you have "haulage bashers". They collect as much traction as possible.'

I ask her what she means by this.

'Mode of traction,' she says.

I ask her again what she means.

'Motive power,' she says, sounding exasperated.

'I'm still unsure,' I say.

'The type of engine!' she cries. 'Then you have the "number crunchers". They've started as kids at the end of the platform. Some of them cheat, if they're with someone else who has seen the number but they haven't. They've just had the number read to them. There's a morality about these things. The idea is to finish off a series: to see every example of a particular class of a train engine. Some people also take down carriage numbers, too.'

She regards me closely to make sure I'm getting what she's saying. 'You've also got "footplate riders". They like to go up in the cab of a steam train. Actually it's wonderful. You get different views when you're with the driver and the fireman. I was in one for forty minutes in Australia. It was at night. Brilliant. I was just lucky they let me.'

Charlie stops her 'rail enthusiast' briefing, for a fraction of a second. She is really quite animated, gesticulating wildly. Her mind leaps about as though a thought not told that instant might disappear for ever. 'It's not just trains. It's canals, buses, trams, trains carrying breakdown cranes, plinth trains.' These, she tells me when I ask, are trains put on plinths like the old steam train we saw in Pristina. 'Coal-tipping wagons, narrow-gauge railways, rail museums. It's very important to see the museums. Then you've got gauge, signals, railway models, miniature railways in gardens. Oh, you can have all sorts of gricers: train gricers, bus gricers, tram gricers.'

'There are so many areas of interest, it's complicated,' I say, managing to slip in a few words.

'Oh yes, and if anybody gets in the way of the picture they can get very angry,' she says. 'Very angry indeed. If they're taking a picture of a steam train coming by and middle-aged women are waving from the windows, they get cross. They're ruining the authenticity of the picture. They'll go as far as cutting trees down to get the right shot.'

The legendary Boocock is passing along the carriage as she says this. There is a lot of getting up and down among the group to take different positions for pictures. He overhears what Charlie has just said.

'Some call it gardening,' he says, with an air of nonchalance.

'It's beyond the pale! They're cutting the bush back!' Charlie retorts, raising her voice and sounding a little mad. She's hit full-steam-ahead in her Rail Enthusiasts: An Insider's Guide briefing and, despite his mystical standing, Boocock is interrupting her spiel.

Boocock, maintaining his ice-cool demeanour, looks at me, raises an eyebrow and moves on.

'People can't cut trees down. It's not fair,' Charlie says, once he is out of earshot. 'As long as you don't affect other people's lives – that should be the rule. In Argentina, there was a tree screening a bath used by the wife of a man who came out shouting. The tree had been cut down for a picture of a train.'

I try to imagine this scene: a red-faced Argentine shaking his fists at a group of trainspotters with long-lens cameras perched by a track in the depths of South America, guilty of having just chopped down the tree protecting the modesty of the red-faced Argentine's loved one.

'Gricers are too single minded. Intelligent but obsessive, but on the whole harmless,' Charlie says, as cameras click like a swarm of crickets to capture a siding with more rusting old carriages.

And with that – and another swarm to catch the old train depot by the fork in the line outside the capital, once again – we pull in to Pristina.

Were Kosovo and Serbia on friendly terms, we might have caught a train northwards to Belgrade. However, as they are not, there are no trains between the two countries, other than a local service between Mitrovica, the northern city where many of the Serbs in Kosovo live, and a border town close to Serbia. This line is under Serb control, which seems odd given that it runs within Kosovo. Politics and trains, as I am increasingly to find, are often intertwined.

We spend a day in the capital learning more about the huge divisions that still define the region, starting with a visit to Gazimestan, the famous hill just outside Pristina where a monument from 1953 commemorates those who died in the battle between Serbia and the Turks that took place in surrounding fields in 1389. The Turks triumphed, taking Kosovo, yet over the years this battle became a symbolic cornerstone of Serbian identity. It was at this windswept hill that Slobodan Milošević gave a rousing speech calling for Serbian unity on the 600th anniversary of the conflict, in 1989. The speech stirred Serbian nationalism and antagonism against the Muslim community in Kosovo, and is regarded as an important prelude to both the break-up of Yugoslavia and the violence that followed during the Kosovo War.

The words of what is known as the 'Kosovan Curse', attributed to Prince Lazar, the Serb leader who died in the 1389 battle, are inscribed on the stone walls of the monument:

Whoever is a Serb and of Serb birth
And of Serb blood and heritage
And comes not to the Battle of Kosovo
May he never have the progeny his heart desires!
Neither son nor daughter
May nothing grow that his hand sows!
Neither dark wine nor white wheat
And let him be cursed from all ages to all ages!

Charming stuff. Afterwards we meet the British ambassador to Kosovo. His name is Ian Cliff and he's a rail enthusiast. Ian has got wind of our visit and he's curious about the party of train fans passing through his patch. So before we catch the train south to Macedonia, a few of us have tea with the ambassador.

Cliff is jockey-sized, with a flapping shirt that seems too big for him, grey hair that also flaps to one side, half glasses and baggy slacks. Everything about him seems relaxed and loose-fitting.

'Three days after independence in 2008, Serbia took control of the northern lines,' Cliff says, immediately 'talking railways' and explaining the situation around Mitrovica.

We are sitting in the rooftop cafe of the Sirius Hotel, with sweeping views of the modern buildings of the city centre as well as a derelict Serbian Orthodox church.

'If Serbia and Kosovo could create a joint railway company then maybe there could be a link from Pristina to Serbia.' Cliff sounds doubtful as he says this; such an agreement would appear to require a big forward leap in diplomacy.

The ambassador fills us in about the country: 'Some of the poverty in Kosovo is almost at African standards. In rural areas there is a lot of grinding poverty. About seventy per cent of the population is under thirty. The problem is that people come through education with high aspirations, but there are no jobs.'

He tells us about the displacement of Albanians during the Kosovo War: 'One million people were deported in three or four months. Then after the war they just walked back.' This was because there had been much damage to the lines during the fighting. 'They had been herded into trains. It was slightly reminiscent of the Jews in the Second World War. They mainly went just over the border in Macedonia or to Albania.'

One local guide had told us earlier that he had not felt comfortable getting on the train to Peja, as it had been his first train journey since his deportation.

'After the war the British KFOR repaired the main train line in Kosovo,' Cliff says, flipping his fringe to one side with a sweep of a hand. 'There are plans to refurbish the damaged stations.'

The ambassador sips his tea, pauses and gazes across the rooftops of Pristina. He seems pleased to be able to impart 'train information' to 'train people'. He scratches his head and says, 'Oh, and did you know that the station at Peja was the Serb intelligence headquarters during the war?'

We didn't. It's a 'train nugget' to tell the others.

Cliff seems satisfied by the response of his audience of rail enthusiasts to this – and his other nuggets – though he cannot remember the PIN for his gold credit card, so we pay for the tea. We part and the ambassador flaps off in the direction of the embassy, a breeze catching his shirt as he almost sails away along the pavement.

'When I was married, I was a doormat,
but now this doormat is a magic flying carpet'
Pristina, Kosovo, to Skopje, Macedonia

Our train to Macedonia the next morning is Italian made – by Fiat in 1980 – though it was used in Sweden and rebuilt in 1993, says Boocock. He is truly a demigod when it comes to the provenance of a locomotive. Like a master sommelier assessing a rare wine, he seems to savour the whole experience, as though breathing in the very essence of the train.

He surveys the grotty grey seats.

'A little worn,' he pronounces.

After this update, Boocock disappears to a far end of the carriage.

The line upon which the carriages are travelling is, we have also learnt from the local guide, standard gauge and was built in 1874 by the Compagnie des Chemins de Fer Orientaux under Turkish guidance; the Turks wanted to connect Istanbul with Vienna, eventually achieving this in 1888.

We are on the 07:10 to Skopje, where we are due to arrive at 09:52. It is a grey day and a few of the rail enthusiasts (myself included) are slightly hungover from cheap Kosovan wine and shots of raki the night before. The weather seems to match our early-morning mood. We move southwards beneath a mushroom-coloured sky, passing a power station, a scrapyard and a series of rusting wagons. Graffiti on a wall says: *R.I.P. IGENTZZ.* A bedraggled piebald dog watches our progress from the trackside.

The Bill Clinton Sporteve stadium comes and goes. The minaret of a mosque shoots up beyond a concrete depot. Another piece of graffiti says: *URBAN WOLF*, while someone else has scrawled: **** *SERBIA*. And not long after that, we hit undulating green countryside.

At around 9 a.m. we cross the Macedonian border, stopping beforehand by a platform sprouting weeds at Hani Elezit station. Here a Kosovan immigration official boards and stamps our passports; the stamp has a neat little picture of a steam train to show that we left by train. We change trains to another with a green locomotive built in Yugoslavia during the 1980s, according to Alan from Ffestiniog Travel (Boocock is busy talking to others), and stop at a station on the edge of Macedonia, where officials take almost an hour checking our passports after collecting them all – thus delaying the train. No undesirables are discovered among the rail enthusiasts. The Macedonian officials hand back the passports without stamping them.

We continue, twisting between hills and alongside rivers. I make friends with Margaret, a seventy-something, widowed former teacher from Surbiton, now living in Cambridge. She has fluffy white hair and a whimsical disposition; the Miss Marple of our group. She's travelling alone and reading a novel called *The Page Turner* by David Leavitt. I ask her what it's about.

'A gay couple – about a man who turns pages for a conductor, his lover. It's about gay love, but there's nothing too dirty,' she says.

She pauses. Talking about the book seems to have triggered a thought. 'Did you see the porn channel in the room at the hotel in Pristina?' she asks.

I hadn't.

'I mean, what can you do? You're flicking the channels and it's there!' she says.

I had not expected this turn in conversation.

Margaret begins to tell a story about a holiday she once had in Vancouver: 'I was totally lost, near Chinatown. I was worried. I didn't feel safe.' She pauses for dramatic effect. 'So I picked up a man. I asked him for help and we went for a coffee. I've been on three holidays with him since: Namibia, Iceland, St Petersburg. I can sit with him and laugh. We email each other. He's ten years younger than me and lives in Cardiff.' She rubs her fingers together. 'He has money. He's on a good little earner. Oh yes.' She pauses. Then she lowers her voice. 'When I was married, I was a doormat, but now this doormat is a magic flying carpet.' She grins and gazes out of the window.

We soon arrive at the new main station in Skopje, whereupon a few of us walk over to see the city's old station. Charlie and Johnnie have got wind of this 'station museum' and are determined to pay a visit.

Skopje was hit by a devastating earthquake at 05:17 on 26 July 1963, and the hands of the clock on the station have been left at 05:17 as a mark of respect to those who died in the quake. The City Museum is housed in what was once the ticket office. Inside there are displays about the earthquake and how most of the eighteenth- and nineteenth-century architecture of the city was destroyed. A yellowing cutting from *The Sunday Times* dated 28 July 1963 is in one cabinet. 'When I drove into the devastated tourist city of Skopje at daybreak today, Yugoslav army rescue teams who had worked all night by searchlight had just dug the 262nd body out of the huge piles of rubble which fill almost every street of this ancient Macedonian capital,' writes reporter Antony Terry. Altogether, more than 1,000 people died and 200,000 were left homeless.

The disaster struck during the rule of President Josip Tito, who rebuilt the city with mainly ugly communist-style blocks, we discover. Since gaining independence from Yugoslavia in 1991

– avoiding the bloodshed of other parts of the Balkans – the country has been steadily tearing down the most depressing Tito-era architecture, a programme that has accelerated in the past five years. From the old station we walk along the River Vardar, inspecting grand new government buildings, new bridges flanked with figurines of heroes of the past, and a giant, recently completed statue of Alexander the Great, who is believed to have come from the territory of the Former Yugoslav Republic of Macedonia (FYROM), as the country is officially recognised by the United Nations. This incredible burst of construction, complete with new Alexander-the-Great-style galleys converted into restaurants and bars on the river, is regarded as an explosive expression of national identity: post Yugoslavia, the new Macedonia is established, on the map and here to stay.

Skopje is where I part from the rail enthusiasts, many of whom I have got to know well. They are going onwards by train to Albania, but I am travelling to the other side of the globe – to see what the future might hold for train travel. It's been fun while it lasted, and I'm grateful to all for my immersion in 'rail enthusiasm'. Every loco, every track – just about every siding or old wagon – seems to tell a story, as do so many of those on board.

I now know a *gricer* when I see one, and how to tell the difference between a *haulage basher* and a *track basher*. I now have a decent inkling of what makes a rail enthusiast tick and I've realised something: there's nothing especially odd about the hobby.

I've been on safaris with holidaymakers peering avidly through binoculars at distant grey spots that might be elephants, buffalo or wildebeest. I've seen twitchers on birdwatching breaks cooing with delight after catching a fraction of a second's glimpse of a lesser spotted woodpecker or a ruby-throated hummingbird. The only difference is the subject: trains... and lots of them. Big trains, small trains, old trains, new trains, with a smattering of stations, depots, narrow-gauge tracks and forks in the line thrown in. Trains. Simple as that: lots and lots of trains and train things. And for the less obsessive, of course: the chance to see interesting countries in a pleasant and relaxed way, far removed from the usual tourist hordes.

On the final night we dine on 'peasant pots' of pork in a rich mushroom sauce at a restaurant with an ironic, nostalgic Tito theme. *FIRST PICTURES OF MARSHAL TITO* runs the headline on the cover of a copy of *Life* magazine that is pinned to a wall. He wears a dapper cream suit and a puzzled expression; as well he might have at the time, as the future of Yugoslavia was far from certain.

We raise glasses of fizzy Skopsko local beer – rail enthusiasts enjoying downtime in a little-visited corner of south-eastern Europe (cameras and notebooks in bags beneath the table) – and I think about the train adventure ahead.

3 | CHINA: FAST NOODLES AND REVOLUTIONS

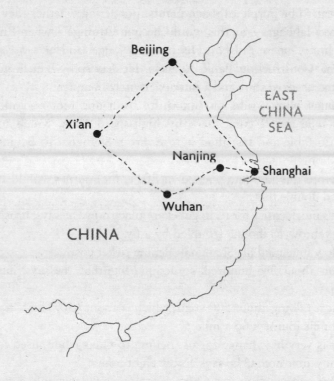

Beijing

Xi'an

Nanjing

Wuhan

CHINA

Shanghai

EAST
CHINA
SEA

OUTSIDE THE FORBIDDEN City on Tiananmen Square, it's a pleasant early evening in May. A breeze stirs, catching the red national flag near the golden facade of the Imperial Palace, upon which the visage of Chairman Mao gazes serenely. He's wearing a trademark buttoned-up jacket and looks like the archetypal benevolent ruler surveying his subjects – across the site of the bloody protests against his Communist Party in 1989, just 13 years after his death.

I am standing by a fence lined with pink flowers and what appear to be purple cabbage plants, pondering whether they are indeed cabbages – as this would be quite strange – when I meet my first Chinese rail fan. His name is Jangei and he works for China Construction Bank, he says. He has spiky hair, a green jacket, checked shirt and a hurried, twitchy manner.

Jangei blinks, rubs an ear, shifts from one foot to another, and tells me, 'I come here by high-speed train. Much more comfortable and fast than before. From Shanghai to Beijing in five hours.'

Before this fast line opened in 2011, the journey would have taken double that.

'It's much easier for us to get every place now,' he says, brushing an eyebrow, as though troubled by a fly.

How much did his Shanghai–Beijing ticket cost?

'Oh about five hundred, something like that,' he says, jutting his jaw.

He is talking about 500 yuan, which is about £50. This is for an 819 mile journey: 6p a mile.

'It is very big change for us. Beijing to Guangzhou, used to be twenty-four hours,' he says. 'Now eight hours.'

This journey, from the Chinese capital to Guangzhou, a city in the south, is the longest high-speed rail line in the world, covering 1,428 miles. Further tracks beyond Guangzhou are planned southwards to Hong Kong, possibly to be completed as early as

2017, thus creating a symbolic link between the centre of Chinese power and the former British colony, where demonstrations against government control of the media and other aspects of life have been held so often in recent times.

'Now I think China will change very fast,' Jangei says, holding still for a moment. 'Politics…' he adds mysteriously. His voice trails off. 'We have a good government,' he comments loudly. Then his eyes dart behind me. 'I think it is very dangerous,' he says in a quieter voice. 'This is our government place. In Tiananmen Square, if we talk politics, or something like that…' He does not complete the sentence.

He twitches and pauses. 'Facebook, you know, it doesn't work around here,' he says, as though that explains everything. 'Come – let's go for a beer.'

We walk down a dark, tree-lined side street; the light has dimmed rapidly. As we do, Jangei asks me if I am a journalist. I say I'm a tourist. He casts a sideways look.

'Here. Inside,' he says.

We are at a shop with a single fluorescent light; a sign saying, *BEER, COFFEE, DRINKS*; and hanging strips of plastic in the doorway, as at a butcher's. Jangei is shiftier than ever; his conversation seems to have been leading up to this point.

I go with the flow.

We enter a grimy, cramped space with an empty counter and a fridge. A hunched woman known to Jangei wordlessly ushers us beyond the fridge into a windowless back room with pistachio walls, another fluorescent light, and a red rose in a vase on a small table with a circular board marked with colourful symbols. This board appears to be a drinking game. A sticky, laminated food-and-drink menu is produced. Jangei jabbers to the woman, who disappears and returns with two bottles of Budweiser. She opens these and Jangei fills a small tumbler with beer. He downs the tumbler in one and bangs the empty glass. I copy him.

He wipes his hand across his mouth. He has stopped fidgeting and now holds a steady stare. There is no one else in BEER, COFFEE, DRINKS, and this is its only room.

'*Ganbei*,' he says. This, apparently, means 'cheers'.

Our 'shots' of Budweiser proceed quickly, with me following Jangei's lead. The bottles won't last long.

Jangei talks about his family: 'I have a child. If I have a second one, I lose my job. I would like to have a second one, but one is also good.'

He engages in a bit of chit-chat. I tell him about my train journeys planned for China. Jangei tells me he wants to travel by train from 'London to Roma, or something like that'. Washington DC is another place on his holiday list. I mention that I once visited Shanghai. He asks me which hotel I stayed at. 'That is very expensive hotel,' he says, seeming to consider the matter.

We finish our beers.

'Tea,' says Jangei. 'In China, when drink beer, must have tea. Tea means friendship.'

The menu is confusing; I order a cup of the cheapest tea. Shortly afterwards two steaming pots of tea arrive. I look again at the menu: these pots are 230 yuan (about £23 each), rather than £3 for a cup. I look at Jangei again. The bill for all of this will be more than £50, the price of a Beijing–Shanghai train fare. His manner has changed. He's super calm now, with a quizzical expression, as though he's trying to read my thoughts.

I tell Jangei I won't pay the full bill as I only ordered a cup. His mood switches once more. He turns angry. He makes a show of throwing some yuan notes on the table. 'So I will pay for the tea!' he says.

I place 200 yuan (£20) on the drinking-game board. Jangei looks at it and shrugs. I leave and he follows into the front chamber. I cross through the butcher's strips of plastic. He steps halfway out to watch me go and I turn to take a picture of him in front of

BEER, COFFEE, DRINKS. He darts inside before I manage to do so. This is the last I see of Jangei.

I have, I realise, just been conned by a Chinese rail enthusiast (of sorts).

China: it's a long way to go to catch a train. From Macedonia to Beijing is about 6,600 miles. On these rail journeys around the globe, I'm going to do a fair bit of leaping about. But that's the way it is with rail interest, as I'd discovered from my friends back in Kosovo: you select each trip and savour the ride, like dining out at a series of good restaurants. Charlie, Mike, Johnnie and the others collected their train journeys over years, building up a back catalogue of experiences. If I am to get into the 'train zone', if you like – if I am to approach Boocock levels of train Zen, though I cannot quite see that happening – I won't do it in one great go. I need to bide my time: hop here and there; take to the tracks and see where they may lead. Besides, I don't want to suffer rail fatigue by setting off on one enormous journey. I intend to come to each trip fresh, with a sense of adventure as I walk down the platform and step on board.

Heading to the Far East so early in my quest, however, I have an aim in mind. The spread of high-speed tracks in China has been one of the transport tales of our times. Throughout Europe, lines are linking up – there are EU plans for a trans-European high-speed rail network with 'corridors' of tracks – but the big rail story, where you can really see the future of trains, is in the People's Republic of China. Or so it would seem, based on the pace of construction of bullet-train tracks and shiny new stations. With centralised control – and, crucially, nobody daring to get in the way – a vast new web of lines has come into being in the past dozen years. The country almost appears to be gripped by the kind of 'railway mania' that swept Britain in the mid nineteenth century.

Into the haze
Beijing to Xi'an

At Beijing West station, the morning after my encounter with 'Jangei', I'm about to find out what it's all about. I show my passport to a female officer in a blue uniform and a peaked cap with a hammer-and-sickle symbol, and step into a cavernous hall with neon signs indicating a KFC and a McDonald's. At first glance, it might be a station just about anywhere in Europe. There's a disappointing international conformity. Then I notice all the noodle shops. In between the familiar fast-food logos, long rows of colourful stalls sell stacks of noodles in plastic pots as well as boxes of tea, bottles of liquor and vacuum-wrapped packets of Peking duck. I go to one and buy some beef and onion noodles; it's possible, I've been told, to heat the noodles using hot-water taps positioned between the carriages. There is a rite-of-passage feeling to this purchase. Passport: check! Ticket: check! Noodles: paid for! Ready to go! I'm about to become just another one of the massive country's 1.3 billion noodle eaters.

Signs are, usefully, in both Chinese and English: *LUGGAGE ATTENDANT... BOOKS... STORE... VIP WAITING ROOM.* Security is tight, with guards with jackboots and guns keeping an eye on matters. There's a reason for this. Earlier in the year, knife-wielding terrorists believed to be seeking independence for Xinjiang (or they could have been Uighur Muslims, a Turkic ethnic group, no one is quite sure) killed 29 people and injured 140 others at Kunming's train station. This event shocked the nation and authorities brought in airport-style ID and ticket checks at stations across the country.

In waiting room number ten – not for VIPs – I take a seat next to a shop selling toy bullet trains, Hello Kitty watches and pictures of revered Chinese generals. My train has a final destination of Baoji, although I will be disembarking after about six hours in

Xi'an, just to the east of Baoji. This is to be the first stop-off on my speedy tour of China, travelling from Beijing to Xi'an, then onwards to Wuhan, Nanjing, Shanghai and back to Beijing, completing a giant circle. It's a total distance of about 2,500 miles and I'm doing it in a week. Having only ever visited China for a day or two before, it's an introduction to the complicated country from the tracks up: fast, fast, fast, all the way.

Everything moves quickly.

This includes my fellow passengers heading for the ticket barrier. The Chinese notion of queuing does not, it is fair to say, correspond with the British. An announcement is made that the train is boarding. The entire population of the waiting room arises and bulldozes towards an automatic barrier that does not work if you have a 'manual only' ticket, as I have. I back out through the football-stadium-style crush, being treated to a rich assortment of what can only be Mandarin Chinese curses, find the 'manual only' ticket gate, give my 'manual only' ticket to the 'manual only' inspector, who is wearing a natty peaked cap with a red and gold band, and make my way to a sleek, eel-like train with CRH written on its side. This stands for China Railway High-Speed. It is electric and this particular train is a G-class running on a standard gauge track (for those who really want to know).

I'm in second class, in a blue seat with a polka-dot pattern and a window view. The passenger next to me sits down and proceeds to tuck into a McDonald's chicken wrap and hash browns. He sips a McDonald's coffee and ignores me. He's wearing a leather jacket that he never removes, plus a pair of heavy-framed tinted glasses. There is, I cannot help feeling, something sneaky about him.

We depart at 08:10, precisely on time. And as we venture, swiftly, towards Beijing's suburbs, I begin to get a sense of the sheer size of the country – as well as some of its pressing problems. It's an eye-opening start. Through my window, inhuman tower block aftcr inhuman tower block soon appears, rising murkily through a haze of orange-brown sky. This haze, I quickly discover, never goes away. Sure, there had been smog at Tiananmen Square, but it's only now, as we slide out of the city, that its pervasiveness strikes me. In this cindery gloom, the blocks – many of which are still being built and are surrounded by cranes – look especially forbidding: ugly, unrelenting, soul-sapping and all very Big Brother. What's it like to live in the shadowy suburbs of Beijing, gazing out across the misty cityscape – one of 1.3 billion people in a country where speaking out too much might land you in prison or cause you to simply disappear?

I raise this here as, in the run-up to my visit, I have been following an Amnesty International campaign to highlight the plight of more than 220 lawyers and activists who either went missing or were detained for speaking out about human rights earlier in the year. The Chinese Communist Party paper, *The People's Daily*, had recently accused them of being part of a criminal operation to 'undermine social stability'. Lawyers from the Fengrui law firm, based in Beijing, had been rounded up – including the prominent lawyer Wang Fu, who text-messaged friends to say that her house was being broken into late one night. This is the last anyone heard of her. Fengrui had been defending human-rights activists as well as the prominent Uighur academic Ilham Tohti.

Happy train travels! Seeing China from its high-speed tracks seems somehow to take you a step away from usual tourist affairs – the pandas, the pagodas, the Great Wall – and closer to the reality of life viewed from your window. Amnesty International's assessment of China runs thus: 'The authorities continue to severely restrict the right to freedom of expression. Activists and human-rights defenders risk harassment and arbitrary detention. Torture and other ill treatment remain widespread and access to justice is elusive to many. Ethnic minorities including Tibetans, Uighurs and Mongolians face discrimination and increased security crackdown. Record numbers of workers have been on strike demanding better pay and conditions.'

Fume-bellowing factories, tumbledown warehouses, ramshackle junkyards and electricity depots zip by as we begin to gather pace. The driver shifts smoothly through the gears, and the train begins to float along. A digital monitor at the end of the carriage shows our speed: 290 kmph (181 mph). Yet more grim Manhattans of concrete and steel arise, before we break into farmland with long, thin, rectangular plots of land.

Television screens in the carriage show Communist Party officials attending a press conference, then flashing cameras at the unveiling of a new car model at what seems to be a trade show. Neighbours behind me slurp noodles and crunch on prawn crackers. The smell of both fills the air. Mobile phones ring. Tweets bleep (even though Twitter is also banned in China). Elderly men noisily clear their throats in a manner that would be unacceptable back home. During one especially violent spell of coughing, it's as though a hacking competition has begun. If they weren't so dreadful, the lung-wrenching, guttural sounds could almost be considered comical: it's as though I'm in a carriage full of human bullfrogs (with twenty-a-day smoking habits).

After a stop at Xinxiangdong, I take a walk along the train. There appear to be four classes of carriage. These consist of 'business class' (extremely comfortable, fully-reclining, scoop-shaped seats, with slippers provided), 'premier class' (ruby-red leather seats with satin-esque throw cushions, not fully reclining), 'first class' (similar to premier, but not quite as fancy), and 'second class', where I am amid the hackers. There may also be a 'third class', as some carriages seem to have seats with slightly less legroom, although I may be imagining this and, as my Chinese is limited to *ganbei*, I'm having to rely on what I see.

The train has 15 carriages in total including a buffet car. Here, I buy a 'VIP Executive Ready Meal' – the noodles can wait. This

VIP lunch comes in a moulded plastic tray with sections that contain salty beef and potato, sticky white rice, sweet and sour chicken, spinach (or something like spinach), and a thin vegetable soup. A toothpick is provided with *toothpick* written on it. The price is 45 yuan (£4.70). I sit at a red wooden table, opposite a middle-aged woman in an aquamarine-and-sequin outfit who is slowly eating sunflower seeds. She nods, smiles and pops a sunflower seed in her mouth, looking out at a little river cutting through paddy fields. In the middle of this river a white stork stands dead still, not bothered in the slightest by the bullet train. I try my VIP meal. It's spicy, pleasingly strange and makes a happy change from overpriced, cardboard sandwiches back home. We pass Luoyanglongmen, then pause at LingBaoXi. I nod goodbye to my dining companion, and return to my second-class seat.

The man with the tinted glasses has vanished – and so has the guidebook I left in the pocket on the back of the seat in front. Maybe he took it. Maybe someone else did. Who needs a guidebook anyway? Cartoons flicker on the television screen. Factory stacks and cooling towers scud by. The train sways gently as we hit 300 kmph, then creep upwards: 302 kmph, 303 kmph, 304 kmph… This top speed is 190 mph, although the trains could go as fast as 219 mph, were it not for speed restrictions. A head conductor of some sort skips down our carriage – she's wearing a burgundy miniskirt and knee-high boots and has a microphone hooked to her ear, as if she is about to appear on *The X Factor*. Outside, a car factory, a shanty town of corrugated abodes and a dusty plain appear in the mist. Then a massive construction site emerges, as though a whole new city is being built.

Amid this hive of activity, the train slows and stops. We have arrived in Xi'an, in its 'North Business Development Zone'.

I know this because I have been met by Sally, my contact in the city, and she's told me so. I've arranged to be collected at the station, shown round for a day and taken back to my next train.

This is sightseeing on the quick, but it's not just the sights that interest me.

'This development zone, we do this because of the railways,' says Sally, who is, I soon learn, a single mother, originally from Inner Mongolia. She's short and well wrapped up in a scarlet scarf, even though it's not all that cold. She wants to tell me... everything.

'High-speed trains come in 2012. It is half the price of flying to Beijing: 515 yuan.' This works out at £54. A journey on a slow, overnight sleeper would, she says, cost just £31.

'Around the station we are building. High-speed trains make China change. Everywhere is smaller. Everywhere is connected, like a big family. There are more choices for different holidays. Everyone has the right to enjoy their free time. In China you have first-tier cities: Beijing, Shanghai, Guangzhou and Chongqing. These have become very expensive places in the last fifteen years. Then you have second-tier cities: Lanzhou, Taiyuan, Yinchuan, Qinghai and Xi'an. Deng Xiaoping [who led China from 1978 to 1992], he developed the south of the country, because it was close to the ports. Now develop north of country.'

We are in Shaanxi province, one of 23 in China. This province is rich in gas and coal reserves in the north, while Xi'an, the capital, is known for its textiles, electronics and for factories connected to the 'National Defence System – they make aircraft, rockets for space, things like that'.

Sally says that iPhone 6s are extremely popular, that mortgages have become commonplace in the past ten years, and that 'there is a big gap between the rich and the poor'.

'There has been corruption. Some people want to take investment money for themselves. They have been caught, according to CCTV News. This is good thing. Deng Xiaoping said it does not matter if it is a black cat or a white cat: if it catches the rat, it is a good cat. In the 1980s and 1990s, the first people make a lot of money easily. Deng Xiaoping, he allow this. He said we should mix with the world and if some people get rich, we can get rich together.'

I'm just about following her. But there's another saying attributed to Xiaoping that's perhaps more pertinent to this journey: 'A socialist train coming with a delay is better than a capitalist one that comes on time.' It sounds as though this 'truism' was an excuse for stagnation during previous regimes. These days, however, the socialist trains seem to be pretty punctual, too.

Judging by the Aston Martin and Lamborghini showrooms in downtown Xi'an, there are some very rich people indeed in this communist country. Sally and I drive about the fancy malls and hotels of downtown Xi'an to see the attractions.

At the 64-metre-high, seventh-century Great Wild Goose Pagoda ('the only leaning pagoda in China'), I ask her about Tibet. Sally just looks at me and laughs; talking about Tibet with foreigners is obviously not a good idea.

We drive to the marvellous, mesmerising Terracotta Army, where I buy a book about the 2,300-year-old figures – considered by some to be the eighth wonder of the world – and have it signed by one of the farmers who discovered them while drilling for water in March 1974 (and who appears to have long since retired and moved into the publishing world).

I see a Tang-dynasty-style show at the ornate Shaanxi Grand Opera House, where I'm fed dumpling after dumpling served with slices of tongue-like meat with plum sauce – all washed down with fizzy Snow beer. On stage, women in gold and blue costumes dance to jolly Tang hits such as 'Breeze Dancing on Water' and 'Girls Look Forward to a Nice and Happy Life'.

I go for a walk from my hotel to watch a flag-lowering ceremony by the town hall – marching music echoing across a square – and to see elderly men cracking whips to keep spinning tops going in a park.

Then the next morning, Sally takes me to a museum with propaganda posters including one that is part of a current Communist Party campaign and depicts a mother using a basin of water to wash her feet, with a child who asks whether she can help clean the mother's feet too.

'Children can sometimes be very selfish in China,' Sally says. 'They are spoilt as they are only children. They are given everything. Sometimes they are so spoilt they do not know how to consider others. So we need to relearn our doctrine, to consider our parents, to pay them respect.'

The single children are a result of the one-child policy mentioned by Jangei – although this has been relaxed in the countryside to allow two, says Sally. She also explains that when two city-dwelling single children marry, it is possible to request permission to have more than one child (apparently because their families' offspring rate is already low). A report in this morning's English-language *China Daily* newspaper quotes figures from the National Health and Family Planning Commission showing that 26,000 couples living in Beijing had made such an application so far that year, which does not sound all that many in a city of more than 21 million.

'Ha na, ja mah, na, jah!'
Xi'an to Wuhan

That's Xi'an. I won't dwell on it; you don't have time for lengthy reflections on a high-speed rail tour of China. Onwards!

After exchanging email addresses with Sally, I'm back by the tracks almost before I know it – about to head for Wuhan, a car-manufacturing and cigarette-producing city with a mere ten million inhabitants.

At the station, a man holding a plastic bag is taking pictures of the bullet train with his mobile phone. I appear to have found a

Chinese trainspotter – possibly even a Chinese gricer, judging by his dishevelled look. I ask if he is one.

'Ah ha ha ha za la,' he answers.

He hasn't the foggiest clue what I said, nor have I of what he's just related (I really should brush up on my Mandarin Chinese).

During the four-hour journey to Wuhan I become acquainted with some very noisy neighbours. As we move away into the apartment-block haze that already seems so standard on the edge of any Chinese city, I realise that the man sitting next to me will neither keep still nor shut up. He is in his thirties and has a buzz cut, yellow teeth and high cheekbones. A set of keys is attached to his belt. He jiggles his legs as though this is a nervous habit. Doing so rattles the keys, creating a tinny sound. His chatter goes on and on; I cannot count beyond five during the pauses in his communication with two friends across the aisle.

'Her, ter, der, cling! Her, der, der, der, ter, ter, cling!' he yells – or something along those lines. Loudly. The whole time.

I'm sure it's a very interesting conversation.

This continues for the entire journey, broken only by my neighbour knocking over his flask of water, a feat he achieves four times thanks to his leg-jiggling (once splashing the book I'm reading). His female friend across the aisle is even noisier. She is drinking a can of Tuborg beer and gesticulating wildly. What's in my friend's flask, I wonder.

For lunch, and a break from the party, I go to heat my noodles. This turns out to be a semi-traumatic experience. The idea is to fill your noodle pot under a boiling water tap. As I am about to do so, a small elderly female attendant begins jabbering at me. The way she does so makes it sound as though I am on the cusp of some sort of emergency.

'Ha na, ja mah, na, jah!' she says. Rapidly.

Language, if you do not have any, can be a problem in the People's Republic of China.

She grabs my noodles, somehow indicates that I must wait for an orange light to turn on, and fills my pot at the right moment. I thank her and go back to my seat. As I return, I find my jiggling neighbour examining the label on a bottle of Perrier I took from the Xi'an hotel. Without looking at me, he replaces it on my table. Perhaps he was checking to see if it was a type of beer. Then he and his Tuborg-drinking friend pause for a while, watching me eat my noodles.

So passes my time on the train from Xi'an to Wuhan.

Despite its size – it's the biggest city in central China – Wuhan feels like a backwater. Not many tourists visit, and were it not for the high-speed line I doubt I would have ever gone. My new contact, Frank, is no-nonsense about the city, informing me bluntly that there is only one tourist attraction, the Yellow Crane Tower. He has a high opinion of this tower, telling me: 'I dare to say that, if people see it, they will feel fantastic.'

Frank does not offer to take me there; he's an unusual sort of guide. He's just going to drop me at my Shangri-La hotel and collect me for the train on to Nanjing in the morning. He is skinny and his hair has a dyed-red tint.

Frank likes the city's new bullet trains, which were introduced four years earlier. Wuhan has had trains of some description since the late nineteenth century. 'I think it keep pace with the world,' he says. 'Improve development of the city. Save lot of time. Your time is money. Everyone wants to do things very fast, right?'

We cross a bridge over the Yangtze river; the Yangtze and Han rivers converge at Wuhan. It's an especially pollution-clogged afternoon. 'Wuhan has the worst air,' Frank says. 'When I was young, five years old, I could see blue sky and clouds.'

But not since then, seems to be the implication.

After dropping my bag at the hotel, I go for a stroll along narrow, chaotic, fuggy streets where elderly folk play mah-jong and little shops sell Singer sewing machines. There are many skyscrapers and numerous fashion shops. I find 'Walking Street', which the hotel concierge had recommended. People are indeed walking on Walking Street, past even more fashion shops. Just when I'm wondering whether I should cut my losses and call it a day, I stumble upon the 1911 Revolution Museum.

This is where Wuhan comes into its own.

The city, I find, was where rebels successfully overthrew local Qing dynasty officials, leading to the establishment of the Republic of China on 1 January 1912, and the abdication of the six-year-old 'Last Emperor' of China, Aisin Gioro Puyi, on 12 February 1912. Railways, I am surprised to learn, played a key part in this revolt. In May 1911, the debt-ridden Qing government ordered the nationalisation of railway lines that were owned by private investors. This sparked widespread discontent and is referred to in China as the 'railway crisis'. Strikes and protests were held, part of what was known as the Railway Protection Movement, culminating in the uprising in Wuhan on 10 October 1911, when there was mutiny in the Qing army.

There you have it: no railways, no revolution. The emperors might still have been in charge and history would have been rather different.

This is perhaps – I'll concede – a *slightly* simplistic take on Chinese history.

Nearby, I take in a wall by a block of apartments upon which a series of sayings has been inscribed. *Extravagance leads to insubordination, and parsimony to meanness. It is better to be mean than to be insubordinate*. This is attributed to James Legge, a nineteenth-century Scottish sinologist who translated many Chinese classic volumes into English. He's also responsible for: *The wise find pleasure in water; the virtuous find pleasure in hills. The wise are active; the virtuous are tranquil. The wise are joyful; the virtuous are long-lived*. And for: *When the solid qualities are in excess of accomplishments, we have rusticity; where the accomplishments are in excess of the solid qualities, we have the manners of a clerk. When the accomplishments and solid qualities are equally balanced, we then have the man of virtue.*

Wondering what on earth Legge was on about – and how the great Scottish sinologist would have categorised those who 'find pleasure in railways' – I get an early night, followed by an early train to Nanjing.

This server cannot regulate that command
Wuhan to Nanjing

On board I meet Joe. He's sitting next to me. He's a financial investment student and he's travelling to Nanjing to see his girlfriend. He has widely spaced eyes that taper towards his ears, and a neat side parting. He's more than six feet tall and dressed in black. We strike up a conversation after I go to the dining carriage and return with a 'sautéed beef fillet with hot green pepper' brunch. The menu had been in English as well as Chinese and other dining options included: 'new farming braise in soy sauce beef noodles', duck tongue, stewed lotus root, 'oaten cake' and 'the spaghetti'.

My steaming beef fillet with hot peppers catches Joe's attention. 'Not the best Chinese food,' he says. 'Because it is on a train.'

Chinese train food, apparently, has a bad reputation, though I quite like it. I ask Joe where he learnt English.

'First it was as a child. I listen to music. Then learn at school. I want one day work for American bank.'

He enjoys the country's new bullet trains: 'It make much more comfortable. A symbol of new China. Please eat!'

I do, and as I tuck into the (very) hot peppers, Joe tells me his dreams. 'A big house! A lover!' he begins. 'Some friends, and I can do what I want and have much time to do what I want. Not to have to work. To do reading, sports, travel. First in China, then foreign. I have already been to England. My dad take me there when I was eight years old. My father was lecturer at university in Newcastle. I went for one month. I don't remember much except very large grass in a park and that even a small boy play football very good.'

Joe is interrupted by an announcement in English. These come from time to time on the Wuhan–Nanjing train. We have arrived at a station: 'Please keep an eye on the gap between the train and the platform.'

Joe says that his favourite pop groups and singers are Westlife, the Backstreet Boys, James Blunt and Michael Jackson: '"Billie Jean" – very good!'

He is not a member of the Communist Party. 'I am happy,' he says, referring to the way the country is run. 'But not all people are. They make much complaints, but they don't work hard. So bad situation remains. They hate the bad situation, but they don't make change.'

We zoom through paddy fields, some with farmers wearing conical hats. We slip through tunnels. We see tower blocks in the haze. We have arrived at Nanjing.

Joe heads off, and I take a taxi to my hotel near the city's Confucius Temple. I am on my own in this ancient capital of the Ming Dynasty (1368–1644), also capital of the Republic of China from 1911 to 1937.

I take another taxi from the hotel to see the mausoleum of Dr Sun Yat-sen, one of the main revolutionary figureheads and the first president of the republic. He had been in exile – in Denver, Colorado – at the time of the October 1911 railway-inspired uprising. The mausoleum is at the top of a towering set of stone steps and within a pretty park with unusual sculptures of elephants and camels. So this is the resting place of the 'railway hero' who helped depose the Chinese dynastic line and is worthy of any train lover's interest.

Afterwards, I stop by Confucius Temple, take in another Chinese saying or two ('I hear and I forget. I see and I remember. I do and I understand') and, with the main tourist attractions 'done', I go for pork noodles by Qinhuai river, watching rickshaw men in lurid lemon-yellow outfits eating their own noodles during a break. The Qinhuai looks sublime in the early evening, with light from the lanterns flickering on its placid coal-black surface and little tourist boats lined with red bulbs scooting here and there. Golden dragons adorn the walls of traditional homes with curl-topped roofs that pack the waterfront.

I drink a Snow beer and read the papers. I have copies of *China Daily* and *Shanghai Daily* from the Wuhan–Nanjing train and they make curious reading.

A man in Henan province has broken the world record for continually spinning his body for 14 hours (claiming to the reporter that he could read a book while turning circles). An eight-year-old girl from Chongqing has had a hairball the size of a newborn child removed from her stomach (she had, apparently, developed a habit of eating old hair). Two students from Yunnan province have been 'expelled over professed love' – whatever that might mean. A man in Shaanxi province has poisoned his neighbour's sheep for eating his pear tree. A mobile-phone thief in Beijing has swallowed five sewing needles hidden in his collar upon arrest but lived to tell the tale. While in Shandong province, men are signing up for 'childbirth torture' at a maternity hospital so they can empathise with wives about to go into labour. To achieve this, electric shocks are fired into the abdomen. 'It felt like my heart and lungs were being ripped apart,' says one participant.

You couldn't make it up.

In Shanghai, restaurants are in the news. A 'driver's licence' for restaurants is being introduced: 'Under the initiative, an eatery responsible for a death through food poisoning will lose its entire annual quota of 18 points and will be closed.' Deductions of 12 points will be made for food poisoning affecting 'fewer than ten people'. In a separate scheme, authorities are cracking down on restaurants with an opium habit: 'Putting poppy seeds containing morphine into food is illegal but some restaurants and snack bars still add it to their dishes to keep customers coming back for more.'

As far as railways are concerned, China Railways Group has just secured a government contract worth 24.2 billion yuan (£2.4 billion) to build a Huaihua–Shaoyang–Hengyang line in Hunan province covering 215 miles. The deal is regarded by *China Daily* as a sign that the government is 'lifting investment to tackle slacking economic growth'. Trains, it would appear, are being used as a key economic catalyst, just as they were in nineteenth-century Europe. To put things in perspective, £2.4 billion is roughly equivalent to the GDPs (Gross Domestic Product) of Swaziland and Eritrea and slightly more than those of Guyana and the Maldives.

I poke my noodles and look at them afresh after the opium-poisoning story. They are very good indeed, though I'm not hallucinating, yet.

A final article catches my eye. The Beijing Chaoyang People's Court has sentenced Yang Xiuyu, a popular microblogger, to four years for 'spreading rumours online'. This only merits a small space at the bottom of a page, and it's yet another reminder of the reality of life in a country with censorship. I have long given up trying to look up information online using Wi-Fi at hotels as I'm sick of the message that *this server cannot regulate that command*.

'Politics is very sensitive, my friend'
Nanjing to Shanghai, a journey on the airport magnetic
levitation train, and then on to Beijing

I don't spend long in Nanjing. I'm soon on a bullet train speeding onwards to Shanghai, a journey of 1 hour 40 minutes. My circle of one section of the centre of the People's Republic is almost complete.

On board, I sit next to Mr Lin, who wears a brown striped tie and has darting, lizard-like eyes. He tells me about the country's Air Quality Index. Today's measurement is 116, which is 'not too bad', though it still looks quite misty.

'Two hundred is very bad,' Mr Lin says. 'Three hundred is severe pollution. We check the index every day. Every half day they change it.'

Flights had been delayed at Shanghai airport the previous day because of the thick fog caused by pollution, he says, while many highways had also been closed.

Mr Lin has never been abroad – only five per cent of Chinese citizens have passports – though he has an interest in the wider world. He says that those who want to can easily get around the official ban on certain websites: 'Facebook, there's an app to get you on to that, my friend. Twitter, it's the same. The authorities know that people use Twitter. They are not very strict. What they do not want is anything political.'

He pauses, then whispers, 'Politics is very sensitive, my friend.'

Railways came late to China – many years after they were built in India and Japan – as the Qing dynasty was sceptical of the newfangled devices for getting about. There was a belief that steam trains were inventive but impractical, and would interfere with feng shui. British merchants built the first line in Shanghai in the 1860s, but the Qing court considered the tracks 'strange' and had them dismantled. However, the benefits of railways were soon recognised, with privately owned local lines opening around the country, including a link between Nanjing and Shanghai in 1908 (using standard gauge). After the 1911 uprising, Dr Sun Yat-sen oversaw the creation of a national railway network for the new republic. Disruption during the Second World War and the foundation of the People's Republic of China set back the laying of lines. Then came Five-Year Plans and the Great Leap Forward in 1958, designed to bolster the economy, with trains a big part of the plot.

But it is post 2007, when the first high-speed trains were introduced, that the story has taken off. Since then, the total track length in the country has increased from 48,729 miles to 64,465 miles (at the time of the Qing dynasty's collapse there were 3,128 miles). It is estimated that more than 2.5 million passengers now travel on China's fast trains each day.

Many of them travel through Shanghai, one of the world's largest cities, with a population of more than 24 million, and home to China's most important stock exchange as well as the busiest port on the planet. It is a very big place and I am here for a day, during which I visit a silk factory, go for an afternoon stroll amid the haze and the skyscrapers on the Bund (where I meet several 'Hello, sir, you like lady' touts) and enjoy an evening at a jazz bar with septuagenarian musicians at my delightful old hotel. I'm at the Peace Hotel, where Bill Clinton, Steven Spielberg and J. G. Ballard have stayed; their pictures are in the lobby.

In the morning I take a taxi to catch the super-speedy, super-smooth Maglev (Magnetic Levitation) train to Shanghai Pudong airport. This lays claim to being the world's fastest train and it covers 19 miles with a top speed of 431 kmph (269 mph). It's a silver bullet train with orange and blue stripes, and with station notices warning that *striding over caution line is forbidden* (just in case you were thinking of striding in front of the world's fastest train). Platforms are guarded by shivering police in blue peaked caps; it's a nippy day on my visit, and quite a few passengers are eating sausage McMuffins from the station's McDonald's.

The train has *SHANGHAI TRANSRAPID* written on its aerodynamic nose. Inside, the seats in 'economic class' are royal blue and we are soon zooming along. The train has been going for over a decade (it was introduced in 2004) but the Chinese still appear to be getting used to it. Once the McMuffins are consumed, cameras come out and selfies are taken as the digital monitor clicks upwards to 431 kmph. I try to get a decent shot out of the window but all my camera seems to pick up is a blur of trees and electricity pylons, although I do get one in-focus snap: of a B&Q home-improvement store next to some apartment blocks.

The journey takes a dizzying seven minutes each way, which is just as well as I'm in a rush to catch the train from Shanghai to Beijing. Afterwards, I take a taxi to the intercity station (the ride taking a fair bit longer than seven minutes, over a distance of about a mile) and I arrive at my bullet train to the Chinese capital.

So begins my final Chinese bullet-train ride. On board, I proceed to drink a Snow beer and eat another VIP Executive Ready Meal. It's a five-hour journey, principally marked by watching a group of drunk American guys get even drunker in the dining carriage as we get closer to our destination. They're singing songs at the start and singing them louder by the end. The attendants in the dining carriage, which they have totally taken over apart from one table of mah-jong players, seem terrified. All sorts of bottles that are not for sale on board litter the carriage. The group seems as though it consists of Ivy League types, perhaps working for multinational corporations; lads on a weekend tour. I have no desire to get to know them as I'm not feeling up to the banter, but one of them grabs me by the shoulders as if I'm a long-lost buddy. I'm holding a couple of Snow beers to take to my seat. Maybe he thinks I'm one of his tribe.

'From the window, man,' he says. 'From that window I observe everything.' He's pointing outside into the dusky evening murk. 'I can absorb information continually, man. I'm like a video machine taking it all in. Do you see it, man? The horizons are changing, the colours, the patterns, the clouds, the smog and all those buildings being built.'

Funnily enough, it's not a bad summary of the Chinese bullet-train experience.

At Beijing's Railway Museum on my final day in China, I find out more about the history of Chinese trains, taking in displays on the latest locomotives and seeing one of the country's oldest remaining locos, *The Rocket of China* (1881).

Train museums, as Charlie said back in Kosovo, are important – if you're a rail enthusiast. And the one in Beijing is a corker, found in Beijing's first railway station, dating from 1906, on the south-east corner of Tiananmen Square. Beyond its stripy facade, information panels explain how railways 'went to worse from bad' during the Qing dynasty, and tell me that the top speed of *The Rocket of China* was just 32 kmph – quite a lot slower than Robert Stephenson's *Rocket* of 50 years earlier (if I'm reading the information correctly).

Cabinets are crammed with 'main valves of air compressor on steam locomotive', 'number 15 automatic couplers', hydraulic lifting machines, railway signs adorned with busts of Chairman Mao and old station clocks. Upstairs there are models of the latest G-class bullet trains, a virtual-reality machine that allows you to take a high-speed 'ride', and videos praising the new fast-train line into Tibet – which, like the railway to Hong Kong, takes on a political dimension, though that is not mentioned overtly, of course.

On the top floor you do get a little bit of politics. A display proclaims that: 'Since China began opening up to the outside world in particular, the Chinese railway industry made unprecedented historic advance on the path of socialism with Chinese characteristics, which not only plays an extremely important role in promoting the development of economic society, but also left a mark on the world history of development of railway.'

I cannot, however, find a section on the dreadful high-speed train crash of 2011 in Zhejiang province, during which one train was struck by lightning and lost power only for another to speed through malfunctioning signals and collide with it. The result was at least 40 deaths, many serious injuries and the sacking of the then railways minister; safety has since been made a priority, with trains now travelling slower than the fastest possible speeds of 350 kmph.

Nor can I find any information on Japan's pioneering work on high-speed railways that led to the introduction of *Shinkansen* bullet trains to coincide with its staging of the 1964 Olympics – half a century or so ahead of China. But there is plenty to keep a rail enthusiast going... including a shop selling model trains, naturally.

Outside, I take a stroll around Tianamen Square. It has, I reflect, been an unusual, *very fast* few days in China. From Beijing (with its train-loving conman) to Xi'an and its growing forest of station-side skyscrapers, via the history of the 'rail revolution' in Wuhan, the 'rail revolutionary's' tomb in Nanjing, and the world's quickest train in Shanghai, I have breathed in the new China from its new high-speed tracks, and I have got a feeling for the pace of the country's rapid 'progress', its manifold difficulties and its ongoing bout of train mania. There's a frenzied atmosphere with the construction of lines going ahead full throttle, and with trains seemingly regarded as a magical way forward that somehow pull together and modernise the vast nation – even attracting a Chinese trainspotter or two (if only I knew what on earth they were saying).

On this last day, I go to see the pandas and the Great Wall – well, you've got to, really. Now I'm off to another big country, where there were no Qing rulers mistrustful of funny-looking locomotives – and trains arrived a little earlier.

4 | INDIA: TAKING THE TOY TRAIN

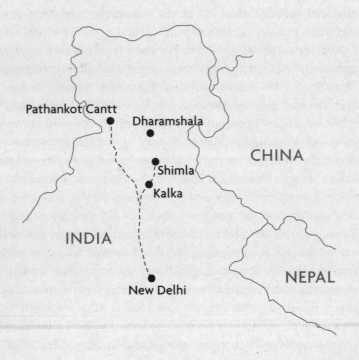

RAILWAYS MEAN A lot to India – and a few statistics, plus a dash of train history, help explain why.

To start, there's the sheer scale of them. More than 1.3 million people are employed by Indian Railways, carrying an estimated 20 million passengers and 1.3 million tonnes of freight a day along 68,000 miles of lines (quite a distance further than in China, despite its recent construction boom). To cope with this enormous load, there are approximately 14,500 daily train services. These call in at around 7,000 stations.

The creation of this giant web of trains has been the work of many years – not without mishaps along the way. The first track in India was laid in 1853 between Mumbai (then Bombay) and Thane, a small town in the countryside. This was a distance of just 21 miles and it was the brainchild of Lord Dalhousie, India's fierce governor-general from 1848 to 1856. He did not hide the fact that he saw railways as a means of reinforcing control of the country during the British Raj. The lines would also open up avenues of commerce, allowing resources such as cotton and coal to reach ports for transportation back to Britain. In turn, the sale of export goods manufactured back home would bolster the profits of the British East India Company.

Hundreds of thousands of coolies (cheap unskilled workers) were employed on low wages to construct these early tracks. Many suffered terrible deaths, particularly on an infamous section through the Western Ghats mountain range, an initial obstacle on the way out of Mumbai, which was considered on completion to be one of the engineering feats of its time. Lord Dalhousie, who liked to blow his own trumpet, had grand plans: 'The complete permeation of these climes of the sun by a magnificent system of railway communication would present a series of public movements vastly surpassing in real grandeur the aqueducts of Rome, the pyramids of Egypt, the Great Wall of China, the temples, palaces and mausoleums of the great Moghul monuments.'

So the railways came and within 20 years there were more than 5,000 miles of lines. Their military purpose was quickly put to effect during the quashing of the Indian Mutiny of 1857, while the coolies working on the railways themselves revolted against their bosses in 1859 – in protest over late payment of meagre wages. They too were put down, though conditions were subsequently – slightly – improved, and by 1901 there were 24,750 miles of train tracks.

This rapid growth revolutionised travel in the country and proved hugely popular, even if nationalists such as Mahatma Gandhi later regarded railways as a symbol of imperialism. After Indian independence in 1947, rail construction continued as the population boomed from around 360 million then to more than 1.2 billion now (India is expected to overtake China as the most populous nation soon). Images of passengers hanging on to carriage roofs hitching free rides and crazily cramped commuter trains were to follow, as were backpackers in the mid to late twentieth century, many taking to the Hippie Trail to seek spiritual enlightenment from the country's (occasionally infamous) gurus.

To get a feel of just how big trains are in India, the current number of Indian Railways employees is more than that of the populations of Mauritius or Cyprus (however daunting it may be to imagine a large-ish island entirely populated by conductors, engineers, train drivers and various other train folk). As an employer, the organisation is now said to rank eighth in the world. The top four spots are held by the US Department of Defence (3.2 million), the People's Liberation Army of China (2.3 million), Walmart (2.1 million) and McDonald's (1.9 million). Guns, guns, groceries, burgers – and a little further down the list, trains.

Oh yes, and there is something else about trains in India – something that every keen rail enthusiast knows (or ought to).

They do not run on standard gauge tracks. The track gauge across most of India is 5 feet 6 inches. This covers 75 per cent of Indian railways and is regarded as a 'broad gauge'. It was the brainchild of Lord Dalhousie, who feared that tropical storms could be a threat to trains on standard gauge. He had initially wanted an even broader gauge of 6 metres, though engineers said this would be too wide.

As well as broad gauge, there are some sections of track that run on 'meter gauge' (1 metre wide), and others, especially in the mountains, where narrow gauge is used. There are two types of this narrow gauge: 2 feet and 6 inches or exactly 2 feet.

Intriguing, as I'm sure you'll agree (some might even venture to say: exciting). Railways in India open up a whole new train game.

The Dalai Lama's cardiologist
New Delhi to Kalka

With these thoughts in mind, not so long after my Chinese jaunt, I find myself at New Delhi station. It is 7 a.m. and there are a lot of people about. I have walked the last few hundred metres to the station as the traffic jam was so bad the taxi driver thought this option would be better. Out of the cacophony of horns from lorries and autorickshaws – many of which have *BLOW HORN* written on them, a feat they are achieving with aplomb – I enter the forecourt of my first Indian station.

It's already baking; the temperature the previous day had touched 40°C, prompting some Delhiites to open fire hydrants to cool off in impromptu showers of water. Porters in red shirts cluster near a taxi rank, a few eyeballing me with hopeful expressions. Skinny men in colourful polo shirts are gossiping by a higgledy-piggledy sea of yellow-topped autorickshaws; drivers waiting for fares. Railway Protection Force Officers in khaki uniforms and berets stand guard.

I stop to look at an information panel in English that says the station dates from 1926. It was created by the East India Railway

Company to help cope with growing demand for train travel, to provide a more relaxed place to board trains than the already busy Old Delhi station. When New Delhi was inaugurated on 13 February 1931, Viceroy Lord Irwin and various bigwigs came through the station to see the newly completed imperial capital – work on which had begun in 1911, overseen by the British architects Sir Edwin Lutyens and Sir Herbert Baker.

Above the panel is the front of an old steam locomotive decorated with golden dragons; its name is *Deshbandhu* ('friend of the nation'), which refers to Deshbandu Chittranjan Das, a much-loved freedom fighter from the period of British rule.

Those with an interest will perhaps like to note that this locomotive is an Indian Railways WG class that was built in 1950 with a 2-8-2 wheel configuration for broad-gauge tracks. I hesitate before adding that 2-8-2 means the loco had pairs of unpowered wheels at both the front and back of the locomotive, as well as four pairs of wheels powered by the steam engine above – and coupled, or tied, together – in the middle. At least, I think that's right.

I'm really going to have to watch myself (in case I get into this train stuff just a little too much).

Beyond the ticket office, chaos reigns. Porters scramble. Passengers throng towards platforms. I follow a crowd and find myself at platform two. My train is long and sky-blue with dented panels partially covered in splattered flies. I'm on the 07:40 to Kalka, a journey that will take about four hours travelling due north through the state of Haryana, covering 190 miles. From Kalka I am to catch a famous narrow-gauge train onwards into the foothills of the Himalayas, ending at Shimla, the summer capital of British India and current capital of the state of Himachal Pradesh. This will take more than five hours over a mere 60 miles, with an arrival time of 17:20. It's said to be one of the most spectacular rides in India – some say, the entire world.

Litter is strewn across the platform, mainly heaps of fast-food packages as well as an occasional pile of papers, as though someone's suitcase has exploded. Porter prices are listed on a wall. Hauling a 40 kg bag would cost 60 rupees (about 60p), while 'carriage of sick person on a stretcher' is 120 rupees (£1.20). I step past a dog sleeping in a patch of sunlight, oblivious to the hurly-burly all around. Further along, a man is also fast asleep, with passengers carefully avoiding his head and outstretched arms, but otherwise paying no attention to him whatsoever.

And so I board the express train to Kalka. As I am to take only three trains in India – the two up to Shimla and an overnight sleeper back – I've decided to do it in comfort. A first-class ticket, bought in advance, to Kalka in an air-conditioned carriage is £12.55 – hardly a maharajah's ransom. I settle into a turquoise seat with a red-yellow-and-lilac swirly 1980s style pattern. The windows have aquamarine shades that have been pulled down a third of the way, allowing a view but blocking the sunshine. The air conditioning is strong. People have plugged electronic devices into sockets halfway up the carriage walls, making it look as though we are in a high-tech mobile unit of some kind (although cartoons and soaps flash up on screens).

I am sitting next to a polite teenager who introduces herself as Visha and who is travelling with her mother to stay with grandparents in the cooler climate of the Himalayan foothills during the summer.

Copies of *The Sunday Guardian*, *The Sunday Times* and *The Hindustan Times* are distributed to each passenger who wants one. I read an article in *The Sunday Guardian* about a big clear-up under way at New Delhi station. Cleaning squads have been introduced in an attempt to ensure the removal of the 12 tonnes of garbage estimated to be produced each day in the station. Meanwhile, waiting rooms free of 'paan-spits' have been established; paan-spits are the buckets for the red-coloured spit produced by those who chew areca nuts. The station is one of the busiest in the country, handling more than 500,000 passengers on 350 trains each weekday, I learn; as this is a Sunday it is much quieter than usual. The cleaning blitz on the station is part of a nationwide campaign launched by Prime Minister Narendra Modi to create a 'Clean India' by 2 October 2019, to mark the 150th anniversary of Gandhi's birth.

'Cleaner?' says my neighbour, who has noticed me reading the story. Visha makes no further comment, arches a doubtful eyebrow (she clearly does not consider New Delhi station to be in the slightest bit cleaner), and puts on some earphones to listen to tinny pop music with a Bollywood beat. Just about everyone is wired up some way or other.

We head off, seats facing backwards, in the direction of Kalka. A welcome announcement is made in English, highlighting the rule that 'no smoking is permitted *ever* in the washrooms'. A pot-bellied ticket inspector with gold-striped epaulettes, an Indian Railways badge, a clipboard and a bushy moustache checks our tickets.

My neighbour on the other side of the aisle places three mobile phones neatly on the table before him, looks at them to make sure they are just so, then picks up one and starts playing a computer game. He also has a moustache, and is wearing a tent-like lime-green polo shirt. He is so large that his neighbour in the seat beyond is hard to make out. All that is visible is part of a turban that dips forward now and then as a hand reaches for a teacup next to a flask. It is as though the bulbous lime-green belly has sprouted a tea drinking claw.

This is the set-up in FIRST AC CHAIR CAR, which is how the carriage is billed on the outside. We are on a Shatabdi Express, a class of fast train that runs during the day in India. 'Shatabdi' means 'century' in Hindi; the name was given to commemorate the centenary of the birth of India's first prime minister, Jawaharlal Nehru, in 1989.

Indian trains are complicated. I know this because even experts on Indian railways admit as much. 'The Indian rail system is one of the most complex in the world,' says the Indian Railway Secrets website. Other than Shatabdi Express trains, the website goes on to explain, there are also Rajdhani Express trains. These travel long distances and go overnight, with sleeper carriages; I am to return in one of these to New Delhi. Then there is the Duronto Express, the fastest of all train classes in India, with the most expensive tickets. This one has an average speed of 82 mph and takes 16 hours 20 minutes between Delhi and Kolkata (formerly Calcutta), 28 hours 20 minutes between Delhi and Chennai (formerly Madras), 29 hours between Kolkata and Bengaluru (formerly Bangalore), or a whopping 44 hours from Delhi to Kerala.

Add to this, Garib Rath trains (with air conditioning but cheaper than Shatabdi or Rajdhani), Jan Shatabdi trains (cheaper still than Shatabdi but without air conditioning), Sampark Kranti Express trains (a sleeper service with air conditioning that connects the regions to the capital), Superfast Express/Mail trains (which travel long distances at an average speed of 55 mph), regular Express trains (which make more stops than Superfast Express trains, so are slower), normal passenger trains, metros and monorails... and you can begin to appreciate just how complex Indian trains are. Mix in the various different classes of travel, always differentiated by whether air conditioning is offered or not, plus whether carriages are sleepers, and you begin to lose yourself in a world of Indian train nuances that can only, you imagine, be properly understood by the master controller of Indian Railways, tucked away in his no doubt air-conditioned office, somewhere in the depths of New Delhi.

This is what Indian trains are all about though, as I am quickly discovering: the details.

A layer of caramel-coloured pollution hangs over the edge of New Delhi as we roll northwards; nothing like as thick as the fug in China. Kids rest on a crumbling wall next to breezeblock buildings, idly watching us pass. These structures are covered in creepers, as though nature is on the point of taking over the suburbs. In sections between the low-level houses, yards full of rubbish compete with the spread of vegetation. A shirtless man on a rooftop stops repairing an aerial to watch our Shatabdi Express. Cows munch on weeds by the edge of the track. Ramshackle rickshaw depots lead to dusty school playing grounds, then a shanty town of corrugated-roof houses and a wasteland piled high with rubbish heaps that look like sand dunes in a desert, if you squint your eyes.

Everywhere there are people: hanging out washing, scolding children, striding towards corner shops, gossiping, leaning against trees, scooping food from bowls, lying flat out, fastening bags, washing clothes, placing towels on heads (for protection against the sun), squatting cross-legged in doorways, gesticulating, pontificating, arguing, smiling, waving, gazing, letting time slip by. The unimaginative and soulless, grand-scale town planning of China of my last journey has gone, replaced by a cornucopia of vibrant life. Folk are getting on with matters, down by the tracks.

After the city, the countryside is parched. Termite mounds rise from patches of jungle, looking like ancient monuments to some secretive ant-God (perhaps). Buffalo drag ploughs across fields. Steam billows from the cooling tower of a power station.

An attendant wearing a burgundy shirt and a pinstripe waistcoat brings tea and a breakfast tray. This is an event. Like the 'arm with the turban', I am given a red flask of hot water and a cup with a teabag. Visha declines hers and watches me as I pour the hot water and drink the tea black (I don't like 'creamer' sachets).

'That is very unusual,' she comments. 'No sugar either. Unusual.' She returns her concentration to her music.

Breakfast consists of two slices of bread, a jam 'blister pack', a 'butter chiplet' [sic] and a 'tomato souce sachet' [sic]. The quantities of each are written on a paper menu on the tray, so that you are able to query the allocation of one slice of bread, should such a travesty ever befall you, when in fact you know that you ought to be allotted two. Creative flair has been permitted on the packaging of the bread: *Hearty brown bread! The original taste of brown bread! Egyptians were the first to add yeast to bread transforming flat bread to something lighter – around 10,000 BC man first started eating a crude form of flat bread, a baked combination of flour and bread*. Meanwhile, the ketchup is marked *enhance your taste ketchup*, and the sugar is referred to as *superfine sugar*. Only the best in FIRST AC CHAIR CAR. I eat the butter chiplets. They taste like buttery lukewarm hot dogs (so I add a bit of tomato souce).

I discover from the attendant, who comes to clear the trays, that the train has 15 carriages, 13 of which are second class (with 78 seats each) and two of which are first (with 50 seats). The train is 25 years old, he says. In a fit of rail enthusiasm, I ask him what type of locomotive powers the train.

'Oh no,' he replies, looking at me askance. He doesn't know the answer.

At this, the man with the lime-green polo shirt introduces himself as Rakesh Wason. He is a 'wholesaler of ladies' fashion' who has been visiting Delhi from his home town of Chandigarh 'for business purposes'. He tells me that the Indian economy is 'a bit up-down, up-down' and that he likes cricket. Then he shows me a picture on his phone. It's of Rakesh with a policeman in Manchester, where he visited relatives before going on to London to watch events at the 2012 Olympics. Another shot is of him standing next to a Network Rail sign, and another by a Virgin train. Without much difficulty, I seem to have unearthed an Indian rail enthusiast.

'Virgin was very good,' he says. 'I prefer to go business class. On a Saturday, if you want to upgrade it is just £15.' He says this as though he is letting me in on a secret. 'I paid £30 for the two of us and had the free coffee and snacks.'

Mr Wason is a fan of Brighton, not so sure about Birmingham, and loves Madame Tussauds: 'The Queen, Margaret Thatcher, Obama, Benazir Bhutto, Indira Gandhi: very good!'

Adopting his conspiratorial style once more, he advises me to go to Madame Tussauds to see the waxworks for myself. As he is doing so, the turban beyond his belly pokes outwards, like a hermit crab emerging from its shell. It is attached to the head of a thin, bearded man with a broad smile. He gives me his card. His name is Professor J. P. S. Sawhney, a cardiologist from Delhi. He too is a rail enthusiast – they seem to be everywhere.

'Trains!' he says, leaning forwards so he can see me. 'Switzerland has the best trains. Stockholm to Oslo: this was also a very good experience. Picturesque, beautiful place. US: trains are not very good. The quality is poor. In India there is the *Palace on Wheels*, you know.'

The *Palace on Wheels* makes up yet another category of Indian trains: using plush old-fashioned carriages of the sort once popular with the maharajas of Indian royalty. I've decided to give the service a miss as it seems too touristy.

Professor Sawhney and Mr Wason say that they always try to travel first class on Shatabdi trains.

'I was going to fly this time, but there were no seats,' says Professor Sawhney. 'There were no seats on this train either. So I called a patient at the Ministry of Railways. I was then confirmed a ticket. My client prepared this.'

Mr Wason had been in a similar situation; however, he found a seat via a different method: 'I had to pay double. Today is my wife's birthday, so I had to go urgently.'

Professor Sawhney surprises me: 'The Dalai Lama is my patient.' Shimla is close to Dharamshala, where the Dalai Lama lives in exile from Tibet, and I'm planning to see the mountain-top town. 'I was with him for six days as he had a problem: one of the arteries was blocked,' the professor says. 'It was a wonderful experience. He gave me a book with his autograph.'

The professor had provided the Dalai Lama with advice on his diet, including a recommendation to eat more bananas, to which the spiritual leader had particularly taken. 'We had many talks about his teachings: truthfulness, simplicity, honesty, all those things.'

Professor Sawhney returns to health matters: 'Heart disease is the biggest killer of mankind. For the Indian population the big problem is the lack of exercise. And we are overeating, like the Americans.'

Mr Wason keeps quiet during this.

'You can live off about one quarter of what you eat. We can eat milk, meat and eggs but also take lots of fruit, vegetables and nuts: almonds, walnuts, cashew, pistachio. Soya milk: it is good. And don't use too much oil when cooking food.'

Professor Sawhney gives me the telephone number of the Dalai Lama's main doctor, Doctor Dorji, whom he believes will be able to arrange an audience with the spiritual leader; I'm intending to travel by vehicle from Shimla to Dharamshala (there are no direct trains). Then Professor Sawhney takes my pulse using a device attached to his mobile phone. I am running at 71 beats a minute. Satisfied that I am not about to drop dead, the professor retreats, crab-like, behind his neighbour's belly. I appear to have been given the all-clear by the Dalai Lama's cardiologist.

The subject of diet exhausted, Mr Wason takes over once again.

'You know, I used to be a wedding photographer,' he says, apropos of nothing. 'For seventeen years I was in that line, but it is going way down. Everyone knows how to take pictures like this. Digital cameras: who needs wedding photographers?'

He doesn't sound especially disappointed by his career change.

We are on the outskirts of Chandigarh and kids are playing cricket on a dusty pitch next to an electricity plant.

'Le Corbusier: French,' says Mr Wason. 'He created this city. One and a half million people. Very beautiful city. I went to take a look and I am still there.'

Le Corbusier was responsible for overseeing the new city in the 1950s, designing a grid pattern of streets that makes Chandigarh quite different from the chaotic labyrinthine set-up of most Indian conurbations. It is divided into 91 sectors, each assigned to four zones – A, B, C and D – which are separated by broad boulevards. In sector 17B, there's a science museum and the National Portrait Gallery, with many pictures of the country's freedom fighters against the British. Meanwhile the Nek Chand Rock Garden, a space filled with eye-catching, world-famous sculptures by the artist Nek Chand, is in sector 1 in the city centre.

It all sounds a bit *Truman Show*. The original architect for the city was a less rigid, more relaxed Pole named Matthew Nowicki. Sadly, he died in a plane crash before his plans could be put into motion. This was when Corbusier stepped in, creating his science-fiction-like, futuristic vision.

Mr Wason is full of praise for the city: 'So clean, so well ordered, so easy to get around.'

We pull into Chandigarh station. Mr Wason and Professor Sawhney disembark. Mr Wason insists on taking my picture with my camera, so he can show off his photography skills. I join him on the platform. He drops down on one knee and fiddles expertly with the zoom lens, while telling me where to stand. We all shake hands, and then I return to my seat in the carriage and the train moves on, passing an enigmatic, guru-like man in a blue robe, matching turban and long white beard. He smiles at the train, looking as though he's stepped out of the pages of a J. R. R. Tolkien book.

Then we travel through jungle and the train starts to climb. The foothills of the Himalayas begin here.

I go for a wander. There are two toilet choices: 'TOILET WESTERN STYLE' or 'TOILET INDIAN STYLE' (a hole in the floor). Neither is exactly wonderful. The second-class carriages seem to differ mainly in that they have three seats on one side of the aisle and two on the other, thus making them more cramped than first class, which has two seats on either side.

I return to FIRST AC CHAIR CAR and glance through the papers. They're packed with mischief. *The Sunday Guardian* shows a picture of Prime Minister Modi and China's President Xi Jinping taking a selfie in Beijing. Modi, who is on an official visit, has used his phone and appears to have taken President Xi Jinping by surprise. The Indian prime minister is said to be a fan of selfies, and this is the first time anyone has dared to try the stunt on the Chinese president. Another article describes a father-and-son team from Patiala who have just built a termite-proof wooden 'wonder car'. The Chennai Super Kings cricket team has 'demolished' Kings XI Punjab in a 'clinical performance'. This report is next to a 'WAG of the Week' picture of a bikini-wearing girlfriend of one of the players. The front page of *The Sunday Times* runs a story headlined: *ALCOHOL CONSUMPTION IN INDIA UP 55% IN 20 YEARS.* During this period, only the Russians and Estonians have increased their drinking more, according to the Organisation for Economic Cooperation and Development.

That's one of the things about being on trains: you have the time to read bits and bobs, to patch together an understanding of a place through its incidentals (and India's English-language newspapers are overflowing with those).

I close my eyes and feel the train rising further still. I doze for a while, and when I wake we are entering a city. We are about to arrive in Kalka.

Footplate ride in the Himalayas
Kalka to Shimla

So what type of train brought me to Kalka? What type of loco? I take a snap of the front of the train at Kalka station, in true rail-enthusiast style. By now, I have no shame. It is a WAP-7 30248. The body is a mishmash of green and blue colours with rusty streaks and a heavy grille on the front window. I have no idea what the numbers mean and I cannot find the driver, though I later check on the internet and discover that *someone has posted a film of this very train on YouTube*.

Unbelievable.

It is, if Mr Akshay Gupta is to be trusted, a Duronto Express locomotive. So, although we were on a Shatabdi Express train, we were being pulled by a Duronto Express loco. Simple. At the time I take a look, Mr Gupta's 31-second YouTube film has attracted almost 1,000 views.

There are clearly a fair few Indian trainspotters out there.

I cross a platform and come to a train that is internationally renowned. New Delhi–Kalka was the warm-up for the main act: Kalka–Shimla. This is a narrow-gauge train with a two-tone red-and-pale-yellow livery, and a bustle of passengers attempting to board. I go to the front to take another picture – I might as well try to have one of each ride, and this one is especially photogenic. It is, after all, nicknamed 'the Toy Train'.

As I do so, I meet Peter Jones, a lanky, local-government licensing manager from Bromham in Bedfordshire. Like me, he has come to India to ride this train. Like me, he is also capturing a few images on camera.

'Oh, I used to be one,' Peter says when I ask if he's a trainspotter. 'When I was sixteen, seventeen, eighteen. Now I just like trains. We still regularly go on steam and diesel outings. Annually.'

Peter goes on to explain that he was brought up close to a famous scrapyard for steam trains and carriages in South Wales: the Barry scrapyard, run by the Woodham brothers. This was when his interest in trains began. The Woodhams had contracts with British Rail to dispose of withdrawn carriages and steam locomotives, and in the 1960s they had collected so many steam locos that enthusiasts would come from far and wide to see them. As the scrap metal from carriages was easier to extract – and as there were many more carriages than locos – the Woodhams had concentrated on carriages first, leaving the locos for later. This is where the rail enthusiasts stepped in. While on their train pilgrimages to Barry, many visiting enthusiasts decided to buy the locomotives with the aim of restoring them to working order, so the Barry scrapyard is important in trainspotter circles.

Chance encounters can lead to chance train knowledge.

Peter is in another carriage. Mine is packed to the rafters with passengers, luggage and parcels. I'm in second class on the *Himalayan Queen Express*; there is no first class on this service, although there is on other Kalka–Shimla trains. I'm on a narrow, hard, faux-leather bench-seat, sitting next to a man with glasses and a pale-blue shirt with a pen poking out of a pocket.

Opposite me a twenty-something American couple are whispering to one another and eating curry with rice from plastic trays that have been handed to them through the window as we wait for departure. The American woman has dyed orange-red hair and wears large spectacles, while her companion sports a stubbly beard and is in a baseball cap with *CAL* on it. They look 'alternative'. We are the only westerners in the carriage, which is enclosed so you cannot walk into connecting carriages.

With a blast of a horn, we move off, the carriage swaying and creaking. We ease past a railway crossing where a skinny man is in charge of a downtrodden camel laden with baggage. Cows with ribs like staircase rails poke about in rubbish in a gutter. Battered old corrugated-iron buildings, roofs secured with stones, line the track. They've got a house-of-cards look, as though the slightest wind might bring them down. We enter thick, tunnel-like jungle that opens out now and then to allow glimpses of hillside with purple jacaranda trees. This train begins at 640 metres and rises to 2,060 metres through the Shivalik Mountains, passing through precisely 102 tunnels.

My neighbour introduces himself. His name is Jyotirmoy Dutta, aged 40, a 'central-government supervisor, securities department' from Kolkata. He has very little English but communicates the basics as the train slides out of the jungle back to a neighbourhood of rundown housing.

'This is slum area,' he says, then shuts up. He seems pleased to have made an acquaintance; he's already given me his email and phone number, should I ever visit Kolkata and be in need of assistance. He proceeds to gaze out of the window.

The couple opposite have been listening to our stilted encounter. They introduce themselves as Aimee and Ben from San Francisco. She works for a tenants' rights group, while he is a lawyer.

'It's all about the balance of power,' says Aimee. 'We need to shift it in favour of tenants. There have been two hundred per cent rent increases. Displacement. Wealthy foreigners are coming from out of town. Chinese.' Combined with the wealth generated by some Silicon Valley companies, it is putting pressure on the renting residents of San Francisco.

They are about to embark on a nine day trek through the Spiti Valley. They had also been on the New Delhi–Kalka train. 'It's a totally different experience to the US. Really great. We were surprised that we were fed,' says Ben. 'In the US there's a car culture. Sure, there's a train infrastructure but it's mainly for freight. They're slow. It's an eight-hour drive from LA to San Francisco, or a fifteen-hour train. So nobody takes the trains.'

They had bought their curries by mistake, after someone on the platform asked them if they were having food on board; they had thought it was part of the service. 'We didn't mind,' says Ben. 'We just said, "yeah".' The meals had cost them 300 rupees (£2.70).

Ben begins to talk about English football (he supports Reading FC) and cricket, which he enjoys for its 'relaxed nature: you don't have to pay attention the whole time, you can have it on in the background – the commentators are a refreshing change from Americans shouting and yelling'. I don't think I've ever met an American cricket fan before.

With Ben discussing goals scored by John Salako and saves made by Brad Friedel, the scenery becomes increasingly dramatic as we ascend, cutting through cedar forests and breaking into open patches with clear views across the Himalayan foothills. It's the most beautiful part of the ride yet, with mist hanging on the horizon and shafts of sunlight filtering through, turning the landscape vivid green. All eyes of those still awake (several passengers are fast asleep, with the sound of gentle snores emanating across the carriage) are on the hills. Blackbirds sail high in the sky. Villages cling to mountainsides in colourful clusters of single-storey buildings. Farmers with bags balanced on heads stop to watch us pass. The train snakes upwards at such a gentle pace you could almost run alongside. On bends, it's possible to look back along the train behind; this is the best moment for pictures, and you can stick your head out of the window. At one end of the carriage a door has been left open to allow in extra air. We pause at Kumarhatti station at 1,579 metres, where there's a poster of Gandhi on a wall, before rising onwards. In places the mountain shoots down below so steeply that a few metres from the track you might tumble to a terrible death.

The Kalka–Shimla Railway was completed in 1903, and opened by Lord Curzon, the viceroy of India. There had been a dozen years of planning and building, with the tunnels being the most time-consuming aspect. Shimla – or Simla, as it was then known – had been the summer capital of British India since 1864, so this was a key project. With temperatures in pre-air-conditioning days so high, the decision had been made to move the British administration from Calcutta to the mountains, initially making use of a (slow) road that Lord Dalhousie had ordered to ease trade with Tibet. A technical report on the feasibility of a railway was conducted in 1890, with engineers keen to replicate the success of another important mountainous narrow-gauge line, completed between Darjeeling and New Jalpaiguri in 1881 (its import lying in its transportation of a much-loved commodity back in Britain: tea).

As well as the Kalka–Shimla Railway's 102 tunnels, construction also required 800 bridges and 900 curves. This was a logistical nightmare – and one part of the track involves a sad tale. Workers, overseen by a Colonel Barog, had attempted to cut a tunnel through a section of mountain, but there was a problem: the colonel had misjudged the points at which the ends – being dug simultaneously from both sides of the mountain – would meet. Humiliated by his mistake, he is said to have gone for a walk with his dog and shot first his dog and then himself. The replacement tunnel is now known as the Barog tunnel and, on the Shimla side, this is where the train stops for a short while, at Barog station, to allow passengers to buy snacks from stalls on the platform.

As we pass through the Barog tunnel, kids in the neighbouring carriage howl like wolves (as they do in all the tunnels) and the drivers blast the horn a few times. I buy a bright-yellow lentil lunch when we arrive at Barog, and somehow convince the drivers to let me join them in the cab of the train for a couple of stops.

This is my first 'footplate ride'; Charlie back in Kosovo would, I think, be quite jealous.

Being up front puts a whole new perspective on the journey. The main driver wears a blue shirt with a few buttons undone and a string vest beneath. He has a gold watch, and a smartphone pokes out of a pocket. He sits on the right. A younger man in a similar shirt is to the left. His job is to switch on the headlights in tunnels, and to sound the horn as and when he sees fit. The main driver's task is to control a lever determining acceleration. Our standard speed is 14–16 mph (22–25 kmph). I perch on a shelf-like seat behind them and watch. Apart from the main driver telling me that the fan in the cab is not working and that the locomotive was made in 2014 and is number 705, we do not exchange a word.

From the cab there's an even greater sense of the twists and turns. We rattle and squeal along. Indicators on grimy monitors show *engine rpm* and *lub oil temp*. The man on the left flicks the light switch with great show as we enter and depart a tunnel. The horn is blasted many times. There are bleeping sounds. Through the front grille peaks appear as we curve round cliff faces. The gradient of this track is one in 33.

On the floor by my feet is a curious, loop-shaped object with a metal key attached. When we stop at a station, where I get out to return to the carriage, this loop is handed to a stationmaster, whereupon the driver is given a different loop, known as a 'token'. This is a method, developed in the nineteenth century in Britain, used to ensure that trains cannot collide with one another on the single track. I have bought a book entitled *The Toy Train* by local historian Raaja Bhasin that helps explain this and other safety precautions. Bhasin describes how signals can only be altered using a key attached to each token. He goes on to say that each linesman between Kalka and Shimla is responsible for nine kilometres of track. If an obstruction such as a landslip or fallen tree is discovered, firecrackers are placed on the rails in each direction. These will explode when a train's wheels pass over them, thus warning the driver to apply the brakes.

Crackers in more than one sense perhaps, though it seems to work.

There are two principal historical points of interest at stations along the Kalka–Shimla line. The first is the Tara Devi station, where the British Central Investigation Department used to conduct much-resented checks on passenger names to monitor the movements of freedom fighters. The second is the halfway station of Solan, where we pass close to the Solan brewery. British troops stationed in India during the Raj had a taste for beer, but attempts to create breweries had failed, so beer in the mid nineteenth century had to be shipped in from the UK. The problem was that it did not always survive the long journey. This is, as Bhasin points out, why Indian Pale Ale was invented: it was a type of beer that lasted the trip better. Several further breweries were attempted in India, but the one at Solan, with the freshwater supplies from the mountains and its connection to the Kalka–Shimla train, was the breakthrough. 'When the railway line arrived in 1903, it ran right through the brewery,' says Bhasin. Cases of bottles would be sent on wagons across the country.

No trains, no beer – or, at least, not as much as was needed.

At Tara Devi, my neighbour Jyotirmoy Dutta disembarks, after tapping me on the shoulder: 'Do you mind selfie?'

He has been quiet for the journey, listening to Ben and me wittering on about the qualities of Gillingham FC's Andy Hessenthaler and an exciting 2–1 victory for Reading FC against Norwich: 'We came from behind. Then we played Cardiff and that was terrible. Alex Pearce scored an own goal and got a red card: he won't like to be reminded of that.' Ben really does know a lot about the English football league.

Jyotirmoy takes selfies with me and the Americans.

'So very good! This is best!'

He hops off the train and heads off to carry out securities department work, clinging to a backpack, a suitcase and a copy of *The Sunday Times*.

Not so long afterwards, we pull into Shimla – the end of the line.

Up in the mountains
Shimla

Some places are 'railway towns'. Crewe felt like that, of course, as it would not have existed without its railway. Shimla is another.

I am to spend three days adapting to mountain life here at Shimla, which some regard as the real centre of power during the Raj, as so many officials passed more than just the summer months in its pleasant environs. One fifth of the world's population was once governed from this out-of-the-way spot in the hills. And the railway was a crucial tie to the outside world.

Shimla station hangs on the edge of a precipice, close to the heart of the old town and facing a curve of mountain dotted with precarious-looking properties. More than 800,000 people live on the various slopes that count as Shimla, many in an incredibly packed section known as Little Shimla, where I sincerely hope there is never a major earthquake, as the consequences would be dire.

It feels like a railway town not only because trains have long provided such an important connection. It is the 'train sounds' of Shimla, which are unlike any I have heard elsewhere. Standing in the city centre, where the main government buildings are to be found, horns echo upwards across corrugated roofs and down narrow lanes. Drivers are not shy; the blasts emanate every minute or so, with trains coming and going with regularity. They have a soothing, comforting quality, accompanied by the rumble of wheels and slither of steel on the tracks. Through the thin, cool air beneath the pale-blue sky, trains are going about their business. A dash downwards from the statue of Indira Gandhi by The Ridge, the main square, and you could be at the platforms in minutes, soon heading to 'reality' down on the plains.

Just up from the station, you come to the Oberoi Cecil Hotel, a prominent structure with parts dating from the 1880s, where many Toy Train visitors have rested over the years. It is also where Rudyard Kipling took a room and wrote some of his stories, quite possibly including *The Man Who Would Be King*, which has a section describing the 'very awful' conditions on Indian third-class trains, where passengers are sometimes carted out dead in hot weather. The protagonists meet in one of these carriages and discuss the 'politics of Loaferdom, that sees things from the underside where the lath and plaster is not smoothed off', with the narrator memorably describing his new companion as 'a wanderer and vagabond like myself, but with an educated taste in whisky'.

Kipling visited each year from 1885 to 1888 during his annual leave from work on a newspaper in Lahore. This was before the Kalka–Shimla trains: 'My month's leave at Simla... was pure joy – every golden hour counted. It began in heat and discomfort, by rail and road. It ended in the cool evening, with a wood fire in one's bedroom, and the next morn – thirty more of them ahead! – the early cup of tea, the Mother who brought it in, and the long talks of us all together again. One had leisure to work, too, at whatever play-work was in one's head, and that was usually full.'

The ghosts of the railway-building British occupy these hilltops.

I'm staying at the Cecil, close to the Mall, with its promenade of little wooden shops and Scandal Point – a junction associated with a maharaja said to have had an affair with a viceroy's daughter. Viceregal Lodge, the mock-Tudor summer residence of the British viceroys, where Nehru and Gandhi came in the 1940s to negotiate Indian independence, is just round the corner.

My grandfather, Neville Chesshyre, who was brought up in a military family, came to Shimla as a child in the 1910s, and once told me that he remembered only two cars in the town: one belonging to the viceroy, the other to the commander-in-chief of the army. Now most streets, other than the Mall, which is pedestrianised, are jammed with vehicles.

My grandfather also remembered that there were coolies, four to each rickshaw. Amazingly (to me, at least, being a novice visitor to India), a sign above a shadowy doorway at Shimla station still says: *COOLIE SHELTER*. On a walk back to the station one day, I go to take a look. Surely it has been kept up as a historical curiosity to remind modern travellers of how things once were.

Before I even arrive, I realise it is nothing of the sort. On the way to the station, a hunched elderly man heaves two large bags on his back, with an ample-sized, able-bodied couple strolling a few yards behind. It is an extraordinary sight.

Down in the station I find the coolie shelter is a dimly lit room with a wooden bench along the wall and a dozen rolls of bedding next to bags of possessions. This is the home of the coolies, the porters who carry bags to hotels up the steep hill; the days of people-carrying rickshaws are long gone.

Mr Karim is tall and gaunt. He has a ramrod-straight stance and is wearing a red porter's vest and enormous trainers. He is aged 65 and has been a coolie for 40 years. I ask him if it is hard work at his age.

'No! Strong!' he says, straightening his back.

He says that the coolies are paid 50–100 rupees (about 50p–£1) for a typical load.

He clicks his heels, military style, shakes my hand, and strides to the edge of the platform. A train is arriving.

I watch Mr Karim go, then look at the old red locos at one end of the station. There's a giant turntable here so trains can be serviced at one spot, then spun round and returned to sidings. Monkeys dance along electricity wires and on the station roof (do not try to eat anything in the open at Shimla station: the monkeys will have it). I poke my head into the empty *REFRESHMENT ROOM (VEG)* and regard two half-asleep officials in the peculiarly named *ELECTRIC COMPLAINT ROOM* (perhaps for complaints sent by email) next to the quite separate *COMPLAINT-CUM-SUGGESTION ROOM*. Then I return up the hill to the comforts of the Oberoi Cecil Hotel.

Meeting the colonel
Dharamshala, and Pathankot Cantt to New Delhi

The temples of train-less Dharamshala are splendid: a riot of gold, pink, saffron and blue; thick with incense; humming with intonation; busy with pilgrims in flip-flops and cross-legged burgundy-robed monks... Though Dr Dorji and the Office of His Holiness are unable to arrange an audience with the Dalai Lama. He has, apparently, 'taken to his room'.

On the way there, however, I lay eyes on another legendary name. While eating lunch on the terrace of Wildflower Hall, just outside Shimla, I happen to sit two tables from Sonia Gandhi, wife of the former prime minister Rajiv Gandhi (who was assassinated in 1991), and her daughter Priyanka. She is, I gather from the hotel manager, overseeing the interior design of a nearby Himalayan home for Priyanka and the only snatch of conversation I make out is: 'The televisions: we can't get them to work, you know.' She's talking to someone who appears to be a foreman on the project. She has a moon-like forehead and upright stature, and is dressed in a flowing milk-coloured sari.

After this brush with Indian 'royalty' – and my tranquil time in the hills (where you do not have to be Buddhist to appreciate the deep spirituality of the setting) – I go to Pathankot Cantt, the closest main station to Dharamshala for New Delhi, to catch the sleeper train back to the capital. It is to leave at 21:23 and arrive at 05:00.

I sit on a bench on a crowded platform near motorbikes wrapped in sacks of straw for protection during transportation and a pile of old-fashioned traveller's chests. Birdsong comes from the rafters. Mosquitoes buzz by my ankles. A tea-seller shambles up and down calling out: 'Chai! Chai!'

A filthy red, white and blue train comes: the Rajdhani Express to New Delhi from Jammu. I board and enter the first-class sleeper carriage. The fare for this overnight journey is £26. The average annual income in India is about £400. I'm blowing a month's salary.

In my cabin, which has a single bunk, I meet Mr Malhodra. He is a retired colonel from the Indian army, 'seventy-plus' and, when I ask his first name, he replies, 'Is it not enough that I give you my last name?'

He is lying on the bottom berth, tucked beneath a wine-red blanket, next to a tattered wine-red curtain. He has a frog like face and a habit of shaking his head from side to side. He is wearing khaki pyjamas (perhaps they are old army issue). He is coming from Jammu, where he visited the Hindu shrine of Shri Mata Vaishno Devi on a four-day pilgrimage. His suitcase is chained to a loop – placed there for this purpose – beneath his bed. He has been taking trains since 1964.

'Steam engines, I remember,' he says. 'They look nice, but speed slow. A lot of smoke.'

A tray of food is delivered to our door by an assistant. It's for me: a tray of vegetable curry with rice and roti bread. As I eat, Mr Malhodra talks.

He likes croquet, dislikes cricket, can bear volleyball and considers the train food to be 'too heavy'. He is a man of definite opinions. The narrow-gauge train in Darjeeling has 'scenic views and tea gardens en route: very nice'. He has a daughter who works as a physiotherapist and lives in Tennessee, where he once visited: 'I didn't like the place much. East or west, home is best. I don't like leaving my house.'

He shows me the locks on his briefcase, as if to ensure that I know that the briefcase is locked. He tells me I may turn on the light on my top bunk, if I like, during the night. My food tray is collected and Mr Malhodra indicates that I should go to sleep.

So I climb to my bunk and listen to a brief phone conversation Mr Malhodra has with his wife: 'Journalist from London. He took my interview.'

I fall asleep to the rumble of the engine. We are right next to the locomotive. Horns blow. Fittings creak. The Indian night slips by.

There you have Indian trains: I love them. You meet a lot of people, and they take you places.

For the sake of good housekeeping, the locomotive on the Rajdhani Express was Swiss built, of indeterminate age, with a top speed of 110 kmph and 'easy, easy' to drive (I know this as I asked Sunil Tigga, the driver, at New Delhi station). It was also a WAP-7 30294. There are many YouTube films of this one: it appears to be quite legendary.

One last tip-off: any rail enthusiast must visit the National Rail Museum in New Delhi. It is a shrine to old steam locos, with enough to see to keep even the most knowledgeable Boocock happy.

Indian Railways' nickname is 'Lifeline of the Nation'. Go to India and you'll soon find out why: the chaos yet the order, the characters, the clamour, the grime, the joy taken in a simple ride.

It was the same – with a twist – for Mark Twain on a journey from Calcutta to Lucknow in 1895, as he describes in his travelogue *Following the Equator*: 'The train stopped at every village; for no purpose connected with business, apparently. We put out nothing, we took aboard nothing. The train bands stepped ashore and gossiped with friends for a quarter of an hour, then pulled out and repeated this at the succeeding villages. We had thirty-five miles to go and six hours to do it in, but it was plain that we were not going to make it. It was then that the English officers said it was now necessary to turn this gravel train into an express. So they gave the engine-driver a rupee and told him to fly. It was a simple remedy. After that we made ninety miles an hour.'

Indian trains do seem to go by their own rules.

Now I'm heading almost due south, about 2,000 miles, to a nation with train lines just as colourful, offering an important new lifeline to a place that is beginning to open up to the world.

SRI LANKA: ON THE REUNIFICATION EXPRESS

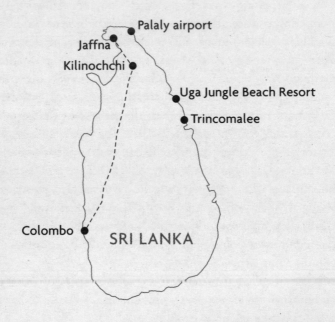

TRAINS, POLITICS AND trouble seem to attract one another. Back in Kosovo, the line to Serbia remains shut, while memories of tracks being used to deport hundreds of thousands of ethnic Albanians are still strong. In China, where the 1911 'railway crisis' led to the overthrow of the Last Emperor, current schemes to connect Beijing to Hong Kong by bullet train, as well as the already-completed fast link to Tibet, have taken on powerful political meaning. In India, British imperial rule was, as Gandhi observed, underpinned by the laying of tracks; while today's trains into Pakistan and Bangladesh are journeys that continue to cover sensitive ground (though I did not feel any of those tensions on my 'toy train' to Shimla).

In Europe, railways have long been intertwined with both politics and nationalism. Some believe that Belgium and Germany might have fallen apart during crucial periods of the nineteenth century were it not for trains. Bismarck, the first chancellor of Germany, is known to have constructed tracks in the hope of binding his vast country and creating a sense of national unity. In Britain, railways were key to the success of industrialisation, creating the wealth to fuel the British Empire and shaping the Victorian era. More recently, the entrance to the Channel Tunnel in Calais has witnessed flare-ups between security guards and hopeful immigrants to Britain fleeing unstable countries, many trying to sneak on to trains, while the much debated project to construct a high-speed line from London to Birmingham through the picturesque countryside of the Chilterns has politicians of all colours up in arms.

Where there are trains, there are usually stories behind trains – and most of the time they're contentious.

In Sri Lanka it's no exception.

'This is a time of hope and change'
Colombo to Jaffna

It is 05:15 at Fort station in Colombo. The sodium lit streets of Sri Lanka's capital are quiet on the way in by taxi, though many of the city's autorickshaws – and their catchy (if sometimes gloomy) slogans – are already on the move: *Peace comes from within... Who flies not high, falls not low... Crazing and desire will ruin your life.* And my favourite: *Don't let them chang you* [sic].

In the humid early-morning semi-darkness outside the station my attention is caught by a flash of gold near the whitewashed facade of the station's entrance. This comes from a statue of Colonel Henry Steel Olcott, an American from New Jersey who founded the Colombo Buddhist Theosophical Society in the nineteenth century. A fresh garland of flowers hangs round his neck. Olcott, a military officer and journalist, is a much-revered figure in Sri Lanka for his efforts to safeguard the rights of Buddhists during the time of British colonial rule, says a plaque. The religion was seen as an important expression of the country's identity during the period of British control from 1815 to 1948, when independence was granted. This statue, in its prominent spot outside Colombo's main station, seems to be a symbol of defiance to the old colonialists.

A little bit of politics... and I haven't even stepped on my train.

In the narrow ticket hall a handful of bronzed backpackers mill about. They're blond and in their twenties; possibly Scandinavian. Two of the men wear sarongs. They seem to be confused about their tickets to Kandy – and they do not appear to be rail enthusiasts. Male trainspotters, in my albeit limited experience, do not generally wear skirts.

On my platform, there are no westerners, though the cramped space is crammed with people and bags. A colourful kiosk sells sweets and papers. A little doorway opens to the neon-lit Cafeteria Smak, which promises to be 'full of natural goodness'. A sleepy-eyed Railway Protection Force officer, with a blue peaked cap, olive uniform and polished shoes, stands by the empty track. A leather belt cuts into his prodigious waistline, and a metal chain hangs in a loop from a button of his shirt, disappearing into a pocket. Perhaps it is connected to a watch or a whistle.

He speaks some English.

'Are the trains generally on time?' I ask.

'No,' he says.

'Is this train on time?'

'I don't know,' he says.

At least he gives a straight answer.

I am about to catch a train northwards to Jaffna, a distance of about 250 miles. Until a few months before my visit, this had not been possible. The line between Colombo and Jaffna had been closed for 24 years due to the troubles that beset the Indian Ocean nation during its bloody 26-year civil war, which ended in 2009. Fighting between the Tamil Tigers and the Sri Lankan Army had long made the journey unsafe. Rebels had blown up a train in 1985, killing 12 civilians and 22 soldiers, wounding 44 others. The service kept on for a while but was closed indefinitely in 1990.

Now, after repairs to the tracks since the fighting stopped, the trains are back – an important symbolic moment in Sri Lanka as the city of Jaffna is the cultural and spiritual centre of the country's Tamil population. When the inaugural train rolled into Jaffna station in October 2014, it was accompanied by the then president Mahinda Rajapaksa amid great fanfare: drumming, piping, singing and dancing. Rajapaksa had joined the train for the final 27 miles of its journey. Many regarded the 'new' railway as a moment when the Tamil-majority north and the Sinhalese-majority south literally came together, drawing a line beneath the troubles of the past. This is also seen as a pivotal time for developing tourism in the north, bringing this part of Sri Lanka to the wider world.

Quite a lot of politics... and I still haven't stepped on my train.

I ask the officer what he thinks of it all.

'Tamil people come here and Sinhalese people go there,' he says. 'They transport their things. This is very useful, in fact.'

This seems a fair enough analysis. I thank him and go over to Cafeteria Smak, where I queue to buy a couple of 'fish buns', unsure exactly what they are. These are handed to me in a paper bag and feel quite light.

Back on the platform, the train has arrived. It is pale blue, shiny, long and has a snub-shaped nose. Chaos has broken out with everyone rushing to board. I find seat number 21 in Carriage A and settle down to watch the madness calm down outside and start up again within the train. I seem to be amid a dozen or so involved in an early-morning family party of some sort. There are many plastic boxes with flatbreads and curry smells. Food is soon being consumed on red plastic plates. Flasks of tea and bottles of fruit juice are handed around. This is to continue for most of the 6 hour 10 minute journey. It is my happiest train yet, and we haven't even left the station.

The train departs at 05:55, only five minutes late, passing the office of both the Stationmaster (Operating) and the Chief Stationmaster (Administrative). My guess is that the chief doesn't have to get his hands too operationally dirty dealing with the public – that's why he's got the top job, sitting in his office, possibly keeping up to date with the latest cricket scores. Just about every single notice in Fort station is sponsored by a company named Fashion Bug, including the exit and toilet signs. *GENTS WAITING ROOM. FASHION BUG, KEEP THE TRAIN STATION CLEAN: FASHION BUG, TICKETS TO KANDY: FASHION BUG*. One way or another, the words 'Fashion Bug' seem to seep into your brain.

For those keen to know, the train is a Sri Lanka Railways Class S12; a diesel multiple unit, which I recall from my train schooling in Kosovo means that the engines are under the carriages as well as in the locomotive. This one was built in China in 2012 (I managed to get a snap of the number at the front and have been able to look it up on the internet via my mobile phone). The service is named the *Yal Devi*, which is Tamil for *Queen of Jaffna*.

There's no harm in checking out these things, I suppose.

My seat is in a first-class air-conditioned carriage and cost 1,500 rupees (£7.20). We are soon trundling out of Fort station – built by the British in 1877, though the first trains in Sri Lanka came in 1864 – and humming and faintly rocking across a metal-framed bridge above a wide, muddy river. A kindly, grey-haired man wearing a white uniform with epaulettes checks the tickets. Beyond the bridge, thick jungle encloses the tracks, with fronds and leaves scraping against the windows. It's almost as though the train has yet to establish its right of way.

The jungle opens onto a shanty town of decrepit breeze-block buildings with corrugated roofs. Some do not even have roofs; instead tarpaulins have been hoisted above, held down with old bricks or whatever the owners could lay their hands on. Just as in India, poverty appears to be taken for granted. Women hang washing on lines not far from great mounds of decomposing litter. Yet within a minute or so of such scenes, a modern neighbourhood emerges with a Porsche showroom and smart apartments. A commuter train heading to Fort station chugs by, the doors left open on each side and many faces peering out. A Buddhist temple flashes past: red, gold and green, with curving columns and figurines. At just about every level crossing, dozens of mopeds and autorickshaws are waiting – and at most, there are smaller Buddhist shrines.

The sense of bustle and beaver-like commerce is strong. According to the World Bank, Sri Lanka is striving to become an 'upper middle-income country'. The economists' latest findings show that the GDP per capita is £2,147 (or £179 a month). This is up from £564 in 2002 (or £47 a month). So financial matters appear to be heading in the right direction, although the World Bank also points out that 36 per cent of the population is living in poverty, with the highest numbers in the former Tamil Tiger conflict zones in the north and east.

From the train tracks, a series of images begins to accumulate: piles of smouldering rubbish, mango trees heavy with fruit, herons by a riverbank, a man asleep in his autorickshaw at a station, lakes with lotus lilies, thick fog above a banana plantation, a plain of paddy fields, a stray dog at a siding, thin white birds perched on fat brown cows (pecking and picking out ticks), shiny Honda motorbike showrooms, impenetrable-looking jungle, peach-coloured clouds, clattering bridges, schoolkids in bright white uniforms... The scenery shifts and mutates as the *Queen of Jaffna* rolls on.

Before arriving in India, in 1896 Mark Twain visited Sri Lanka, or Ceylon as it was known during British rule. The purpose of his grand world tour, involving so many early train journeys and described in *Following the Equator*, was to raise cash by giving paid talks along the way and publishing his travelogue at the end. The creator of Huckleberry Finn, who first worked as a printer after leaving school, had invested US$300,000 in a typesetting machine – the Paige Compositor – that was supposed to revolutionise printing. It did not. It was far too fiddly. Only two were ever made and it was a devastating financial blow for the author. Twain's US$300,000 is about US$8,000,000 in today's money, and was just about all he had.

I have brought a copy of *Following the Equator*, which I'd begun in India, with me and it makes a good 'train read'. On his ship from Sydney to Sri Lanka, Twain describes enjoying watching cricket being played on deck: 'They enclose the promenade deck with nettings and keep the ball from flying overboard, and the sport goes very well, and is properly violent and exciting.' When he arrives in Colombo for a short stopover before a change of vessel onwards to Bombay, he is struck by how 'utterly Oriental' the country is with its tropical vegetation, 'proper deadly snakes, and fierce beasts of prey, and the wild elephant and the monkey'. It is unclear whether Twain takes to Sri Lanka's train tracks, although on one journey outside of Colombo he is impressed by the colours of peoples' clothing: '... a splendid green, a splendid blue, a splendid yellow, a splendid purple, a splendid ruby, deep and rich... [a] radiant panorama, that wilderness of rich colour, that incomparable dissolving-view of harmonious tints'. He is ashamed to be dressed so boringly himself and he is also shocked to see some children from a missionary school dressed primly and piously in clothes reminiscent of a 'summer Sunday in an English or American village'.

The bright white uniforms of the children I see all these years on are perhaps not quite so prim and pious, but they strike a chord with his words. And it is a little sad to imagine Samuel Clemens, as Twain was born, traipsing about in these parts to see the sights at Galle Face – in his early sixties, with a shock of grey hair, bushy eyebrows and moustache   jotting down his observations, while dwelling on the dreadful typesetting machine that had him chasing round the globe to claw back a few bucks.

I eat my fish buns; the ongoing curry fest has made me hungry. Fish buns consist of soft, white, triangular-shaped bread in the centre of which a spicy potato and fish concoction is to be found. They are tasty and I could see them catching on back home. Afterwards, I take a walk along the carriages. I count seven including a dining carriage with an empty kiosk and no food for sale. It seems the idea is that passengers bring their own meals here to eat at the tables, although the whole carriage is deserted when I pass through. Second class is little different to first, but minus the air conditioning. Someone in second is playing music on an electronic device. The refrain goes: 'Everybody jump now! Everybody dance now! Everybody jump now! Whoa, whoa, whoa!'

Not far away are two westerners, the only others on the train. I ask if they are tourists going to Jaffna. They are not. They work for Unicef, the intergovernmental organisation that acts on behalf of children. Their office is in Kilinochchi, about 40 miles south-east of Jaffna, where they will be disembarking. Una heads up Unicef in Sri Lanka, while her colleague Christian is chief of education.

Unicef has a team of 65 in Sri Lanka and a budget of US$12 million; 25 per cent of children are 'malnourished or undernourished'; the maternity mortality rate is 3.4 per 1,000 births; and in the late 1990s more than 30,000 children were 'involved in sex favours, but it's cleared up now' – all of which is relayed to me at speed by Una. She is from Kilkenny in Ireland and is dressed in a colourful blouse that would have had Mark Twain's approval, with a butterfly brooch attached. She has glasses, short hair in a neat side parting and a wry sense of humour. Christian wears a white shirt and designer stubble. He is from Germany, and says little. They've been to Colombo to meet the education and health ministers as they want to get various programmes – fittingly for our setting – 'back on track'.

Sri Lanka has a new government headed by President Maithripala Sirisena, a liberal-leaning politician who has replaced former president Rajapaksa, who was in power for ten years from 2005. Rajapaksa is accused by Sirisena of having overseen widespread corruption during his time in office. International human-rights groups also say that Rajapaksa gave the go-ahead to the indiscriminate shelling of Tamil civilians at the end of the civil war, allowed the torture of imprisoned Tamil Tigers and permitted the widespread harassment – and probably worse – of journalists critical of his rule. One of the biggest cases involves Prageeth Eknaligoda, a prominent writer and cartoonist who contributed to an anti-government website. He went missing in mysterious circumstances in 2010, and no one has heard of him since.

This is what I know already. But before Una, Christian and I move on to politics, we keep the conversation to trains.

'What do you think of the *Queen of Jaffna*?'

'Very useful,' says Una. 'We used to go by road and it took ten hours. By train it's five hours. The roads are not bad, but they have heavy traffic.'

However, she has a complaint: 'The toilets are clean here, but there are cockroaches, as I have just witnessed.'

Una has a precise, no-nonsense manner. She has worked in Sri Lanka for 18 months.

'Where were you posted before?'

'Panama and West Africa: Togo and Sierra Leone. Thirteen years in West Africa,' she says.

West Africa is in the middle of the Ebola crisis at the time of my visit. 'Are you glad you're in Sri Lanka now?'

'Oh no, I wish I was out there to help,' she says.

We pass a field of brown cows, each and every one with a small white bird on its back, poking about for insects. They make odd couples. As do Una and Christian.

'It's a bit bumpy,' says Christian, piping up for a moment. He's referring to the track.

'"It's lovely," is the correct UN answer,' Una swiftly cuts in.

He falls silent once again.

'This is a time of hope and change,' Una says, turning to the rapidly altering circumstances of the island. 'In times of change, children need to understand that change. They will lead the united, peaceful approach. If you don't address prejudice and ethnic suspicion by the age of ten or twelve, it's no good. We forget that children will be politicians when they grow up. But children don't vote so people don't focus on that. One hundred per cent of children in Sri Lanka go to school up to the age of fifteen: they're a perfect audience.'

She pauses for a moment and looks out of the window. 'Wow, look at that over there.'

Christian and I do. The sun has turned into a red ball, glowing through thick fog that hangs over the jungle. It's a beautiful sight – almost menacing in its raw, ruby intensity.

One of Unicef's jobs is to help parents find children who went missing during the conflict with the Tamil Tigers. 'Many are tracing their kids, but most had been recruited into the LTTE,' says Una.

LTTE stands for the Liberation Tigers of Tamil Eelam. The name 'Tamil Eelam' was given to land in the north and east of Sri Lanka that the Tamil Tigers hoped to take to create an independent state. The LTTE forcibly recruited many of their ranks, including children, creating much fear and hostility towards the rebels within the Tamil community itself.

'They are most probably dead,' says Una. It is believed that up to 100,000 people died in the 26-year conflict.

Many small children, I learn, were picked up in the street by other families during the confusion of the height of the troubles. As they were unable to speak their parents' names, they were adopted.

'Every now and then DNA is used, and a child is found. The sad thing is that it gives people hope.' The reality is that such hope will be misplaced as most children were killed.

This is just one of the many ongoing issues facing the Tamil-dominated parts of the country. Since the war ended in 2009, there have been huge upheavals in the north and east, as tens of thousands of people had been left homeless by the conflict. Most have since been resettled from refugee camps, although many homes are still under construction, so the return to 'normal' is far from complete.

Una and Christian are travelling by Land Cruiser from Kilinochchi, which was once a Tamil Tiger stronghold, up to Jaffna later in the day. They have a meeting tomorrow with the chief minister of the northern province. They want to persuade him to end corporal punishment in schools, starting with making them 'smack free'.

'Kids copy violence. If they think that hitting solves things, then they will hit,' says Una.

Trying to draw him out a bit, I ask Christian where he worked before coming here.

'Myanmar. Three years,' he says – and leaves it at that.

'Whereabouts in Germany are you from?'

'I did not live in Germany.'

'Oh, where did you grow up?'

'France and Switzerland.'

And that's the end of that.

I leave them as the sun is turning tangerine above a lake of pink and white lilies – and return to the party in Carriage A.

Teetering termite mounds, long red-dirt roads, banana plantations, dogs that turn and howl at the big blue train as though still unused to this strange apparition so recently introduced to their lives – that's what's going on outside. Inside, my neighbours are standing up and chatting to one another as though they're at a social gathering in a living room.

Sri Lanka's official name is the Democratic Socialist Republic of Sri Lanka. I flick through my copy of the *Daily Mirror*, picked up at Fort station, where the main story of the day comes from our destination. President Sirisena visited Jaffna yesterday to announce the return of some of the territory confiscated by the military from landowners in the north during the civil war – this land had been seized to create an area known as the Palaly High-Security Zone. Yet it is the language that Sirisena uses that stands out: 'Karl Marx has explained very clearly that the root cause of the fight between the landlords and the proletariat was the ownership of lands. Therefore, we politicians must pay our attention to resolve land issues all the time.'

Back in the UK, if you put the Labour Party's difficult-to-work-out Jeremy Corbyn to one side, it is hard to imagine a mainstream politician going about quoting Marx and referring to the proletariat – and it's a striking reminder of the 'democratic socialist' side of the country (Sirisena is a former member of the Communist Party of Ceylon). Travelling on the *Queen of Jaffna*, I feel as though I'm moving to the heart of the country's ongoing debate: the source of the stories that are making its front-page headlines.

The ethnic make-up of Sri Lanka is thus: Tamils, of which the vast majority are Hindu, are about 11 per cent of the population; Sinhalese account for 75 per cent and are mainly Buddhist (Sirisena is Sinhalese and a practising Buddhist); about nine per cent are Muslim; and the remaining five per cent includes a mixture of people such as Indian Tamils, a distinct ethnic group brought to Sri Lanka to work by the British. There was already much Tamil–Sinhalese tension in the aftermath of British rule in 1948, but relations deteriorated in the mid 1950s when an act was passed making Sinhalese the official language, while failing to recognise the Tamil language; the Sinhalese majority had been fed up with the well-educated Tamil minority holding many positions of power in the civil service and universities, and this was their way of doing something about it. The act inflamed matters enormously.

The next key moment came in 1958, when widespread anti-Tamil riots took place. Afterwards, tensions grew year by year, with open discussion about creating a separatist Tamil state. The Liberation Tigers of Tamil Eelam came into being in 1976, led by Velupillai Prabhakaran, who had previously overseen another group named the Tamil New Tigers, founded in the early 1970s. The civil war is said to have begun in 1983, after the LTTE attacked an army convoy in Jaffna, killing 13 soldiers. The backlash against this led to riots in which more than 3,000

Tamils died. At the same time, relations between the Tamils and the Muslim community were also deteriorating, reaching a low when Prabhakaran expelled 24,000 Muslims from Jaffna. He also ordered the 1989 assassination of India's Rajiv Gandhi, whom he believed to be anti Tamil. Prabhakaran's death in May 2009 came at the end of the civil war, when the LTTE had been pushed to a tiny strip of land on the north-east coast. Hundreds of civilians caught in the crossfire died in the final days of the conflict there.

The treatment of the Tamil minority – which is the majority of the population in the north and parts of the east coast – is seen as key to the future of Sri Lanka. In reply to the president, Mr C. V. Wigneswaran, the chief minister of the north (who Una and Christian are going to meet), is quoted in the local *Daily Mirror* as saying: 'Our people have suffered nearly thirty years and have lived at so-called refugee camps and welfare centres as paupers. They are crying for their legitimate lands to be vested in them and unfortunately the process is extremely slow. The paramount duty of the government is to reconstruct not only the buildings and infrastructure but the pride and dignity of the northern people as there was a time where schools, temples and hospitals were bulldozed.' Not enough land is being returned, and it is not 'proper for the armed forces to cultivate lands that belong to people, forcibly depriving their livelihood'.

Meanwhile the *Daily Mirror*'s editorial is not pulling its punches over the issue of corruption in Sri Lanka: 'President Sirisena pronounced the end of a party political era where politics had become a big business like heroin or liquor and most politicians came in to plunder the resources of millions of suffering Sri Lankans. President Sirisena said the principles of the new era would be good governance and democracy, accountability, transparency and social justice with the politicians being aware that they are not kings, lords and masters but feet-washing servants of the people. Anyone who did not or could not live according to these values and principles must quit the government and go into whatever profit making or criminal business they desire.'

A great deal of politics... as the *Queen of Jaffna* rattles northwards.

Meanwhile, elsewhere, an 'Ayurvedic massage clinic' in Mount Lavinia had been closed down as it turned out to be a brothel; a bus driver had been suspended for driving through a gap at a level crossing and narrowly missing the Galle express train; 54 fishermen from Tamil Nadu had been arrested for fishing in Sri Lankan waters; and David Beckham is reported as saying: 'I let Victoria dress me ninety-nine per cent of the time.'

I look out of the window, where the jungle is thick with vines; it's easy to understand how the Tamil Tigers operated undercover for so long. A startling bird with a blue-and-red body and black-and-white-tipped wings soars by (I later learn this is a Sri Lankan magpie). White butterflies in their hundreds flicker above a paddy field. And I try to imagine living in a country where major papers refer to their politicians as 'feet-washing servants of the people'. I think I like the idea of that.

Beyond Anuradhapura station – where a lot of people get off, not a lot of people get on, and there's a Priests' Waiting Room – I become acquainted with the party people of Carriage A.

Raj Varatharaj sits down next to me. He has heard me talking to a man in the row in front who has been telling me all about his brother, who lives in Milton Keynes and sells 'whisky, beer: he has shop'. Raj seems to have organised the party in Carriage A. He lives near Los Angeles and is of Tamil origin, visiting Jaffna with his wife, children and relatives to attend a wedding. He grew up in Jaffna and is a civil engineer responsible for work on bridges and harbours in California. He studied engineering at university in Sri Lanka before winning a scholarship to the University of Oklahoma. 'My brother lives in Switzerland, it is so lovely in Switzerland... when I went to live in Oklahoma, I was so disappointed.'

There are four Tamil families that are joining up for the wedding, one of which is from Australia, where the couple are to live. It is an arranged marriage.

Raj loves the *Queen of Jaffna* and remembers travelling on it as a child, before the service was shut down in 1990.

'The whole war is over,' he says. 'Now we can plan ahead. Tamils had forgotten about pre-planning their travel. We could not say: "We will be here, and we will do this on that date. I'm going on the train and we can do that." Now there are trains, it is different.'

In other words: the wedding in Jaffna would have been impossible without the reopening of the railway. The marriage had been postponed especially so the group could travel together.

Raj looks American: jeans, shades, polo shirt, gold Casio watch, short back and sides. He says that being on the other side of the globe has allowed him to regard the troubles in Sri Lanka with clarity: 'There are factions on both sides. There are so many bad memories of each other. From the US I can see this: you guys are crazy, if you really want to move forward and forget about the past, don't be severe, forget about the hatred of each other, but don't forget the lessons to learn.'

A stone cracks into the bottom of the carriage. We are on a bouncy section of track, with bumps and jolts. The jungle is even thicker. We pass a military barracks; it has a castellated wall and two soldiers stand guard at an entrance facing the railway. We are beyond Kilinochchi, where Una and Christian disembarked. I wonder whether this is part of the Palaly High-Security Zone.

Raj discusses the ongoing effects of the civil war: 'There are 80,000–90,000 war widows in the north and the east. It's a massive problem. There are lots of young women without a husband – some with children.' He pauses and gazes into the jungle, as though imagining the former rebels who camped out there.

Raj is concerned that one day violence might erupt again. However, overall he has an optimistic outlook, while remaining realistic: 'Winning the hearts and minds of the people is going to be difficult. People are still bitter now, but there is more hope for reconciliation.'

Jani, Raj's wife, joins us. She is in a Twain-friendly pink dress and is smiling broadly, with a red bindi on her forehead. She also grew up in Jaffna. 'Everything is perfect now,' she says, referring to the country's troubles and the reopening of the Colombo–Jaffna line. 'It's wonderful: looking out of the window. The kids don't value or notice. They just watch *Harry Potter* on their iPads.'

We have our pictures taken together, exchange emails; Jani recommends the Mango restaurant in Jaffna; and we arrive at our final stop.

Up north
Jaffna

Jaffna station is modern, naturally. Most of it was blown up during the conflict. Adverts for mobile phones and banks are pasted on walls. A display case shows the bombed-out shell of the original station: mouldering walls with bullet and shell marks, frames without windows and tall weeds on the track. This stands next to a picture of the shiny white station: *DREAM BECAME A REALITY*.

I have a couple of days in the city, before travelling by plane from the Palaly High-Security Zone's airport to the east coast to stay at a beach resort operating in an area once controlled by the Tamil Tigers. Yes, I know, planes are bad, trains are good, but I want to see how the *Queen of Jaffna* is playing a part in bringing together new 'tourist areas'; some tour operators are already offering train-and-plane options in Sri Lanka's north and east.

So what do you do after catching the train to Jaffna?

You probably stay at the Jaffna Heritage Hotel. It's early days for tourism in the city, with just a handful of hotels and little pandering to overseas tourists. The Jaffna Heritage Hotel is the exception (for now), on a street with a run of non-governmental organisations and UN offices. Plain rooms with good air conditioning, a small pool that no one uses in a garden with a lawn, a little lounge with sketches depicting local life ('a typical Jaffna woman in her traditional appearance') and a waiter who knows how to find you a beer and have it taken to your room in a paper bag (even though alcohol, which is legal in Jaffna, is not on the hotel's menu at the behest of the owner). The alternative, for the serious rail enthusiast, is the Green Grass Hotel, which has rooms overlooking Jaffna station and serves a highly recommended crab curry.

It's a short walk from Jaffna Heritage Hotel – past an old-fashioned tailor's using ancient Singer sewing machines, corner shops overflowing with colourful vegetables, a sign outside an NGO depicting a rifle with a line drawn through it (no guns allowed), a stray dog or two, and a cow wearing a blue-and-red bandana while munching on litter – to the city's big attraction. This is the Nallur Kandaswamy Temple.

There has been a Hindu temple here since AD 948; the current temple is from the eighteenth century. Intricate figures with bulbous eyes and bellies are carved into the orange stone that towers upwards, alongside birds and lion-like creatures baring teeth. The sky is powder blue, and there is something brilliant about the juxtaposition of the orange and the blue. Male visitors must remove shirts on entry. The idea, an elderly man with a toothy grin tells me, is that your heart and soul are opened to the gods. Both men and women must remove shoes. No photos may be taken when inside.

By great fortune I enter as a *puja* ceremony to celebrate Murugan, a Hindu god of war, is in full swing. Pipes squeal and drums beat as a procession follows a figure made of pink and red flowers mounted on a silver peacock 'throne' on a platform fixed to two wooden poles, held aloft by ten shirtless men in sarongs. This task is conducted in shifts as the throne is so heavy; those taking over tend to grimace when first feeling the weight. Incense fills the air. Devotees dressed in white shuffle behind as the ceremony, over half an hour long, weaves onwards between tall golden columns. Bells toll. Drums quicken. At the end, after placing the throne in a chamber that is quickly closed to prying eyes, many followers lie prostrate on the ground or kneel with foreheads pressing on the stone floor.

The city's other big sight is its Dutch Fort, completed during the seventeenth century. Sri Lanka has a long history of foreign interference: the Dutch forced out the Portuguese (who had bases on the coast dating from 1505) in the mid seventeenth century; while the British defeated the Dutch in 1796, assuming full control of the entire country in 1815 following a successful campaign to see off a local king and take Kandy. In the early seventeenth century, the Portuguese had been responsible for putting an end to the ancient Jaffna kingdom, which had ruled in the north since the thirteenth century. The final Jaffna king, Cankili II, had been hung, hundreds of Hindu temples destroyed, and the local population forcibly converted to Roman Catholicism.

The fort is huge and star shaped, with thick stone walls surrounded by a moat. There are views across a lagoon to a string of islands running in the direction of India – at its closest point, Sri Lanka is just 22 miles from mainland India. From the fort's walls I can see empty lots where there were once houses and municipal buildings that were destroyed in the civil war. Within the fort itself, the crumbling stone remains of a Dutch church bombed during the troubles can be found – the Sri Lanka Air Force carried out many attacks on the city when it was in Tamil Tiger hands in the 1990s. The whitewashed domes of Jaffna Public Library are also visible. This is another tourist stop-off as it has become a symbol of Tamil culture and history after being rebuilt following an arson attack by a pro-government Sinhalese mob in the early 1980s. Outside it there is a sad statue of a man who loved the library so much that he had a heart attack and died when he saw the building burning down.

The streets of Jaffna are busy without being overcrowded, full of shiny old Morris Minors and Austin Cambridge cars that have been lovingly maintained over the years. Sri Lankans seem to have a penchant for ice cream and there are three excellent parlours near the Nallur Kandaswamy Temple. These are bustling spots and it is not uncommon to see tables of soldiers in uniform, each with an ice-cream sundae.

From outside the Sooryaa Ice Cream and Bakers Cafe, I flag down an autorickshaw with *Art is long. Life is short* written on it. The gangly driver takes me on a circuit of the city, telling me how he lived for many years in Saudi Arabia to escape the conflict. I see the massive bulk of St Mary's Cathedral, the local base of the Roman Catholic religion. It's close to a hospital that specialises in artificial limbs – needed, sadly, as many landmines remain. From time to time, the gangly driver points and says, 'Old building' or 'Somebody's cow' or 'This is prison'.

He tells me he lives in a suburb and has a garden with a small paddy field, coconut trees, a goat, a cow and chickens. 'Never I buy: eggs, milk, coconut or rice.' We pass the bombed ruins of what I take to be the old district secretariat. A sign outside it says: *Say no to destruction: never again!* The gangly driver tells me: 'My son lives in New Malden' (in England). Then he takes me to the Mango restaurant, where I have an excellent *thali* meal: spicy chickpeas, onion and chilli salad, coriander and pepper soup, butternut squash and coconut, flatbread and rice.

'Twelve years in the Tigers and I was involved until the very last day'
Uga Jungle Beach, near Trincomalee

Jaffna is a curious city, having so recently rejoined the tourist map thanks to its new trains. But I'm soon on the move. The Palaly High-Security Zone is reached via a big roadside checkpoint. It covers about 6,150 acres of disputed land. Yesterday President Sirisena released 1,000 acres to the original owners, but many others want their land back – as Mr C. V. Wigneswaran, the chief minister of the north, had complained to the *Daily Mirror*. There is also resentment at the huge numbers of soldiers who remain in the north and east; as many as 160,000 are believed to be stationed among the camps here.

The roads in the security zone seem better maintained than those outside the zone. Smart flower beds line the turn into the tiny airport, where I wait in an air-conditioned lounge with cricket on the television. It's Sri Lanka versus South Africa; 'Beautifully bowled, totally deceived him,' says Ian Botham, who is commentating. I share the propeller plane with a handful of stiff-backed and untalkative air-force officers, listening to really awful piped music on the sound system.

Planes just can't compete with trains.

I'm making this journey to the east coast as I want both to relax by the beach (after the recent run of rides) and to meet the manager of a hotel that has begun employing former Tamil Tigers. The Uga Jungle Beach Hotel, which opened in 2012, is in an isolated spot that was a no-go for tourists during the civil war. The employment scheme seems forward thinking. If the train to Jaffna is going to be popular with holidaymakers, the city is going to need hotels like Uga Jungle Beach.

Sivabriyan Anandasivan is the resident manager at the hotel. He is a Tamil from Jaffna, in his thirties with a goatee beard, puffy cheeks and a debonair manner. We go for a walk around the stylish hotel, with its comfortable villas, plunge pools and wooden walkways to restaurants and bars.

Over a coffee he tells me early on that his wife is Sinhalese. 'This is quite rare. During the wartime it was quite difficult. She can speak Tamil very well, and I can speak Sinhalese,' he says. They have been married 15 years and have a son.

Of the train from Colombo to Jaffna, he says, 'This is a good move. It links people. There is more opportunity to mingle with other communities.'

Then he tells me about the hotel's staffing policy. 'We have ex Tigers working with us. We give opportunities. They were living in refugee camps – in camps near Trincomalee there were near to three thousand families. They were eager to work but most did not have formal qualifications. We spread the news that there were jobs and some came and asked. Our laundry: most of it is run by war widows. We have fifty-five local staff. Ten are ex Tigers. I am one of the few Tamils from Jaffna in this industry. This area we are in was named a tourist development zone after the war. We bought fifteen acres.'

He believes that the fall of ex-president Rajapaksa signals good times for Sri Lanka: 'The new government gives a chance for reconciliation. Before you could only sing the national anthem in Sinhalese. The new government has said you can sing it in Tamil too. There are no hardliners in the government. There is willing to reconcile.'

Sivabriyan asks where I'm from. 'Ah, London. There is a huge Sri Lankan diaspora in London. In London all the petrol stations are run by Sri Lankans. The Patels, the Indians: the second generation are not willing to take on the convenience shops from their fathers, or the petrol stations. They want white-collar jobs now. But the Sri Lankans are hard-working.'

I'm introduced first to Suganthini, one of the laundry staff, whose husband was arrested and disappeared in 2008. He had left her without informing her that he was joining the LTTE several years before. She was in a refugee camp for three years after the end of the civil war. Then she got wind of the job at the hotel. I ask what her current feelings are about life and Sri Lanka.

'I am doubtfully having hope,' she says.

Then I meet one of the gardeners, who asks not to be named. He is a former Tamil Tiger. He's about 5 feet 2 inches, aged 32, slight and wearing a T-shirt with *British Denim* written on it. He has a moustache and gentle, protuberant brown eyes. He does not look like a former terrorist or freedom fighter (depending on which side of the debate you sit).

He says that he was found unconscious on the final day of the war in the area where the last battle took place: 'Twelve years in the Tigers and I was involved until the very last day.' He had been hit by artillery. He shows me the scar on his knee. A Muslim member of the Sri Lankan Army discovered him and kindly sent him to a civilian camp; there are reports of the disappearance of some of the Tigers taken to military camps for interrogation. He says that most of his friends are dead. He pauses and I'm shown a bullet wound on his left arm, as well as the exit mark.

I ask if he's happy now.

He replies that he is happy that there is not much involvement with the military any more. Military intelligence used to check up on him once a month; now it is once a year. His job within the LTTE involved riding a cargo boat transporting weapons. He was known as a 'Sea Tiger'. His ship had been destroyed by the air force towards the end of the war.

We chat for a while by the kidney-shaped pool. Then the softly spoken Tiger returns to his duties, attending to a vine. Sivabriyan watches him go. 'This kind of thing,' he says, 'it satisfies me, because I'm giving something back to society. I have had the chance of higher salaries but I don't want to go because of the satisfaction here.'

He is not boasting: the words come from the heart.

Trains lead to stories, and the *Queen of Jaffna* has many twists to its tale. When I set off from Colombo, I knew that doing so would be opening up the tricky politics of Sri Lanka – far from straightforward so soon after the civil war. The train to Jaffna is more than just another train; it is – as I have found – a way into understanding the make-up of a complicated nation.

Next up, I'm going west for a ride where I'm expecting plenty of twists and turns, too… in one of the most secretive countries on Earth.

6 | TURKEY AND IRAN: 'WE HEARTILY WELCOME HONOURABLE TOURISTS'

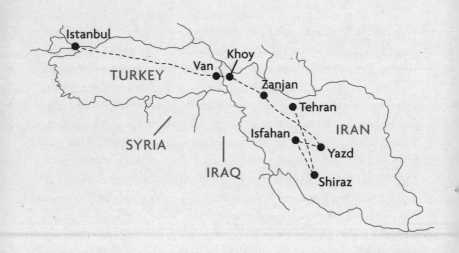

BEFORE DEPARTING ON a journey by rail of more than 2,700 miles from Istanbul to Tehran – with a few detours – a handful of passengers is making a train buff's pilgrimage.

On the hills above the target of our interest we have seen the many splendid sultans' palaces and ancient mosques of Turkey's biggest city; all the usual tourist sights. But as we head down narrow lanes with carpet shops and cafes, a place close to the silvery waves of the Bosphorus is calling. And it's a spot that means a lot in the world of trains into which I am diving.

Orient Express... the end of the line
Sirkeci Terminal and the metro beneath the Bosphorus, Istanbul

The Sirkeci Terminal was the final stop of the old *Orient Express* service that ran between Paris and Istanbul from the 1880s to the 1970s. The group I am with consists of rail enthusiasts who are keen to take a look, and who are about to join a bigger party on a chartered train that will convey us eastwards across Turkey into Iran, where we are to perform a southwards loop taking in Zanjan, Yazd, Isfahan and Shiraz, before ending in Iran's capital. This will be the first charter train of its kind to complete such a journey – with sleeper compartments – in the modern era. Permission for passage has been specially granted by tourist officials in Tehran.

We cross a busy road and come to the distinguished but faded facade of the Sirkeci Terminal, with its stained-glass windows decorated in geometric patterns – similar to those in the mosques we saw earlier and conveying a strong sense of being in the East; no doubt the intended effect of the German architect, aiming to impress long-distance travellers arriving in bygone days. Now, however, the grey-stone outer walls are grimy and the pale-pink paint is peeling. Holes by doorways suggest that lanterns and other fittings have gone missing. A forlorn man sits by a booth with a sign advertising a 'whirling dervishes' show. No one else is around.

None of this matters to us, though – beyond the ticket hall, bathed in colourful streaks of light cast by the windows, we come to a veritable train lover's treat. We step through the curved doorway of the Orient Express Restaurant (opened in 1890) to find ourselves in a dimly lit room with pictures of old steam trains and original *Orient Express* posters. Tables are covered with stiff white cloths. A straight-backed waiter wearing a black tie takes our order of teas, and as he does so I notice a sepia photograph of Agatha Christie, holding a steady gaze and wearing pearls. Christie stayed up the hill at the Pera Palace Hotel while, it is said, writing *Murder on the Orient Express* (published in 1934); room 411, where she resided, has been renamed the Agatha Christie King Room. During the crime novelist's time, guests would be whisked up from the Sirkeci Terminal in sedan chairs.

It is a quiet early-August mid-morning, and the setting remains strongly evocative of the golden era of train travel that the *Orient Express* has come to symbolise. Sunlight catches a window and multicoloured light momentarily bathes our corner table. We are beneath a high ceiling with original cornices and old brass light fittings with bell-shaped shades. The floor is laid with mahogany-coloured wood. Other than the shuffle of the waiters' polished black shoes, there is silence, as though the room is just waiting for a trainful of scheming vicars, poisonous blondes, mysterious Americans and seemingly respectable English country gentlemen – plus, of course, a very particular Belgian detective with a curling moustache and plenty of whirring 'little grey cells'.

A poster by our table dates from 1888 and explains that passengers could board the *Orient Express* at the Gare de l'Est in Paris at 07:30 on a Wednesday and arrive in Constantinople at 06:49 on Saturday, stopping at Munich, Vienna, Budapest and Belgrade along the way. The train is billed as a *service rapide sans changement de voitures et sans passeport entre* and the advert is headed *Chemins de Fer Orientaux*. Meanwhile, another promotional poster shows the connections that could be made from London to Paris, Dijon, Lausanne, Milan, Venice, Trieste, Belgrade, Sofia and Constantinople (the name change to Istanbul came a few years after the establishment of the Republic of Turkey in 1923). London is marked by a Grenadier Guard with a sword, while a moustachioed man wearing a cherry-red fez awaits at the final stop. A dotted line indicates the crossing of the Channel by ferry; though even in those days some dreamt of digging a tunnel.

We sip our teas. The waiter wheels across an amusing old-fashioned drinks trolley with a front shaped like a mini steam locomotive. It seems such a pity, we all agree (as all good rail enthusiasts and train lovers would), that there is no longer a regular Paris-Istanbul service, only the extremely plush *Venice Simplon-Orient-Express* between the cities once a year. The price of a six-day journey in a 'vintage cabin', with overnight hotel stays in Budapest and Bucharest, is £6,340 per person.

Pondering this, we finish our drinks and hand over a few lira to catch a train.

We're not, however, boarding at one of the platforms used by the *Orient Express*. Instead, we leave behind the ghosts of the old Sirkeci station and stroll a short distance to the much newer station of the same name next door. Here, we descend on long escalators to a tunnel beneath the Bosphorus.

This tunnel opened in 2013 and it's the second part of our homage to trains in Istanbul. We are about to travel through the world's deepest underwater railway tunnel, some sections of which are 56 metres below the seabed. It's an 8.5-mile engineering feat that, just like the tunnel beneath the Channel, was first suggested in the nineteenth century; an ambitious sultan proposed the project in 1860.

Down, down, down, we go. Mosaics in passageways depict dolphins leaping in the waves as a train races through the depths. This line is deemed by the Turkish Prime Minister Recep Tayyip Erdogan to have connected the continents of Europe and Asia by rail for the first time (circuitous routes not counting), thus creating a new 'iron silk road' linking London to Beijing. Erdogan made a big deal of the opening as it coincided with the 90th anniversary of the foundation of the republic.

We take in our surroundings. It is, we have to agree in all honesty, a fairly standard subway – a whitewashed tube of space. Nothing special. But then the train arrives and we slide away along the new 'iron silk road', with all those ships, ferries and fish above us, heading east beneath the famous, historically important sea. It is a decidedly odd sensation. What would the sultans have thought of this? Are we safe? (Some have suggested that not enough checks have been made for the tunnel's resistance to earthquakes.) Might there one day be a truly oriental express, all the way to the capital of China and beyond?

In this manner – doing 'train things' – we pass our time in Istanbul.

A very low profile... and meeting the Russians
Istanbul to Van, via Cappadocia and Nemrut

Some may consider rail enthusiasm to be a British phenomenon – a legacy of the days of steam trains across the English countryside before Dr Beeching's infamous 1960s cuts. This, as I have been finding, is wide of the mark. Our chartered train journey from Istanbul to Tehran has been arranged by the German tour operator Lernidee and the vast majority of the 65 passengers are Germans interested in trains; although there are two British couples, plus an Austrian and Swiss train lover or two, and a Russian oligarch with his wife.

I am soon to get to know quite a few of them.

We meet at Haydarpaşa Terminal, which was first built in 1872 and then redesigned in its current form in 1909. From a distance, it looks a bit like a German castle, sturdy with turrets, high windows and neoclassical columns; just as at Sirkeci, the architects were German. It is positioned beside the Bosphorus, with an old steam train painted in black and red sitting in the forecourt: cue a flurry of photos.

Haydarpaşa makes a grand departure point. The empty ticket hall is ornate with frescoes of flowers and urns, marble panels, shiny lamps and original brass clocks. No other passengers are about as the station has been closed to all but a handful of suburban trains, as well as special services such as ours; there are rumours that the building may be converted into a hotel. A crazy little cafe sits to one side; ruby-red walls covered in black-and-white pictures of old matinee stars, with a photograph of Salvador Dalí adding to the eclectic mix, plus a profile of Mustafa Kemal Atatürk above the cashier's booth.

I would have liked to have spent more time here but we are ushered onwards by Lernidee guides to watch pipers, drummers and dancers perform a jolly jig on the platform. Then we board our train, which has been named *1,001 Nights*, although the trip is in fact just 11 nights, with seven spent on board and four at 'first-class hotels'. After five nights in Turkey we are to cross into Iran, to go on holiday for a week in George W. Bush's infamous 'axis of evil'.

Passengers have paid handsomely for this experience – about £5,000. I will put my hands up here and admit that I have been commissioned by a newspaper to write an article about the experience; on this basis, I am travelling free of charge. This, however, has put me in a quandary as journalists have been known to be arrested in Iran after mistakenly being accused of espionage. So I have decided to travel as a tourist who works in the hospitality industry – if anyone asks, as a 'freelance brochure writer'.

This whole scenario has made me nervous, so I have made up my mind not to interview passengers on the trip or to appear to be a journalist. I'll stick to the brochure-writing line. I don't want fellow travellers talking about the British journalist on board when we are in Iran. That said – and making the situation more complicated – there is a German reporter on our train who has declared on his Iranian visa application that he works for a paper. However, he has said that although he is a journalist, he is a *journalist on holiday*, and therefore not officially planning to write anything. To make matters even trickier, this German knows that there is another hack on board – just as I know that he is here. He has, somehow, got wind that I am with the group.

He is a tall man wearing black, with a long grey ponytail, and one of the few passengers travelling alone. I clock him, and he clocks me, within a few moments of arriving at Haydarpaşa. For me, he is particularly easy to spot as he is taking notes. He hangs back slightly from the crowd and nods in a knowing way in my direction. I go over, we introduce ourselves out of earshot of others – and I ask him if he can keep quiet about my presence. He kindly agrees.

In short, my aim is to keep a very low profile indeed, take lots of pictures like a good tourist and not go about asking too many questions. I have to admit I'm more than a bit concerned. Before going, a colleague with many years experience of overseas reporting, and who sits opposite me in the features department of my newspaper, asked how I was planning to explain myself should I be interrogated in Iran. He also pointed out that, a few weeks earlier, three journalists had been arrested and held in the country; an Iranian–American freelance journalist, the Tehran correspondent for *The Washington Post*, and a correspondent for the UAE-based newspaper *The National*. I knew about this and also that there were 35 journalists in prison in Iran at the time I set off (a figure that comes from the Committee to Protect Journalists).

But I am just going on a train ride, not covering anything political. And I've decided to be very careful not to take pictures of anything that might vaguely be considered sensitive – just the tourist sights. Any notes will be written in private in my cabin or hotel room in the form of a diary in longhand, so they do not appear suspicious. No shorthand squiggles, just *sunny morning, scrambled eggs for breakfast* with more interesting bits interspersed in a matter-of-fact way. I'll keep this notebook with me at all times.

Yes, tensions between Iran and the West have thawed of late, but there is no point in taking chances. This is especially so as there is, at the time of my visit, no British embassy in Iran. The last one closed after being stormed by anti-Western protesters in 2011. Members of staff were seized (though swiftly released), the offices ransacked and the British flag replaced with an Iranian one. While doing so, protesters chanted: 'Death to America! Death to England! Death to Israel!'

So this train ride has, for me, a few layers of consideration. I do not want to end up a news story: number 36 on the list of hacks counting their days in an Iranian cell.

Yes, I enjoy a train journey, but not that much.

The locomotive of the *1,001 Nights* is a DE22000 made in Turkey in the 1980s under the licence of General Motors (as I am sure you will be interested to know). The 'DE' stands for diesel-electric, which means that it can be powered by either form of power, as I understand it. The railway carriages, of which there are eight including two dining carriages and one for staff, were built in 2000 for Turkish State Railways, Türkiye Cumhuriyeti Devlet Demiryollari. They are white with red-and-blue stripes. Symbols shaped like an eagle surrounded by a crescent moon with the letters TCDD stamped beneath are to be found here and there. The train runs on standard-gauge tracks. Its top speed in Turkey is 80 kmph.

I am reliably informed of the engine and carriage details by the Lernidee representative Frank Niggemann. He has a quiff and a calm manner, though there are usually a few beads of sweat on his forehead (the demands of 65 rail enthusiasts travelling from Istanbul to Tehran can be many and varied). He tells me that he has always had a thing about trains, and that he used to 'skip boring law lessons on Wednesday afternoons to go to work at a steam-train company, putting letters in the post'. He says that the founder of Lernidee offered trips on the Trans-Siberian Railway during the Cold War, with on-board Russian lessons thrown in. One time, when Frank was in the US, he was wearing a name badge while on a train and a black passenger came up to him and said: 'I never seen a nigger-man who look like you.' In fact his name is pronounced 'neeg-man'. Frank has a good laugh remembering his American trip. As I have been finding, people soon open up on trains.

My cabin has a turquoise seat that converts to a bed on one side and a cabinet with a pull-out desk and a fridge on the other. A few plastic hangers are on a coat hook on the wall. There's a beige curtain, a beige carpet and a simple sink; a shower room is at one end of the carriage. The style is utilitarian, nothing fancy. Despite the price tag, *1,001 Nights* is not for luxury lovers or those after an *Orient-Express*-style affair.

Group dynamics on long-distance trains are interesting to observe, I am soon to realise – but it is more or less impossible, in turn, not to be observed yourself.

Pretending to be somebody you are not – in my case, a freelance brochure writer – is rather tricky. Not speaking German, and therefore not being able to communicate with many of the passengers, is a bonus in this regard.

Yet talk you must – sociability is de rigueur on German rail-enthusiast trips – and I enjoy getting to know my new companions. As we travel through the night in the direction of Ankara, I'm soon meeting a cast of characters.

My favourites are the Russians: Boris and Maria. Boris is in his fifties, looks a little like Goldfinger (as played by the actor Gert Fröbe). He has a penchant for bright shirts, while Maria has a perma-smile and is softly spoken, with an almost angelic voice. She also likes bright, designer shirts, and – like Boris – is on the plump side. Boris is usually on his mobile phone, handling business calls. He carries an iPad, which is frequently used to establish facts, such as the scores in Premier League matches or the price of caviar in Iran compared to Moscow. Using the iPad, he is also reading the story of the travels of Marco Polo.

The Russians are brash, good-humoured and stick out – which annoys some of the Germans, one of whom describes them to me as 'filthy rich', while glaring down the dining carriage in their direction. There is a fair bit of name-calling and rubbing up the wrong way.

'I can't stand that Swiss bitch,' mutters a British woman. She also describes one of the guides as 'faceless... it's an insecurity thing'.

Another of the Brits seems to enjoy giving waiters a hard time in a loud cut-glass accent: 'Coo-hoo! Coo-hoo! Hell-loo! Hell-loo!' Extra bread or another drink is quickly fetched.

Meanwhile, one of the German couples is soon, as we move eastwards, reduced to a red-faced rage about the standard of the cabins and, later, hotel rooms: 'First-class hotel! First class! I do not think so!' They also dislike the train food: 'Awful!' After I comment that a local guide is particularly interesting, they say, 'They are paid to do that! We pay them!' And they become so angered about something to do with the Russians that they simply refuse to acknowledge them, despite being in the same daily tour group.

Agatha Christie would have had a field day.

The Russians are certainly well-to-do. Shortly after meeting Boris, he shows me a picture of a football stadium in Moscow. 'I built that stand,' he says as his phone rings, as it always seems to, and he rattles off some instructions.

'Business is business,' says Maria.

Boris, it transpires, is head of a construction company building a 2,000-home town near Moscow. In order to oversee work while away – he and Maria often take holidays and own a house in Majorca – he has installed dozens of webcams so he can keep an eye on what is going on at any time.

'He trusts no one,' says Maria.

They are just back from a deep-sea fishing trip in Cape Verde, where Boris caught a 98 kg tuna, and where he and Maria visited the grave of their favourite singer, Cesária Évora. One of their party reeled in a 350 kg fish.

'It was like a small car!' says Boris, who is from Kyrgyzstan. He joined the army at 17 and became a major. 'But then *perestroika* happened and officers were very badly paid'. So he started a welding business and rose – somehow – to where he is today. As well as the small town that he is building, Boris has a transport company with 120 vehicles, eight storage centres (with ceilings rising to 22 metres), two plastic-making factories, a chain of pizzerias in Moscow and two Bavarian-style restaurants: 'Big beers! German food! Oktoberfest!' Their vehicles consist of Jaguars (two), a convertible Mercedes, a Range Rover, a JMC pick-up truck and a Lada (for staff). Their house in Moscow has a pool and a steam room. It is also full of souvenirs gathered from around the world.

'Like a little museum,' says Maria.

Western sanctions against Russia have led to contrasting outcomes for Boris's businesses. The storage centres have done well, as those who cannot sell goods have to put them somewhere.

'Thank you, Mr Obama!' says Boris.

People are also wary of depositing money in Russian banks as 'international back-up has been withdrawn'. The result is that people are investing in property.

'Thank you, Mr Obama!' he says again.

Sales from his plastics factory near Moscow have, however, been badly hit. When I ask where he thinks the Russian economy will go from here, Boris replies, 'It's either red or black: roulette!'

Boris would like to retire soon and live in Majorca so he can 'smoke cigars and drink cognac'. It is cheap in Majorca, he says: 'Fifteen yur-oos for a meal.' They would also like to go travelling more. He holds out his enormous arms and imitates a plane.

When I offer to pay for coffees at one of our stop-offs, Boris looks at me carefully. I've kept up my pretence of being a brochure writer.

'Riiii-ch! Riiii-ch! I know you are very riiii-ch, Tom!'

He assesses me with his swimming-pool-blue eyes, grins and lets me pick up the tab.

Our passage across Turkey delivers many tourist wonders. Beyond the enormous concrete conurbation of Ankara, the landscape turns steadily orange: arid, inhospitable countryside populated by shrubs and stones. We stop at a small, dusty station and are taken by minibus to see the extraordinary rock formations of Cappadocia. We visit churches built into tapering, towering rocks that look like fairy chimneys, dating from the ninth–eleventh centuries, at Göreme; enter underground towns with tunnels designed so heavy stones could be rolled into place to block marauding invaders; and marvel at the spectacular castle on a 60-metre pyramid-like peak at Uchisar.

We stay overnight in a 'cave hotel' in the village of Ürgüp. Our comfortable rooms are built into the side of a rocky outcrop, close to a series of Cappadocian winemakers' stores. At dinner, Boris and Maria, who have made friends with an Austrian couple, a retired aluminium magnate and a retired engineer for an atomic-energy company, buy the most expensive bottles of wine. The Russians and the obviously wealthy Austrians – all designer clothing in bright colours, which seems to be the 'look' for well-to-do rail enthusiasts on this trip – get on like a house on fire. The Germans simmer furiously.

We return to the train and roll onwards. Melon fields, walnut groves and vineyards come and go. The scenery turns mountainous and rugged. Sheer cliffs plunge into deep valleys as we weave through jet-black tunnels. We pause for a picnic by a viaduct built by Germans in the late nineteenth century – part of the old Baghdad Railway, eventually completed in the 1940s, linking Berlin to Baghdad, and used as a set in the James Bond film *Skyfall*. It is partly because of this German history that Lernidee arranged the *1,001 Nights* train trip.

Here, one of the Swiss men opens up about his fondness for trains. Hans Peter is a retired Nescafé employee. He has bushy eyebrows and kindly blue eyes that take on a dreamy character when he talks about trains. 'The sound of a steam train is like a concerto by Vivaldi or perhaps Rachmaninoff,' he says, after a couple of glasses of Cappadocian wine. 'I am always happy on a train.' He leans forward, as though letting me in on a secret. 'Most of the men here have an interest in trains.'

As he says this, there is a buzzing sound from the tracks. 'A train! A train!' says Hans Peter. He rushes off to take a picture.

His wife Frieda, an Australian, looks at me and says, 'He's always like this.'

Hans Peter returns. 'The funny thing is, I have thousands of pictures but I never look at them. It's like a woman with handbags.

You know, I do listen to steam trains sometimes – on YouTube. If I feel as though I need a boost, I'll do that. If my wife comes in and sees me, she thinks I'm crazy. Sometimes, though, she'll put on the sound of a steam train for me – that's usually when she wants something.'

'And it works,' says Frieda.

After the picnic, we career through dark, empty land, pausing in the morning to drive to see the magnificent stone heads adorning the temple and mountaintop tomb of King Antiochus I at Nemrut (69–34 BC), a UNESCO World Heritage Site.

As we are walking down the steep path from the summit, Boris is reminded of a time when he climbed Mount Ararat. 'Somebody had written *Brezhnev is an idiot* on a big sign at the top,' he says.

He roars with laughter at this, causing the angry German couple to shoot him dirty looks.

I ask Boris what he thinks of Russia's current president, Vladimir Putin. 'Let me just say that people do not like Gorbachev as he broke up the Soviet Union. He's very unpopular. Putin is liked for being strong,' Boris clenches a fist. 'Strong and he ends the war in Ukraine.'

Given that the 'war'/trouble is ongoing, I'm not entirely sure what he's trying to say, though I keep my thoughts to myself. The subject switches to his daughter, who works for a web-design company in California. Boris pulls out his iPad as we stroll along and shows me a picture. She's turning round, looking flirtatious and wearing tight jeans.

'Nice, huh!' he says – and puts the iPad away.

Nemrut is a pit stop to remember, and so is the next day.

Travelling along the moon-like landscape beside the muddy River Euphrates, the train comes to a sharp halt. Word comes from the driver that a rockslide has blocked the tracks. We back up and are taken by coach to the city of Van, while the rails are eventually cleared – involving a call to Turkey's minister of tourism, no less. The train is to be transported by ferry across Lake Van to meet us.

So for a short while we find ourselves in a novel situation: on a train journey without a train. We are transported by bus, then boat, to the handsome, rose-stoned Armenian church on Akdamar Island, and afterwards to the imposing Van Kalesi, a seemingly impregnable castle looming above the city. We also visit a cattery purring with the unusual local breed of cat (the 'Turkish Van'), white-furred and long-tailed with one blue and one golden-coloured eye: both deeply peculiar and gorgeous.

Under attack and into Iran
Van to Khoy and Zanjan

With churches, castles and cats, we occupy ourselves in Van. Then our train arrives by boat... and we have a party.

Alcohol is banned in the Islamic Republic of Iran. So, in order to avoid mass arrest on arrival, all alcohol must be consumed before reaching the border. In the next five hours, we are to drink the bar dry or else dispose of bottles.

Naturally, one of those options has a greater appeal within our ranks.

Festivities begin at around 7 p.m., although it is possible that the Russians and the Austrians may have started slightly earlier, with cognac in cabins. I am at a table with two elderly German women who speak little English, though I ascertain that their names are Erica and Annelisa, and that Erica has a ballerina daughter who studied at the Royal Ballet School in London, while Annelisa enjoys playing golf.

Beers and glasses of wine are being consumed at a fair rate as the train moves off from Van, amid much jocularity. Frank and the guides are acting as sommelier–waiters, hamming up their recommendations: 'A hint of citrus! An essence of vanilla! From a little Cappadocian vineyard I know!' The realisation that no drinks will be drunk whatsoever at our destination has turned the evening into a version of New Year's Eve, minus the date change.

As the chatter rises, however, the mood suddenly shifts. There's a thumping sound on the side of the train, followed soon after by another loud bang. We are chugging slowly through a housing estate on the edge of town. Then an almighty wallop comes from a dining-carriage window, with a large mark left right in the middle of the pane.

We are under attack. Annelisa returns from her cabin looking ashen; she had gone to fetch her 'drinks card' (we all have one to keep a record of what we've consumed so we can pay later, although the wine tonight is free). The window of her cabin has been smashed by a stone hurled at the train. It narrowly missed her and landed in the sink. Another couple of windows have been smashed in the dining car's galley.

Blinds are pulled down, and some of the group seems frightened, although the 'angry Germans' tell me they think the more nervous should 'show more backbone'. Are we about to call off the trip?

'Kids,' says one of the train's porters, explaining who he believes is responsible for the attack.

'Kurds,' says another.

Either way, it does not stop the train or the party, which continues into the countryside beyond Van with growing abandon as bottles disappear one by one, though I cannot understand a word of what's going on. The Brits (who have got on my nerves for questioning me at length about what 'freelance brochure writer' means: I don't think they believe me), Russians and English-speaking others are in the second dining carriage. I'm in the middle of a German rail enthusiasts' knees-up, heading for the border of an 'axis of evil'. It's a rolling last-chance saloon.

No further stone-throwers launch assaults, and half cut – or, at least, very jolly – we arrive at the Turkish immigration point, where we file into a room at a station to have our passports checked. The German journalist, I notice, is questioned longer than anyone else. Then we board the train and putter to a station near Khoy in Iran, where our passports are to be scrutinised by the Iranians.

We are in for a surprise. It's almost midnight, and I'm worried that I might be singled out. Yet at the brightly lit station it seems as though another party is going on. As we judder to a halt, the sound of drumming and piping rises. Through the windows we can see women in costumes approaching, waving green, white and orange Iranian flags. A media scrum of TV crews and cameramen is waiting. Flashes flicker. Microphones are pushed forwards. Officials dressed stiffly in suits beam as we step onto the platform, while women in traditional costumes distribute roses and little plastic boxes with biscuits, walnuts, sunflower seeds and honeycomb. The pipers launch into a new tune, which has a high pitch, strangely reminiscent of Scottish bagpipes. It is chaotic, confusing and *fun*.

We have arrived in Iran.

A sign says: *WE HEARTILY WELCOME HONOURABLE TOURISTS*. So much for fears of an icy reception. In the dead of night, a festival has broken out to welcome the country's first chartered tourist train. Judging by all the cameras, we appear to be regarded as heralding an important new phase in the country's tourism; perhaps seen as a foreign-currency cash cow that will lift the gloom of foreign sanctions on Iran. Even the soldiers in jackboots and army fatigues are smiling.

Once we are all on the platform, we are taken through a hall with a security X-ray, though officials do not seem to be paying much attention. The main purpose seems to be to delay us for a while, during which the train will be checked by another team searching for irregularities (i.e. booze). Frank has collected passports and given them to immigration officials. In the meantime, we are to listen to the music and a short welcome speech by a local governor, as camera crews fight for position to capture his words. Clutching roses and guidebooks extolling the virtues of tourism in Khoy (though we never get to see the city), we return to our cabins, where we await our passports, while reading about local sights. Khoy is not only the 'city of generals and 1,000 martyrs' but also the 'city of religious authorities, devotion and mysticism' and the 'city of beautiful sunflowers and a history of chivalry'. Pictures show monuments, grand roundabouts, beekeepers, mosques, waterfalls, 'tulip plains' and 'the new fresh fruit and vegetables mall of Khoy'.

There is a rap on the cabin door. Is this a border guard about to interrogate me?

No. It's Frank, with my passport.

I have been accepted into the Islamic Republic of Iran. The stamp says that we are at the Razi border point, just outside Khoy. It's a quarter past midnight as the train moves on: no going back now.

My first daytime sight of the 'axis of evil' is of soft pink light on undulating grassland. Rose-hued mountains rise in the distance. Red and yellow wildflowers line the track. We pause at Mīyaneh station, where hard-eyed soldiers in olive uniforms stare into the carriages. The train, we soon learn, is on an unscheduled stop here; there has been a complaint from an officer.

Frank makes an announcement over the loudspeaker system: 'Local people are not used to seeing women who are not wearing headscarves. So even though we have declared for this journey that the train is a private space, please can women either wear headscarves or close the blinds when we arrive at stations.'

I go for breakfast in the dining carriage. Frank is at a table, looking remarkably calm. He tells me over scrambled eggs that Lernidee used to offer a train trip from Istanbul to Damascus in Syria. A group like ours had been in Aleppo when fighting broke out between President Assad's forces and rebels.

'I got a call from my boss, who said, "Get everybody out, now!"' On the way to the border, the two back carriages of their train slightly derailed. 'Oh my God, I almost had a heart attack. We got everyone into the front coaches and left the other carriages behind.' While the group was at the border, a locomotive was sent to collect the righted carriages.

The stoning at Van and a few complaints from Iranian soldiers are nothing compared to the outbreak of full-blown war, so Frank does not seem particularly perturbed: 'Everything is OK.' The window of Annelisa's cabin had, remarkably, been replaced by the train's engineers while the last-chance saloon was in full flow.

Frank fills me in on the train in Iran. Somewhere in the night we have switched locomotive. We are now being pulled by an IranRunner diesel-electric locomotive designed by Siemens and first put into service in 2010. It is operated by the Islamic Republic of Iran Railways.

Iranian train details: check.

We move alongside a pistachio-green river. The sky is porcelain blue. Wispy clouds cling to mountaintops. An announcement is made that a bureau de change has been set up in one of the dining cars. We queue to change money into rials, the local currency. For 50 euros you are supplied with 1,750,000 rials, including a crisp, blue, one million rial note. This has a picture of the Tachara Palace at Persepolis on the back and *one million rials* written, rather unexpectedly, in English on the front.

Millions distributed, we soon arrive at Zanjan. This is our first major stop. Pipers and drummers are waiting at the station for the honourable tourists from Istanbul. More roses are handed out.

We watch a performance before being driven away in buses, led by a local team of guides from the Azadi International Tourism Organisation. These guides, we soon realise, are both extremely knowledgeable about the line-up of sights we are to see and also, one cannot help but sense, picking up knowledge along the way (keeping an eye on us).

From the off, the journalist from Germany is a particular point of interest; fortunately, thanks to doing my best to act like a freelance brochure writer on a jolly, no one seems much interested in me. In Zanjan, after we visit a curious, subterranean, 1920s public laundry room and are taken to the breathtakingly large brick dome of the Oljeitu Mausoleum, the German journalist tells me he has just been collared in the street by a young man who is clearly a member of the security services and asked him lots of questions: 'What do you do for a living? Which newspaper do you work for? Why are you here?'

The German journalist has taken to joining me from time to time, which makes conversation tricky as I do not want to talk shop about papers. Without being rude, I decide to keep out of his way the best I can. People are definitely watching.

As we are shown the sights, it's impossible not to notice the official anti-Western slant of the Iranian state. Outside the Oljeitu Mausoleum, for example, anti-internet advertising placards line the street; one depicting a satellite dish connected to a grenade as though the World Wide Web and foreign television might destroy anyone who logs on or tunes in. Another picture shows a human brain being injected by a medical needle attached to a satellite dish. CNN and Facebook are singled out for attack.

When you add the almost omnipresent pictures of Ayatollah Khomeini, leader of the 1979 revolution against the Western-backed Shah, there's an eerie feeling for Western tourists in Iran.

It's all a bit confusing: are we, the honourable tourists, really heartily welcomed? There is a distinctive sense of 'be careful' about visiting the country, journalist or not.

Careful we are, especially the women when it comes to headscarves.

'I have never worn one of these before,' says Lisa, a German archaeologist, shifting her scarf. She has been employed by Lernidee to impart her in-depth knowledge of Persian history. She is a former lecturer at the University of Würzburg, and is an expert on analysing samples of ancient clothing; she was recently employed by the Egyptian government to investigate the cloth found in the tomb of King Tutankhamun.

As the tour progresses, it is easy to detect an undercurrent of discontent among the Iranians we meet. Not all locals are happy with the set-up of Iranian society: far from it. One, in a cafe, well away from other customers, whispers, 'Life is life. What can we do?'

Another, clearly angered, says that he is sick of fundamentalists' control of the upper echelons of the country, and of the conservatism of the regime: 'Eighty per cent of the people want to be open to the Western world; it is only twenty per cent who are hardcore about these things.' I am not, for obvious reasons, mentioning his name.

In Zanjan, while waiting for the Russians and the Austrians to complete lengthy negotiations to purchase souvenirs – Boris and Maria have developed a penchant for pots with intricate blue patterns – local kids cheerfully try out their 'hellos' and ask where I am from. Their curiosity and openness say it all: they clearly would like Western ways in their country, no matter what the internet- and satellite-dish-hating ayatollahs say.

On another occasion, a woman, who works at an art and history museum with displays about the sad fate of the Armenians in Turkey, says, 'A friend of mine married an Englishman.' She quietly gives me her email address.

Meanwhile, the only British tourists I meet who are travelling independently – not part of our train group – seem to think that troubled times lie ahead for the country. They are three women in their early thirties, one of whom says, 'We wanted to see Iran while we still could.'

Happy in the Islamic Republic of Iran?
Yazd to Isfahan, Persepolis and Shiraz

We clatter onwards overnight to Yazd. The cabin beds are comfortable and I find it both relaxing to be behind a locked door away from 'observation' and easy to sleep. At Yazd, we are met with yet more drumming and dancing at the station. Accompanied by our ever-watchful guides, we visit the marvellous Towers of Silence. These circular, stone, Zoroastrian structures, created by the followers of the religion begun as early as 1500 BC (no one is quite sure when), are on a pair of hills overlooking the city. Zoroastrians, of which there are about 150,000 globally and 20,000 in Iran, believe that the natural balance of the world would be upset were they to bury their dead. Instead, the deceased should be left in the open to be devoured by vultures and other birds. The Towers of Silence were last utilised in the 1960s, and now different places are used as the towers are too close to the encroaching city.

'People did not want their children finding bits of hands or feet dropped by birds in their back gardens,' says one of the guides.

We visit a striking blue-tiled mosque that Robert Byron photographed in the 1930s during his journey through Iran writing his vivid travel book *The Road to Oxiana*. Copies of his pictures are shown in a little exhibition. Byron was struck by the mosque's 'narrow tapering arch' and 'perfect' fourteenth-century mosaics. He also witnessed a Zoroastrian funeral: 'The bearers were dressed in white turbans and long white coats; the body is in a loose white pall. They were carrying it to a tower of silence on a hill some way off.' I have brought the book along – considered by some to mark the birth of modern travel writing – and one section particularly stands out. When Byron entered Iran, travelling by motor vehicles, horses and donkeys with his friend Christopher Sykes, they agreed to use a code word for 'Shah' so as not to get themselves in trouble with the authorities if overheard. They opted for 'Marjoribanks', which Byron also used in his diary. Keeping a low profile in these parts has clearly been going on for many a year.

Byron waxed lyrical about our next stop, Isfahan, describing the city as being:

'... among those rarer places, like Athens and Rome, which are common refreshment to humanity... the beauty of Isfahan steals on the mind unawares. You drive about, under avenues of white tree-trunks and canopies of shining twigs; past domes of turquoise and spring yellow in a sky of liquid violet-blue; along the river patched with twisting shoals, catching that blue in its muddy silver...'

It is indeed a Very Beautiful Place. The main bazaar is set around a giant city square, with fountains, lawns and alleyways leading into cool passageways teeming with carpet and pottery shops, as well as stalls selling exquisite chessboards with elaborate decorations and skilfully carved pieces. Little cafes with ceiling fans and tables full of locals serve delicious ginger- and mint-flavoured drinks. Chaotic emporiums crammed with antiques line hidden courtyards. Mosques with soaring blue domes and labyrinthine interiors are open to outsiders (though you must take off your shoes). Horses clatter past, pulling old-fashioned carriages with Iranian couples, plus a few Italian tourists from a bus, enjoying pleasure rides. Bridges with geometrically perfect arches span the now dried-out beds of the River Zayandeh.

Within these arches, old-timers gather to exchange stories and lovers meet to whisper sweet nothings.

The Russians and I are taken to a carpet shop by one of the guides. Various colourful examples are unfurled, the most expensive being 10,000 euros. The Russians, I presume, could easily afford a few, but they are unimpressed. They prefer Persian pottery. We leave the shop, and the guide mutters a few Iranian words in exasperation (commissions can be 30 per cent or more).

'He's very angry,' says Maria.

We stay at the Abbasi Hotel in Isfahan, which is on the site of a former caravanserai dating from 300 years ago. Queen Elizabeth II is said to have visited in 1961. The hotel is set around a large courtyard filled with lush gardens and a jumble of cafes and restaurants. At one of the latter, I have a run-in with the Germans. A meal has been arranged and I sit at a table with some of the other guests (avoiding the other journalist).

A dour woman turns to me. 'You do know we speak German here.'

'Ah, yes,' I say.

'Why don't you speak German?' she asks. She has a cold look in her eyes.

I take the hint and leave them in peace, heading out into the darkened city, wondering whether it's the best idea to stroll about in the night in an Islamic state where 20 per cent of the population is not so keen on Westerners. I find a cafe selling 'hen and rice' and eat on my own while reading a copy of the English-language *Tehran Times*, picked up in the hotel lobby. The front-page headline reads: *ROUHANI [the President of Iran] CALLS BRITISH PM'S REMARKS 'INAPPROPRIATE AND UNACCEPTABLE'*. The report is critical of David Cameron's comments that touch on the country's *support for terrorist organisations, its nuclear programme, [and] its treatment of its people.*

It is, of course, hard to visit Iran and not think about those imprisoned for speaking out against the regime or acting in a manner considered inappropriate by officials. Amnesty International keeps long files on the country's many prisoners of conscience. At the time of my visit, one of the most infamous is a 26-year-old British–Iranian woman, Ghoncheh Ghavami, held in solitary confinement for mingling with men while watching a volleyball match. She is, ridiculously, accused of 'propaganda against the regime', though she is eventually released, after several months, following worldwide criticism.

Equally ridiculously, a group of six young Iranians who posted an online video of themselves singing the Pharrell Williams song 'Happy' has been given suspended sentences of up to a year's imprisonment and 91 lashes for producing the 'vulgar' film. If they are found guilty of another 'crime' in the next three years, they will have to serve their sentences. Commenting on the affair, Williams tweeted: 'It is beyond sad that these kids were arrested for trying to spread happiness.'

In Isfahan itself, there have been vicious acid attacks on local women deemed not to be adhering to the country's dress code. As many as 25 people have been targeted in the awful assaults blamed on religious zealots. A handful of arrests has been made but fear has spread and many women dare not go outside. President Hassan Rouhani stepped in to say, 'The women of Iran are pious and know how to dress. A few people should not assume they are the only moral compass in the country.'

I go back to the hotel, where television reports are covering 'Zionist plans to close the Gaza Strip and West Bank as Palestinians prepare to celebrate Eid' in between bursts of rousing marching music and pictures of the Ayatollah.

Iran is, without question, the most complicated country so far on these train adventures.

The *1,001 Nights* train rolls south. We have by now settled into the routines of meals and cups of coffee and tea as we pass through the parched countryside. Soldiers at empty stations eye us with a mixture of wonder and suspicion; their looks seem to ask: *who are these mad Germans?* There do not appear to be many other trains; not many people move along the tracks in Iran. There's a sense of being alone in a dry, inhospitable land, with rugged mountains with jagged peaks often rising in the distance. The soil is tinted pink and the sky is a delicate pale blue. Heat mirages wobble on the horizon. Occasionally we pass rows of trees that look as though they bear nuts. We see little other cultivation.

In the dining carriage, I befriend an unusual elderly Austrian named Bali Fra Ludwig Hoffmann von Rumerstein. He holds the title of Gran Commendatore del S. M. Ordine di Malta, an order of knights with connections to the Vatican. I am not making this up. He is the Grand Commander of the Professed Knights and of the Knights and Dames in Obedience, with the responsibility of spreading the faith of the Sovereign Military Order of Malta. I know all of this as he presents me with his card, which is embossed with a Maltese cross. He is travelling alone, and has been on the Trans-Siberian Railway, 'through the Channel Tunnel', and on the luxury *Blue Train* in southern Africa: 'That was the best. I had a bathtub in my cabin. So I could have a soak and watch the world go by.'

The gran commendatore and I drink coffee and talk trains for a while. Having been on quite a few of late, I now have tales to trade. Rail enthusiasm seems to create a natural camaraderie. The gran commendatore becomes my Iranian train buddy (along with the Russians, of course).

We are taken to sights that few tourists ever get to see, including the archaeological highlights of Pasargadae and Persepolis, homes respectively to Cyrus the Great and Darius the Great, dating from around 520 BC. The rows of soldiers carved in the stone walls of the palace of Darius (visited by Alexander the Great), with their amazingly preserved curly beards and beady eyes, are one of the wonders of the ancient world. Graffiti from recent centuries has been protected for its historical interest. Perhaps the most eye-catching is by a well-known hand: *Stanley:* NEW YORK HERALD *1870*. This was scrawled the summer before Henry Morton Stanley discovered David Livingstone in Africa.

We go to see the ruins of the palace of Cyrus the Great and his tomb. Outside the entrance, a few hundred yards from the tomb, a sign says: *The world should know that all Iran and Muslims' problems are due to the politics of aliens. Of the USA, Muslims generally hate Allies and specially hate the USA.* Not the friendliest of hearty welcomes for the honourable tourists here. The tomb itself is step-shaped with sand-coloured stone, rising almost enigmatically from a shrub-land with an escarpment on one side upon which Cyrus's soldiers would keep a watch on enemy movements. It's hard to believe that this and the somewhat scrappy remaining parts of his palace – including columns and old irrigation channels from bathing rooms – have survived more than 2,600 years.

Then we head further south. The city of Shiraz is without its famous wine (as far as we can see, although some locals suggest it is easily possible to source other forms of alcohol). The wine from the region became famous in the seventeenth century, when it was exported to Europe; now any vineyards that remain are harvested for table grapes, many of which are dried into raisins. We visit the peaceful tomb of the Persian poet Hāfez, with its lush garden and fountain, attend a Persian poetry-reading evening, enjoy the mosques and check out the city's charming, intricate bazaar. At the poetry evening in the lobby of our hotel, just a handful of the 65 train lovers turn up.

The Brit who enjoys cooing at waiters says, 'I don't see many of the Germans, do you? It's rare to see people who are interested and cultivated around here.' She looks over at a tall German man passing towards the lifts. 'Arrogant!' she comments. Then she gazes towards one of the guides, who is waiting by reception in case anyone has any questions. 'She doesn't know how to communicate,' she says.

Who'd have thought that a week on a train could generate so much back-stabbing, so many divisions? I have only touched on a tiny fraction of the snipes, comments and icy, dagger-like looks. To summarise, simplifying somewhat, and leaving me out of it: some of the Germans don't like the Russians; the Russians like the Austrians; the Austrians, in turn, like the Russians; some of the Germans don't like some of the Brits; the Brits don't particularly like anyone; and the Swiss and the Australians keep themselves to themselves.

If you don't get sucked into all the infighting of a train full of Germans, Austrians, Russians, Brits, Swiss and Australians, Shiraz and Isfahan seem like laid-back cities, though it's patently obvious that plenty does go on beneath the veneer of calm (much of it very unpleasant).

0.0 per cent beers
Tehran

Before we know it, we are hurtling back through the night to Tehran, passing desert and darkened nut-tree groves. Beyond apartment blocks, we arrive in the capital at 06:30, where officers in jackboots stare into the carriage and indicate that some of the German women need to wear their headscarves (they'd forgotten). We collect our luggage and part from our red, white and blue train. Some of the windows of the galley on the dining car are still cracked from the hurled stones in Van. We tip the staff – who have put up with us marvellously – and go to see the Treasury of National Jewels.

At the jewellery museum it is against the rules to take anything inside, so for the first time within Iran, I am parted from my camera and notebook. This makes for a nervous tour.

As we are shown the world's largest pink diamond, among many other prized possessions of former shahs, the fear factor of visiting Iran as an incognito journalist suddenly returns. What if a security services official pokes about and finds a 'suspicious' notebook, along with potentially troublesome pictures in my camera? Who knows what I may have captured by mistake over the past week? Might I be accused of espionage on my final day? If I'm 'discovered' and questioned, will the German journalist be asked about me? (I've managed to keep him at arm's length over the past few days.)

But both notebook and camera appear untouched when I return to our coach. I was probably just being paranoid.

We visit Golestan Palace, where we admire the fine white-marble thrones and intricate painting, and where another official notice says: *Do you, Jewish religious leaders, enjoin right conduct and piety on the people.*

What on earth is that meant to mean? It's a garbled message, but it's been a fascinating trip. We're 2,700 miles of track from Istanbul and we've travelled through a region in turmoil – Syria is not so far away, slowly imploding, while the neighbouring countries of Iraq and Afghanistan are well and truly imploded. Yet we have been tourists on a train, charging through an 'axis of evil' that's embracing the outside world... for now at least.

On the last afternoon I take a taxi to see the former US embassy, scene of the hostage crisis during which 52 American diplomats and citizens were held for 444 days from November 1979. I snap a picture of the outer wall, which is now daubed with anti-

American graffiti, including a picture of the Statue of Liberty with the face of a skull. A gun is painted in the colours of the Stars and Stripes. Hands emerge from satellite dishes holding matches that threaten to set alight a garden of flowers: symbolising American propaganda's potential effect on the purity of Iran, or so it would seem.

Yet throughout our visit not a single person has acted in anger against us. At every turn, save a surly soldier or two, it's been friendly faces.

Before we fly to our respective countries, we are staying for a night in a hotel in Tehran, and the Austrians, the Germans, the Russians and I have a final meal, during which Maria gives me a little black-leather container with a picture of Lenin on the outside and four shot glasses inside. Then we all drink to our trip, with 0.0 per cent alcohol beers.

In a couple of weeks' time, those glasses could come in handy.

7 | FINLAND, RUSSIA AND CHINA: THE BIG RED TRAIN RIDE

HERE IS THE plan: fly to Helsinki, where I will meet a Finnish contact for lunch at the city's famous art deco Central Railway Station; catch an overnight train with a first-class cabin to Moscow, where I'll spend a day sightseeing around the Kremlin and Red Square; hop on the seven-night Trans-Siberian service (second-class) on the route that skirts the top of Mongolia and then plunges through Manchuria to Beijing; potter about in China's capital for an afternoon; and, finally, take a taxi to the airport to fly home via Kiev on Ukraine International Airlines (because it's cheap).

Total time away: ten days. Total distance covered by train: 6,319 miles.

This is the big one. Just about every train lover dreams of taking the Trans-Siberian Railway. It's got to be top, or very close to the number one spot, of most must-ride lists: all the way across a continent, from the east of Europe to the Far East, on a train.

I'm adding Helsinki to spice it up. During an enjoyable couple of days in the Finnish capital last year, I visited the Central Railway Station and noticed the tantalising destination names of St Petersburg and Moscow on the departure board. I was on a weekend break, yet had I arranged tickets and visas, I could have sped to St Petersburg for an afternoon; the travel time on Allegro fast trains is 3.5 hours (with a top speed of 130 mph).

The ten-hour Helsinki–Moscow service is called the Tolstoy Night Train – the name alone is too good to resist and the cost is surprisingly reasonable: a first-class sleeper cabin is £100. So, ticket in pocket and full of anticipation for the long journey ahead, I arrive at Helsinki's main station on a sunlit August day, just a week after Tehran.

The Tolstoy Night Train
Helsinki to Moscow

I am met by Maria, my Finnish contact (not Boris's wife). She's standing beneath two columns topped with stone sculptures of muscle-bound men clasping lanterns shaped like footballs. The men have centre partings and extraordinary, long wavy hair.

'The silent pharaohs, Tom!' says Maria, who has a whirlwind style of speech and who is well informed about Helsinki as she is a guide for Visit Finland, the country's tourist board. We met the previous summer, when she showed me round the city, and we have kept in touch. 'Yes, I call them the silent pharaohs! Illuminating the journey of the passengers for the travel ahead, that's what I say! In the early 1900s, trains were a serious business. This was a prestigious place.'

Maria has dark curly hair, almond eyes, Spanish ancestry and has lived in Britain, picking up a distinct East End accent along the way. She is wearing pearl earrings, a white blouse and a necklace with a golden cross. Her stature is diminutive, and she likes to talk a lot (in a good way).

'Eliel Saarinen!' she says, after we have hardly had a chance to say hello. 'This is his grand masterpiece!' She's talking about the station. 'He built this in 1914, then in the 1920s he emigrated to the US and became famous there. His son! Eero! His son Eero was a famous architect too! The Gateway Arch in St Louis: Eero built that! Dulles airport in Washington DC: Eero! The TWA terminal at JFK airport, the General Motors office, the headquarters of John Deere, on the shores of Lake Michigan: Eero! The US embassy in London, the one with the eagle on top: Eero!'

Maria wants me to know it all: fast.

We enter the station.

'Lee Harvey Oswald, Tom! 1959 – he took your train,' she says, beginning another burst. 'He was obsessed with the Soviet Union. He got his visa to enter Russia in Helsinki. He stayed at the Torni and then the Klaus Kurki hotels. He walked through these doors, Tom, past the silent pharaohs! I always think of that.' Maria pauses for a split second. 'You know, I don't think he assassinated Kennedy – it's all a cover-up, Tom!'

There is an aspect of Oswald's visit to Helsinki that has divided historians, I rapidly learn. Some investigating his time in the city sought out and analysed Oswald's documents for his visa application to Russia, and they believe that its issue in 24 hours was suspiciously quick. Usually a visa would have taken about five days. Could this be evidence of Soviet involvement in Kennedy's assassination? Others, however, say that Oswald received special treatment simply because he paid for a deluxe-class ticket. The official stamps came quicker when hard currency was flashed about.

The art deco interior of Helsinki's Central Railway Station is wonderful: grand arches, clusters of tubular lights, columns cut with snake-like patterns, polished-wood benches, ticket desks with lampshades. Original kiosks have been kept, selling newspapers, coffee and snacks. The ticket hall – which Maria describes as 'my office' as she spends so much time in the quiet space between tour groups – is opposite the station's one apparent aberration: a massive Burger King in its old restaurant. This opened a couple of years back, says Maria, and we go inside to take a look. I'm expecting the worst, but find that I quite like the place. Great care has been taken maintaining original features, such as dining booths, art deco lights and a splendid mural depicting a lake above the service counter. The mural is protected from kitchen fumes by special air conditioning and was painted by the Finnish composer Jean Sibelius's brother-in-law, Maria tells me (she really does seem to know everything about Helsinki's main station). Finland's National Board of Antiquities oversaw the transformation of the restaurant into a Burger King, and ensured a sympathetic makeover. It has to be one of the finest fast-food joints in the world.

We get a bite to eat and go for a quick early-evening drink in the station's Pullman Bar, with its *FINLAND FOR WINTER SPORTS* posters issued by Finland State Railways, comfortable booths and windows looking down onto the concourse. I order a beer, Maria goes for an Irish coffee, as she proceeds to provide me with a brief – super-speedy – history of Finland's involvement in the Second World War, including 'the 1939 Mainila incident, Tom!'

During this incident, I discover, the Soviet Union falsely accused Finland of attacking its territory as a pretext to launch hostilities. Maria goes on to tell me about Finland's 1941 return strike on the Soviet Union alongside German troops, when land lost in the winter of 1939–1940 was retaken and the Germans went on, without the Finns, to the siege of Leningrad.

'Now, and back then, the Finns probably realise that it was an alliance of necessity,' says Maria, of the Finnish–German collaboration. 'It was a case of: "The enemy of my enemy is my friend." Remember that the Finnish–Russian border is about 1,400 kilometres long, so it was impossible for the Finns to defend alone.'

The Tolstoy Night Train goes along much of the route the Germans would have followed.

'It would take me a year to tell you everything!' Maria adds. She's referring to the history of Finland in general.

'I am like an encyclopaedia, Tom!' As if to prove this, she reaches into her bag and pulls out a book she's in the middle of reading: *The Rise and Fall of the Third Reich* by William L. Shirer – she's halfway through the tome. 'If I read it, Tom, I remember it!'

And I don't doubt her.

We say goodbye on the platform, and I inspect train number one of my two-train, 6,000-mile journey. The Tolstoy Night Train is red and grey, shiny and modern, with carriage attendants standing squarely by its doors in smart pale-grey uniforms with badges showing the Russian Railways symbol.

The male attendants wear peaked caps and look as though they would be handy in a fight. The women are in pale-grey skirts (some markedly shorter than others), skin-coloured tights and high heels. Some have bleached blonde hair; others have gone for a purple-red look. They sternly regard me as I walk past on my way to coach number 11, where I ask the bottle-blonde attendant if I can take her picture.

'Nyet! No!' she says.

I put away my camera.

She carefully inspects my ticket, nods, and I board a spotless carriage with burgundy carpets. My cabin has a table with a white cloth and a vase with a fake yellow rose, two cartons of grape juice, two bread rolls, a chocolate croissant, a pot of yoghurt, a sachet of jam, a teacup and a pair of slippers. That makes up the inventory of a first-class sleeper on the Tolstoy Night Train, along with a magazine in Cyrillic with pictures of BMWs and Ferraris, and a feature on 'Ram 2500 Heavy-duty' pick-up trucks. These are just about the only words in English. There is also a customs notification warning that you are not allowed to import into Russia 'rough diamonds, precious metals or gems' exceeding the value of US$25,000. No more than 50 cigars are allowed and you must not have on your person more than 250 g of sturgeon-fish roe.

I think I'm OK on these scores.

The train pulls away and we are soon passing a glistening lake that leads to a wide plain of emerald fields with cotton-wool clouds hanging low and still. This pastureland is followed by a silver-birch forest with ethereal light filtering between wispy tree trunks. For a while, we run alongside a road with lorries laden with logs, before cutting into arable fields with whitewashed farmhouses and barns, beyond which we enter yet more silver-birch and pine forest. There is, I soon realise, a great deal of silver-birch and pine forest in Finland.

I'm in the mood for another beer after the one at the station, but as I venture out, the bottle-blonde attendant waves me back to stop me going to investigate the dining carriage.

'Nyet! Nyet!' she says.

Apparently I must wait in my cabin for a ticket inspection by a guard before I can go anywhere.

Then she asks, 'Tea? Coffee?'

Beer, I suppose, can wait, so I say, 'Dah, *spasiba*. Tea.'

She replies, 'Meee-ilk?'

'Dah.'

She pours a tea with milk, says 'pozhaluysta' ('you're welcome'), and returns to the end of the carriage. That's about as deep and meaningful as it gets between us, but she seems to have lightened up after my request for a photograph.

The guard arrives. He looks as though he has either a particularly dreadful hangover or has just risen from a deep sleep; perhaps both scenarios apply. A couple of buttons of his shirt are undone, revealing a gold chain. His greying hair is ruffled and a bump protrudes above his right eye, as though he has stumbled into a door. He glances at my passport and ticket as I ask him the whereabouts of the dining carriage. It is towards the front of the train and will open in 20 minutes, I learn. Dishes include 'fish and rice' and 'beef and potatoes', I am reliably informed. The guard shuffles away.

Two carriages along, I find the dining carriage, where Celine Dion is, appropriately enough, singing 'All by Myself' on a television screen at one end. The carriage is garishly ornate, with red-and-cream-striped seats with a zigzag pattern. Bright yellow plastic cloths cover the tables. Grainy black-and-white photographs of Leo Tolstoy are mounted in gilded frames on the walls: one of him, with his exceedingly long white beard, on a horse in a field; another of him with his family, dining at an outside table. Thick grey and red curtains frame the windows, with pelmets of the sort you might expect in a drawing room. The strip lighting has a yellowy-orange glow.

I order a Baltika beer, a 'sandwich with caviar' starter, and a 'nobility schnitzel and fried potatoes' main course from a middle-aged waiter in a lime-green shirt, opting not to try the 'tongue in creamy sauce with walnuts' (maybe next time).

The menu warns that alcohol will not be served to 'drunk people', and it is easy to see how you could become quickly inebriated with all the shots of vodka, brandies and bottles of champagne on sale. I drink my beer and relax. *Let the train take the strain*, I think, as British Rail's old slogan used to go. The Wi-Fi is not working. Who cares? I can't do anything about it. Why worry? I am heading through Finnish forest to Moscow in a happily mad dining carriage, eating caviar on toast.

Songs on the video channel echo across the stripy seats: 'Your love is like a river, baby. Please don't ever leave... You look so beautiful tonight, oh yeah, oh yeah, yeah, yeah... Take my hand, let's dance the night away, sweetheart, oh my darling, darling love.' I seem to be listening to a particularly cheesy love ballad special. Why not? I click open another Baltika beer and watch as the light fades above the tunnel of pines. The thin blue sky turns lilac, then indigo. A milky three-quarter moon gleams in the darkening Nordic night.

A Finnish immigration official enters the carriage. He regards me for a moment. I'm tucking into the excellent nobility schnitzel (unspecified meat, possibly pork, covered in breadcrumbs), with two cans of Baltika on my table. He approaches with a machine hanging around his neck, looking as though he wants to give me a parking ticket. I am still the only diner. Jennifer Rush is howling on the television about the power of love. The immigration official asks to see my passport. He enquires about my journey and questions why I do not have a Mongolian visa; I explain that I'm taking the Manchurian route to Beijing that misses the country. He seems satisfied and informs me that we are 100 kilometres from the Russian border, currently in the Finnish region of Kouvola. We will stop later at Vyborg station in Russia for a further passport inspection.

A new, ginger-haired, younger waiter brings me a shot of Russian Standard vodka. I might as well toast the journey. He is from Ulyanovsk. 'The birthplace of Lenin! The Volga river!' he says. The name 'Lenin' was adopted by the revolutionary while he was involved in underground communist party work; his original name was Vladimir Ilich Ulyanov, the waiter says.

'Why is there no one else in the dining carriage?' I ask.

'Maybe it is the financial crisis,' he says. 'The rooo-bull is down.'

I go back to my cabin and lie on the sofa in darkness, watching the shadowy outlines of trees shoot by. The people in the cabin next to me seem to have been hitting the vodka too. 'Stretch-ka! Orka! Petratska! Stretska! Nilka! One million grand! Britoko! Orka!' their conversation booms. I wish I could understand what was going on. Every now and then, as in 'one million grand', a few words of English sneak in. 'Ah, Americans! Americans! Ah! Ah! Americans!' They are playing tinny music on some sort of portable stereo. At the mention of Americans, they both burst into laughter and the sound of clinking glass can be heard through the wall.

We draw to a halt and an announcement is made to remain in our cabins. A clatter of boots in the corridor is followed by a rap on the door. A short blonde woman with ice-blue eyes, a green uniform and black patent shoes peers in. I hand her my passport and remain standing, as though to attention. This irritates her and she gestures to sit down. She scans my passport into a machine. She's with a tall man in black with a crew cut.

'Is that your bag?' he asks, pointing to what is obviously my bag.

I say it is.

'What's in it?'

'Clothes.'

'Open it.'

I do and he pokes about a bit.

The woman returns my passport. All seems fine (again I'm travelling as a tourist, not as a journalist, so I'm relieved not to have been questioned about the purpose of my travels).

In a fit of gratitude, I say, 'Next time, I will sit down.'

She fixes her ice-blue eyes on me and says, 'So now you know.' She moves down the corridor.

The tall man farts and to accompany this, incomprehensibly, says, 'It's on the money!' He smirks and leaves.

I shut my door and listen to the officials having a long conversation with the noisy duo next door. There is some sort of complication. Then the boots move away down the corridor.

One of the men next door says in English, 'I have forty-five-euro fine!'

His companion says, 'Crazy! Crazy!'

One of them farts loudly.

The other breaks into a fit of laughter and says: 'Oh-at-ah! Oh-at-ah! Oh-at-ah!' At a guess, this probably means something along the lines of 'Oh boy, that was a bad one'.

A few minutes later, we begin to move. My phone is sent a text welcoming me to Russia and saying that calls will cost £1.40 a minute. I read the first page of Tolstoy's *War and Peace*, enjoying his description of a pompous nineteenth-century prince: 'Dressed in his embroidered court uniform with knee breeches, shoes and stars across his chest, he looked at her with a flat face of undisturbed serenity.' I put the book on the table and pull out the fold-down bed: only 1,357 pages to go, but you have to start somewhere. My aim is to finish the novel of all novels by Beijing.

Heroes, ballet and Nicholas II's folly
Moscow and the Moscow Metro

Morning on the Tolstoy Night Train reveals tower blocks and scrapyards beneath lead-grey clouds. Yeleyana, for that is our carriage attendant's name, brings me very good coffee, bread and a platter of salami, cheese, sliced tomatoes and cucumbers (all included in the price). The scenery is uninspiring: warehouses, electricity pylons, skateboard parks with graffiti saying *FIZZ* and *BROKE*, spaghetti-junction road systems and damp tower block after damp tower block. Louis-Armstrong-style jazz plays over the speaker system, followed by rousing patriotic Russian songs. A tall rocket-like telecommunications tower shoots upwards, then the train slows at a station. Yeleyana comes to my cabin and points at a sign. It says: *MOSKVA*. We appear to have arrived.

It is 08:24, precisely on time. We are at the Leningradsky terminal.

I wheel my bag to the front of the train and attempt to ask the driver, whose name is Vladimir Dmitriev (at least, he writes this in my notebook), what kind of locomotive is used on the night train. Vladimir seems to say that the loco and carriages date from 2014 and are Russian built with a top speed of 200 kmph. The gauge of the track in Russia, and Finland, is 4 feet 11 inches and a bit (almost, but not quite, 5 feet). This is as much as I learn, train-wise.

The station is cavernous and consists of a network of halls with displays depicting soldier heroes, stalls selling chocolate, a Costa Coffee and a TGI Friday's restaurant. In one corner, there's a life-size picture of a burly soldier holding an assault rifle. A hole is in the place where the face should be so you can have your picture taken as a burly Russian soldier with an assault rifle. Real-life thuggish guards with batons and guns stand nearby. A shop offers *I LOVE MOSCOW* T-shirts and colourful Russian dolls.

With all the confusing Cyrillic signs, I am at a loss for a while. I had assumed – wrongly, it seems – that I would be leaving from the same station. But the ticket clearly says that I'm going from Yaroslavsky station, and this is Leningradsky. Where is Yaroslavsky, then?

It's next door. I go out onto a pavement facing a broad street filled with yellow taxis and cars with tinted windows, moving fast. I turn to take in the front of Leningradsky, which is all Corinthian pilasters and neoclassical arches, with a clock tower at the top. It clearly dates from the days of the tsars (completed in 1851 under the instructions of Emperor Nicholas I). About a hundred yards away, I notice another grand, station-like building. So I go over to take a look. This is the Yaroslavsky terminal.

And it's quite a sight to behold, built in what is known as Russian Revival style, harking back to ancient Russian castles and mansions, but carried out on a much grander scale (it opened in 1904). The departure point of the Trans-Siberian Railway – with its massive barn-style roof, vast columns, turrets, carved stone hammer and sickle, and murals of peasants and horse-drawn carts – is a tourist attraction in its own right.

What with Helsinki's Central Railway Station and these two Moscow stations, architectural rail buffs on the Tolstoy Night Train can have a field day.

I'm aiming to leave my bags during the day and return an hour before my train at around 22:45. Through a throng I find a baggage storage room, where it costs almost nothing to drop off the luggage. There is also, here, one of the most unusual railway notices I have ever seen. It is in English and is entitled: *LIST OF PRIORITY PASSENGERS FOR SERVICING IN LUGGAGE OFFICES*. A total of 18 categories of people are on this list beginning with *Full Cavaliers of the Order of Glory*, followed by *Heroes of Socialist Labor [sic] and persons awarded the Order of Labor Glory of three degrees*, and those recognised *For Service to the Motherland in the Armed Forces of the USSR of three degrees*. And so on and so on, for 15 further types of Russian citizen. *Former minor prisoners of fascism* come in at number nine, with *Residents of blockaded Leningrad* at number 12, and *Persons suffered from the radiation as a consequence of the catastrophe at Chernobyl NPP, and as a consequence of nuclear tests at Semipalatinsk shooting grounds and equated categories of citizens* at 17. How on earth this pecking order could be observed by passengers seeking their rightful place in the luggage-storage queue is quite beyond me – I have visions of elderly men with chests drooping with medals arguing with one another and waving documents with proof of their level of 'glory'. All of this is disappointingly academic on my visit, as I am the only one there.

A day in Moscow, about 15 hours in all: what to do? First things first, I take the Moscow Metro to Red Square. It's not far from Komsomolskaya station to Lubyanka station, about a five-minute ride. I head down an escalator, admiring murals depicting scenes that must date from the Soviet period: men and women holding picks and spades, united in comradeship, mining the land. Chandeliers and elaborate cornicing – swirls of flowers and classical figures – are further on. Moscow's underground stations are another good 'train reason' to take the Trans-Siberian Railway.

From Lubyanka, I follow a sunny street with more tinted-window cars to Red Square, where a checklist quality to my day begins. St Basil's Cathedral? Done it, got the picture (lovely onion-shaped domes). The Kremlin? Bought the ticket, seen the brass band and guards marching in the square. GUM department store? Rather wonderful, cavernous place (full of international shops these days).

I take a rest on a bench by the Moskva river, watching a performance artist dressed as Lenin. He's fooling about kicking a ball attached to a cord that hangs round his neck. 'Stalin' sits on a plastic chair, smoking a pipe and waiting for his turn to take the stage. They make a peculiar duo.

After this, I go to the Museum of Contemporary History, where I'm surprised that there is already a display on the troubles in

Ukraine, with information panels in English and a pro-Russian bias, naturally: *With the participation of the Russian side there have been achieved the ceasefire agreement and the gradual de-escalation of the armed conflict.*

And to top off my day, I'm lucky to pick up a ticket (£10) to watch a performance of Pushkin's *Eugene Onegin*, set to the music of Tchaikovsky, sitting in a splendid gilded box at the Bolshoi. At the interval, I drink champagne in a side room with a chandelier, feeling scruffy in jeans as most theatregoers are dressed to the nines. Applause and many bravos break out after the dramatic, sad finale (Onegin does not get his girl).

Then I catch the Metro from Okhotny Ryad to Komsomolskaya station... my 23rd train on my journeys round the globe so far.

My 24th is waiting on the platform at the Yaroslavsky terminal, where crowds of travellers are slumped in just about every available space on the concourse. Around 160 ethnic groups make up Russia's population of 143 million, and many of them can be seen at this key transit point. The trains from Yaroslavsky act as a vital connection to remote regions of the largest country in the world. The station has a frontier feel: we are on the edge of a continent; many thousands of miles and strange lands stretch ahead.

Sadly, no Full Cavaliers of the Order of Glory are at the luggage storeroom when I go to fetch my backpack and pull along bag. I still have an hour to kill, so I go for a beer at a bar with a low ceiling and shaky floorboards, sitting at a table near a furtive, heavy-set soldier in a black beret, who has bundled his possessions into a black bin liner and seems agitated. Trying not to attract the attention of my neighbour, I sip fizzy lager and munch on doughy pretzels, while reading up about trains in Russia and their place in the country's history. Yet again, as I've been finding so often, they seem to have played a pivotal role.

The first railway in Russia was built in 1837. This was a 15-mile line out of St Petersburg to Tsarskoe Selo, the location of the tsar's summer residence at Alexander Palace, and it proved extremely popular with both royals and the public alike. The first long-distance railway, spanning 400 miles between St Petersburg and Moscow, was completed in 1851. This was known as the Nikolayev Railway, after Nicholas I, and the journey took 20 hours, with plush carriages for the gentry and basic third class for the majority of passengers: peasants (or serfs) from the countryside, many of whom bought tickets to seek a new life in the city. In the 1860s the Moscow–St Petersburg line was extended to Helsinki and other lines went to Warsaw, yet it was not until 1916, under Nicholas II, that the Trans-Siberian track from Moscow to Vladivostok on the Pacific Ocean opened, a distance of 5,752 miles.

There were many reasons for this long delay. For years resistance among conservative-leaning bureaucrats proved the biggest stumbling block, along with the anticipated high price tag. Eventually, however, the logic for building the line won through. The argument went that a transcontinental track would be vital to holding together the giant nation (separatist rumblings in Siberia had Moscow worried). It would also allow easier access to the iron and coal reserves of the Urals. Furthermore, the military would be able to mobilise at speed to deal with 'yellow peril' in the east, should any present itself. There was, finally, a jealousy factor: America's transcontinental railway had opened in 1869, while Canada's took its first passengers in 1885. The tsar wanted one, too.

But the early days of the Trans-Siberian Railway come with a historical twist. The track was seen by many as being far too expensive at a time when the country was racked with poverty. What was the point? Why was Nicholas II bothering? Wasn't it just an expensive folly, a profligate waste? The line seemed almost to symbolise the gulf between the aristocracy – blowing millions of roubles on trains – and the public at large, who often didn't have two roubles to rub together.

For these reasons, some historians believe that the Trans-Siberian Railway contributed to political instability in the run-up to the infamous 1917 uprising. Just as in China, with its crucial railway crisis of 1911, trains appear to have fuelled a revolution: perhaps the most notorious rebellion of all time.

Backpackers and borscht
Moscow to Ulan-Ude on the Trans-Siberian Railway

Contemplating this, I walk down the platform, where I am met by a blonde *provodnista* with her hair rolled up in the style of Princess Leia in *Star Wars*. *Provodnista* is the name given to the women – a few, but not many, are men – who attend to carriages on the Trans-Siberian Railway. There are two per carriage, allowing them to work in shifts to cover 24 hours. She squeezes my arm and leads me along the platform, where I am met by the two *provodnistas* for my own carriage. Their names are Margarita and Yeleyana. Margarita has a milky complexion, steady blue eyes and puffy cheeks. Yeleyana has short spiky hair dyed in a shade of red, and a penchant for colourful flowery dresses. Both have deadpan expressions and regard me inscrutably. They make a formidable pair.

My cabin is second class, and the entire journey to 'Pekin', as the ticket states, cost £515 from the excellent Real Russia agency (based in north London). This works out at £73 a night, which must make the trip one of the world's best travel bargains. I had had the option of travelling to Vladivostok, which is the longest Trans-Siberian route and moves entirely through Russia (5,752 miles), or of going through Mongolia to Beijing, with a stop at Mongolia's capital Ulaanbaatar (4,915 miles), but I have opted to take the two-country line that travels south through Manchuria to China's capital (5,625 miles), as its departure coincides with my arrangements. Some refer to this as the Trans-Manchurian route, while the journey past Ulaanbaatar is the Trans-Mongolian – both of which cover the line of the Trans-Siberian Railway that also continues onwards to Vladivostok. All this may sound a little complicated, but it's not really: the 'Trans-Siberian' forks off at various points, forming three distinct pathways to the east.

I make my way down a narrow corridor. In my cabin I find John, aged 27, a 'project manager for online assessment' from Kingston in south-west London. He seems relieved to see me.

'Landed on my feet. Landed on my feet,' he says, which takes me aback a bit.

It transpires that John is nervous about sharing with a Russian, as he has not travelled far overseas before and fears being conned by 'dodgy foreigners' (who might well still join us as there are still two empty berths in the cabin, though nobody does). He asks for tips on where to keep his valuables when visiting shifty foreign climes such as Russia, and I make a few obvious suggestions. He listens to these keenly, fixing me with panda eyes.

John has a short back and sides haircut and appears not to have shaved for a few days. He favours baggy T-shirts along with khaki shorts that can be (and are) converted into trousers when necessary. Two of the doughy pretzels from the station are looped on the top of a water bottle on the small table. He is reading *The Casual Vacancy* by J. K. Rowling and is taking the Mongolian route to Beijing, leaving the train in four days in Ulan-Ude, near the Mongolian border. He will spend some time in Ulan-Ude, as well as in Mongolia itself. I am going non-stop all the way to Beijing, with a chance to stretch my legs for a few hours at Zabaikalsk station by the Chinese border, where the train's bogies (undercarriage and wheels) will be changed to comply with the standard gauge on Chinese tracks.

'I'm going out for a cig,' he says, after listening to my advice. He disappears onto the platform, leaving his valuables in my protection.

John returns shortly and says, 'Whoa, here we go' as the train moves.

Then he tells me his current circumstances: 'I split up with my girlfriend, and I had money saved for a mortgage, so I decided to spend it. I quit my job and planned this trip.'

His savings amount to £6,500, I quickly learn. Romantic affairs had not been working with his ex-girlfriend, whom he says 'reversed my car into a colleague's at work – she admitted full liability but didn't tell me what happened. Her colleague rented an expensive car for two weeks while the small dent was repaired. It cost about £5,000.' This appears to have been the final straw in their relationship.

His intention is to: 'meet some young people, backpacker westerners, like me, and take it from there: that's the plan'.

It is midnight and we are moving through the suburbs of Moscow. Fittings in the cabin squeak and creak. John is eager to tell all about his journey so far, which seems to have been eventful. He began by flying to St Petersburg to meet a male friend with a job in the city. 'Terrified of flying, terrified, I am,' he says, which is one of the reasons he is taking the train to Beijing. 'In Heathrow I was terrified. But on the flight there was this Russian woman next to me. Before we even took off, she was rubbing my leg. "Well," I thought, "this is a good start." That's what it was like in St Petersburg. On Tinder I was getting eights and nines saying hello to me.' John is losing me a bit here. I've heard of Tinder, the dating app, but don't know its ins and outs. 'Usually, it's sixes and sevens.' I nod as though I understand what he's on about. I'm guessing these numbers are a way of rating the talent. He says all this in a manner that seems to suggest that I should get myself to St Petersburg pronto, although we are, of course, heading in completely the opposite direction.

His friend had also recently split from a girlfriend, a Russian to whom John was introduced. 'We got on very well actually. We went out late and I stayed at her place, where I spilt beer on her laptop.' The fact that the Russian ex-girlfriend of his friend did not object to this spillage seems to be regarded by John as a sign of her good character. His friend had been none the wiser about their brief romantic elopement: 'We had to keep it quiet.'

Somewhat contradicting what he said earlier about the friendliness of the women he met in St Petersburg, John adds: 'People in Russia are a bit short of manners. You can't smile at a guy, or a girl. I've been told that's just the way it is.' He also feels as though he stuck out in the city: 'I noticed that people could tell that I was not from round there. They just knew: the jeans, the T-shirt.'

After this burst of conversation, we convert the seats into beds, which we make ourselves with the sheets provided, and turn in for night number one on the Trans-Siberian Railway.

It makes a fine old racket – the noisiest train yet. Brakes squeal, wheels judder, horns wail – almost constantly. Air howls by the window as if a gale is blowing outside. Coat hangers on hooks jiggle against the cabin wall (we later take these down). Distant firecrackers seem to emanate from close to the *provodnistas'* berths, as does occasional clanking reminiscent of scaffolding being dropped into a lorry; I have no idea what is responsible for these noises, perhaps it's just bumps on the track. When a freight train passes in the opposite direction, it's as though a sonic boom has struck. I close my eyes, the sounds of the Trans-Siberian Railway fusing in a train symphony with peaks and troughs. Despite the occasional jolt – I almost leap out of bed at the arrival of one colossal freight loco – I have one of the best night's sleep I can remember.

In bed in the morning I listen to the cacophony for a while. There's no hurry on the Trans-Siberian Railway. It's a very long journey, with plenty of opportunity simply to observe the world around you. John, I soon discover, is a late riser, rarely awake before midday – so I lie in too. It's like being a student again, though I'm still always up at least a couple of hours before my cabin mate, who seems to function at his best after 2–3 p.m. – regardless of time zone, of which there are seven on the entire Trans-Siberian route. His internal clock miraculously assesses its place on the planet and resets its late wake-up call.

With mornings beginning in this fashion, days fall into a pattern. After the late rise, I brush teeth and wash the best I can with the use of a sink by the toilet; there is no shower cubicle. The sink has an infuriating tap that requires you to push upwards to release water. Margarita has to show me how to work this, causing me an early loss of face with the *provodnistas*, who appear to consider anyone who wants to take this train as a tourist quite mad. I have already got off on the wrong foot with the *provodnistas* by misunderstanding that the offer of a cup of tea shortly after arrival is not a kindly gesture of welcome, but a transaction to the value of 60 roubles. This was duly delivered and accepted with a curt *spasiba*. I begin the journey a marked man.

When you have thousands of miles to travel on one long train ride, primary functions such as sleep and eating come to the fore. Days revolve principally around visits to the dining car. This is a few coaches along.

The dining carriage has yellow curtains and a small red-and-white bar with an orange tea towel printed with *CANARY ISLANDS* and a picture of a beach hanging on a rail. Burgundy faux-leather seats are set by simple tables. Proceedings are overseen by a large, pot-bellied, bald man with a piratical countenance, who sits at the best table in the small, cordoned-off bar section. A calculator and an accounts book are laid out at all times on this table. The pot-bellied man pecks at the calculator almost constantly, as though attempting to solve a complicated mathematical equation. When not involved in such business affairs, he reads dog-eared romantic novels with cover pictures of voluptuous blondes and brunettes being serenaded by beaux. From time to time, he goes to the corridor by the galley and performs head swivels and energetic knee-bending exercises. Being on a train so much of the time can be pretty sedentary (as I am to find, though it suits me well enough for a lazy week).

He is assisted by a younger waiter named Igor, who wears either a black Guinness polo shirt or a white sleeveless vest. Igor indulges me when I pathetically attempt a few words in Russian: *pah-mee-dor* (tomato), *veet-chee-nah* (ham), *khlyes* (bread), *koh-fyeh* (coffee), *chai* (tea), *pah-zhal-stah* ('please' or 'you're welcome'). These are the phonetics as I know them, though Igor usually asks me to repeat. He does not have much English so our 'conversation' is limited. He seems to have a soft spot for the *provodnista* with Princess-Leia-style hair who showed me on board in Moscow.

The dining-car trio is completed by a short, smiley-faced, blonde-haired woman who appears to be the wife of the bald calculator-controller. She is always in a good mood, and regularly makes trips for cigarettes between carriages; the faint, telltale smell of smoke enters the dining car shortly after she passes. Smoking rules are loosely observed across the train and I often come across figures having a surreptitious puff.

The carriage is like a little principality. It is also where you get to meet other passengers, who are mainly foreign as most Russians consider the dining-car prices steep. This is where the train lovers lurk, and everyone soon gets chatting. From my very first morning, and across the vast rolling landscape to come, rail enthusiasts are to be found here, often talking trains.

The foreigners are all British and our contingent, I work out after a day or so, is made up of ten. My first companions are Jane and Tony. They are, respectively, a housing association director and a French teacher from East Anglia. She is doing the quick *Daily Mail* crossword and he is reading *The Week*. We are all drinking tea from mugs with unusual Christmas decorations: cartoon monkeys dressed like Santa Claus. We are always served tea in these mugs, as though every day is Christmas Day on the Moskva–Pekin Express.

Jane and Tony are planning to pause for three days by Lake Baikal before travelling through Mongolia for another stop-off. They are sharing with another British couple, friends of theirs, and have had a rough night in the cramped space. Apparently, the other couple is engaged in a minor row about something or other to do with which clothes they packed. Jane and Tony are taking refuge.

Jane and Tony had stayed a couple of nights in Moscow, where they thought the hotels were too expensive. 'We are not rich people, but the cheapest we could find was about £100,' says Jane, who is in a striped top and is the main talker of the two. Tony, who has a long, olive-shaped head and a crew-cut, tends to keep his counsel. 'We were surprised,' Jane continues. 'All those people in top-end cars. Government officials. Mafia. General corruption of the oligarch type.'

Jane had visited Moscow 20 years before: 'I was amazed and a little bit disappointed by how Westernised it had become.'

Such politics and social commentary does not, however, last long. Train talk quickly takes over.

'We're trundlers,' says Jane.

'We're not speed freaks,' says Tony, lifting his eyes from *The Week*.

'We've done the overnight from Vienna to Cologne: that was the height of luxury,' says Jane. 'Bulgaria to Serbia. In Bulgaria it was supposed to be non-smoking but everyone smoked. Good-time girls wearing next to nothing were everywhere. It was shocking.'

'Scenery, greenery,' says Tony, switching subject. He's explaining what he likes to see from train windows.

'A glimpse of the mountains,' says Jane.

'It's the romance of the name: the Trans-Siberian Railway. We could have done with a bit more luxury though,' says Tony.

While I slept like a log, their longest passage of sleep was about 40 minutes.

Interrupting us, Igor arrives in his Guinness shirt and, with a small bow, hands us our bills.

'My plumber said that Russia is very expensive,' says Jane, looking at theirs, as though unsure how much the teas have cost.

The tea, with breakfast, is about 300 roubles (about £3 each). This is for a decent helping of *pah-mee-dor*, *veet-chee-nah*, *khlyes* and *chai*. The Trans-Siberian Railway really is dirt cheap.

Outside, pink and yellow flowers are in bloom by the track. Another silver-birch forest appears. It's a sun-baked day and the dining carriage, without air conditioning, is hot. A buzzard hovers above a river as we cross a rusty bridge. During the night, I learn, we passed the town of Kovrov, which is famous for an old Soviet machine-gun factory that now makes motorbikes and small arms. A factory responsible for railway rolling stocks is also somewhere thereabouts. Tower blocks are said to be decorated with murals of machinery in acknowledgement of the rich history of local manufacturing. I know all this from perusing the excellent *Trans-Siberian Handbook* written by Bryn Thomas, who has travelled more than 31,000 miles on trains in his lifetime. The brilliance of the handbook comes from its methodical marking of the sights in terms of their kilometres from Moscow, with detailed descriptions of destinations along the way. This 'kilometres from Moscow' measure is used on information boards on the train to explain the location of each station. We also maintain 'Moscow time', although the dining carriage somewhat confusingly, but practically, shifts its opening hours as appropriate so we are in sync with a sensible eating pattern. The clock eventually leaps forward from 'Moscow time' to 'Beijing time' upon crossing the Chinese border.

Cities and towns flash by. I read that Leon Trotsky once travelled along these very rails in an extraordinary armoured train in which he spearheaded attacks against the counter-revolutionary forces of the Whites during the Russian Civil War. Trains seem always to take on meaning during a revolution – an unsuccessful one on this occasion. Then we come to Kirov, named after one of Joseph Stalin's right-hand men who was assassinated in 1934, quite probably by Stalin himself. From the Bible like *Trans-Siberian Handbook*, I discover that the town is close to a rail track leading to Kotlas, the setting of Aleksandr Solzhenitsyn's *A Day in the Life of Ivan Denisovich*, describing the horrors of a gulag during the rule of Stalin.

The connection with Solzhenitsyn is thought-provoking. While the role railways played in holding the country together in the nineteenth century is intriguing, Russia's railways have a sinister side. They were, of course, used by Stalin during his many purges, to send opponents who had not been slaughtered to the gulag, so often dying in the grim conditions of the hard-labour camps. More than 20 million people died at the hands of Stalin during his 30-year rule from 1922 to 1953. This is on top of an estimated 20 million who perished during the Second World War. Solzhenitsyn calculated that Stalin may have been responsible for the deaths of as many as 60 million altogether. Some of that number would have been coerced to construct the Soviet Union's railways and roads.

So there's an added dimension to our journey: we are, you could say, travelling along the 'gulag line'.

During afternoons, after a late breakfast and perhaps a bowl of *borscht* for lunch – a purple-hued dish consisting of beef and red cabbage that quickly becomes my favourite – I return to the cabin at around four o'clock, where John may or may not have put away his bed. If he has risen, he is probably listening to music on his iPhone. John wears his pyjamas until it is necessary to make his daily trip to the dining carriage, which he endeavours at around six o'clock, usually accompanied by me. At other times he eats noodles from plastic pots, using hot water from samovars maintained by the *provodnistas*. We greet each other with nods. Sometimes we enter into conversation, though we mostly amuse ourselves. I'm steadily wading my way through *War and Peace*, enjoying the portrayal of nineteenth-century aristocratic life with its soap opera of love triangles. In this manner, days slip by as we pace through the forests of this enormous nation.

Russia, like Finland, I can testify, has a lot of trees. There are also plenty of grassy plains, grain silos, and freight trains carrying grain. These are extraordinarily long and come every few minutes or so.

'I think this is the furthest I've ever been from friends or family,' says John, during a thoughtful moment.

The blur of forests, never-ending plains, hooting horns, trips to the samovar, the unfolding and refolding of cabin beds: the Trans-Siberian Railway has a time warp, *Groundhog Day* quality. It also throws up some wonderfully unusual place names: Krasnoyarsk, Zaozyornaya, Nizhneudinsk, Chita, Omsk. We come to Ilanskaya station. This was where Vitus Bering, the naval explorer after whom the Bering Strait is named, set up a town in 1734. He had been surveying Siberia on the way to Russia's east coast. We are, I'm staggered to discover, precisely 4,375 kilometres from Moscow. The Urals, crossed during one of the nights, are well behind us.

At Ilanskaya, the train pauses for a few minutes and Yeleyana indicates that it's OK to take a look about on the narrow platform. Women wearing blue and pink aprons are selling bread rolls and smoked fish from trays. I buy a fish and a couple of 'fish rolls' (bread with a fishy flavour). I take these to the cabin and give one to John, who is back after hopping off to smoke a Lucky Strike.

'Now my mouth tastes even worse than smoking,' he comments.

They're not exactly great. The fish is no better: burnt on the outside with a mushy texture. We dump them in the rubbish bag.

'Help yourself,' says John, pointing at the pretzels from Moscow, which are still hanging on the top of his water bottle. 'They're a bit stale, but they taste all right.'

I decline his kind offer.

John goes for another smoke between the carriages. He had been nervous about this at first – 'if you see me getting chucked off, you'll know why' – but no one seems to care.

Later on, we get talking to a Russian in a cabin down the corridor. He's a paramedic from Krasnoyarsk, a Siberian city that we called in to at the 4,098-kilometre mark. His name is Alexandr and he's in his thirties, with an olive complexion, dark bags under his eyes and ruffled, oily hair. He is drinking Nescafé iced tea and offers us a cup each. He invites us to sit in his cabin and we converse via a Russian–English translation device on his smartphone.

We establish, slowly, that bears and tigers are to be found in the countryside around Krasnoyarsk. He tells us that he shoots 'two bears a year for security'. There is also a 'good fish lake'. The inhabitants of Irkutsk, another Siberian city on the line, 5,185 kilometres from Moscow, are 'crazy people'. Alexandr is not, we discover on asking him, actually referring to the citizens of Irkutsk but to 'Roma railway people', who he says will try to rob us. He is heading to Irkutsk, despite its crazy people, to buy a wardrobe from IKEA. This, he says, will cost him 34,499 roubles (£492). He would also like to buy a child's duvet for 999 roubles. Alexandr shows us the items in his IKEA booklet.

He discusses politics for a bit: 'I like Putin. Yes, yes, Putin good. Big Russia! Lift! Lift! He brings people work. Business! Lift! Lift!

Ukraine–Russia!' He holds his hands together tightly. 'Russian people not in war.' John and I ask him if he is sure of this. He shrugs his shoulders. 'Maybe a small number.'

John and I go for our regular six o'clock beers in the dining carriage. Each evening we have two Kozel beers (a Czech lager), accompanied by chicken stew, *borscht*, or fried potatoes and ham. We always have a side order of dark-brown bread, which is usually freshly bought from vendors at the last station. Over such a meal, I meet Pete and Ryan, retired teachers from the Midlands, who have a fondness for golf shirts and gold chains. They have taken the train all the way from London's St Pancras station. Pete does not rate the Trans-Siberian Railway.

'Five out of ten for comfort,' he says.

'What about value for money?' asks Ryan, challenging him.

Pete ignores him. 'The tap doesn't work properly in the toilet,' he says.

Ryan, in turn, ignores Pete. 'When I was a kid we never had enough money to go anywhere. Then, in 1996. Yes, 1996.' He says this in a very precise manner, as though the year was a watershed. 'I realised in 1996 that at the age of fifty I could do all these travel things. The internet! Book it!'

They're heading down through Mongolia to Beijing, and then onwards to Hong Kong.

We're joined by Julie and her teenage daughter, from Manchester. They're going via Mongolia to Beijing and then to Shanghai, where Julie has secured a three-month international-relations teaching job at a university. Her daughter does not like flying so they are taking the train in both directions.

'I am now moving at a speed that my brain can deal with,' says Julie. 'Looking out the window, the language, the sounds: it's lovely.'

We tuck in to the thin chicken stew, and politics crops up once more. Having met Russians and been charmed by them – and by the country – Julie has formed an opinion: 'This is not what the press tells us about Russia. Apologies to your profession but I think there's a political agenda behind it all.'

She's talking about anti-Russian press in the West.

'You can't say that to a right-wing paper,' says her sharp-eyed daughter (she seems to be under the impression that I'm representing the 'right').

Julie pays no attention. 'We can't communicate well with the Russians, but at all times we have been made to feel welcome,' she says.

Daughter: 'Please can you make it sound less like you believe in a conspiracy theory, Mother.'

The final pair of Brits do not talk much at all. They are Bridget and Pete, the couple sharing with Jane and Tony, and are finding the conditions cramped. 'My husband made me pack hand luggage only,' says Bridget during a quiet moment when her husband has gone to the toilet. 'Can you believe it! The advice I read was to pack for a whole week.' Apparently her husband hates waiting for luggage carousels at airports. This baggage row appears to be ongoing.

Extra Kozel beers are ordered. Fervent discussion ensues.

On UK property prices: 'House prices go up and my son says, "You bastards, you stole the wealth from our generation,"' says Bridget.

On the Labour Party's Ed Miliband: 'He just looks weird,' says Tony.

On Prime Minister David Cameron: 'Toffs. The working class is still deferential to toffs,' says Pete.

On the state of Britain in general: 'Britain is quaint but broke,' says Julie. 'If I was just finishing uni, I'd want to move abroad.'

We seem to have turned into a rolling middle-class dinner party as we rattle onwards through the Russian *taiga* (forest)... deeper and deeper into the Siberian wilderness, into the coal-black night.

Changing bogies and Chinese trainspotters
Ulan-Ude to Beijing on the Trans-Siberian Railway

At Ulan-Ude, the 5,642 kilometre point, all the Brits disembark. Except me.

We are well over halfway now, beyond the semi-legendary station of Slyudyanka, where it is apparently possibly to go for a dip in Lake Baikal during the time the train pauses at the station. John and I had been too afraid of missing the train to give this a try; anyway, the water must have been pretty cold.

John is in a philosophical mood as he leaves: 'I've been stuck behind a desk for three years. I could have stayed there until I was forty-plus. Got married. Had kids. But people have done that a million times over. I keep saying this to my friends.'

He looks along the platform. 'I don't suppose I'll ever spend so long again on a train, but you never know, you never know.'

Then he brightens up: 'I've left you a Pot Mash in case you're desperate, but I won't be offended if you don't eat it.'

With that, John departs and I enter a new phase of the journey – on my own in carriage number three of the number 19 train to Beijing.

Apart from almost getting into fisticuffs with a drunken Russian, this is the most peaceful ride of all my journeys so far.

The scenery opens up beyond the Soviet-era tower blocks of Ulan-Ude. Wide, perfectly still lakes sit by undulating grass-clad hills. Winding roads taper into the hazy horizon. Piebald cattle graze by the tracks. Settlements of pale-blue wooden houses appear. Layers of pink and red light up the dusk sky.

As the sun goes down over Siberia, I enter the dining carriage and drink a Kozel and eat a bowl of *borscht*. Two Russian men devour stews accompanied by a half bottle of vodka (tidily put away). The calculator-controller reads a new romantic novel. His wife pops off for a smoke. I stay for a while, enjoying Napoleon's campaigns against the Russians in *War and Peace*.

Returning to my cabin, though, the calm is shattered.

I almost have a punch-up. My potential pugilist is a sozzled man with a crew cut, a bowling-ball belly and an attack-dog facial expression. I appear to have caused offence by being presumptuous enough to take to the corridor in his presence. His face is livid. His pupils are like bullet holes. He mutters Russian curses and looks as though he would dearly like to strangle me and throw me off the train.

Margarita witnesses this encounter and shoos the man away. 'Don't worry, don't worry,' she says softly. 'He drinks too much.'

Hills tumble onwards as we make progress southwards. These Russian tracks through Manchuria were controversial at the turn of the twentieth century. The Japanese, who were coming out of a long period of isolation, perceived the railway as an imperial threat to their interests in Korea. The Russians wanted an all-year-round warm-water port (Vladivostok, further to the north, was summer only), so they had cut a deal with the Chinese and built a line to Port Arthur, within China on the Yellow Sea. At the time, China was in the midst of its Boxer Rebellion, so many thousands of Russian soldiers were stationed to protect the railway from potential attack by insurgents. The Japanese did not like the look of Russia's movements. They struck Port Arthur by surprise in 1904, beginning the Russo–Japanese War of 1904–1905. With a slow supply line, Russian troops were vulnerable, and the Japanese army proved formidable. The result was a treaty overseen by President Theodore Roosevelt, in which Russia evacuated Manchuria and recognised Japan as having a sphere of influence in Korea.

Nicholas II came out of it all badly, highlighting what many saw as the rash stupidity of his expensive railways. In 1905, he was forced to see off an internal revolt that was a prelude to greater troubles to come. Yet there is a retrospective point to be made here, as the train historian Christian Wolmar highlights in his illuminating *To the Edge of the World: The Story of the Trans-Siberian Railway*. Wolmar says that there is 'no little irony' regarding the fact that constructing the Trans-Siberian Railway was 'more Soviet' than much of what the autocratic communist rulers would go on to achieve. In other words, the railways gave Nicholas II a bad reputation and contributed to his downfall, but the future politburo would surely have been proud.

Just before the Chinese border, the train is taken to a shed to have its bogie changed. As fascinating as this may be to witness (I know, I know, a true rail enthusiast would have stayed on the train and watched the 'changing of the bogie'), I decide instead to go for a walk around the sleepy town of Zabaikalsk, 1 kilometre from the People's Republic. The bogie change will take at least 2 hours. I've been cooped up in a train for a few days; I want to move about.

I tip Margarita and Yeleyana the remainder of my roubles and buy a 2014 Winter Olympics teaspoon with *SOCHI* written on it from Margarita, who sidles up to me in my cabin, twisting the spoon before her face as though it might hypnotise me into a purchase. I go to send some cards at a sleepy post office. The town is almost empty and those locals I come across ignore me – I'm obviously just 'one of those people from the train'.

Back on board, I am grilled about my Iranian passport stamp by a female Russian immigration official.

'You only tourist?' she asks.

I respond in the positive.

'Thomas Doyle Chess-he-yer,' she repeats a few times, eyeballing me.

My facial characteristics are checked against my passport photo. A man goes through my bag and asks what my mouthwash is, as though it might be illicit hooch of some sort. I am quizzed whether I have been to 'Wesh Reefer'. This, I work out after a while, is how Russian border officials pronounce 'West Africa'. I respond in the negative. They go away, taking my passport with them.

About 20 minutes pass, making me fearful I'm going to be rumbled as a journalist–spy of some sort. The Russians return and ask how I got into Iran. I tell them I went by train. 'I like trains,' I say, playing the rail-enthusiast card. They seem to accept this and depart, handing over my passport.

We roll into China, where we stop at a station looking out across impressive skyscrapers that are quite unlike anything I've seen on the 6,661-kilometre journey so far. The Chinese officials happily stamp my passport, although they seem suspicious about my bag. Then I eat noodles bought from Margarita, having mixed them with hot water from the samovar, and get an early night.

From the border to Beijing is a distance of 2,323 kilometres, though I spend much of this asleep as two nights take up the majority of the journey. From a train point of view, the track is noticeably smoother in China. We also switch to 'Beijing time'.

At Harbin station I make a friend. I'm on the platform getting some air during a 20-minute stop around lunchtime, watching a man with a hammer tapping the train's wheels. This is done to test whether they have picked up any cracks on the journey. Wheels with a true sound are safe; those that do not resonate correctly could be dangerous. I had never known that this wheel-tapping business went on.

A man with spectacles, bright blue and orange trainers and a large grin approaches. He is one of the few passengers in the carriage and I think he joined at the border town. He says 'you and me' and points at the train. Then he uses a translation device on his phone to say, 'I work for the government.' Which doesn't exactly narrow things down much: doesn't everyone in China?

Anyway, we stand together watching the wheel-tapper for a while and he writes his name, Sun Wei, in my notebook.

'See you later,' he says.

I don't, but I do hear him.

In the afternoon, after passing through the usual Chinese haze of many mini Manhattans, factories and cooling towers (China really does seem to be booming to the point of blowing up), I hear Sun Wei singing. His cabin is about three down from mine and he sounds as though he's been hitting the rice wine.

'Ohhhh, oh, oh, travel is the friend of mine!' wails Sun Wei, who is almost completely tone deaf. This is his song's refrain; perhaps he looked up the English words on his phone. I may be wrong, but he seems to be singing for my benefit. 'Ohhhh, travel is a friend of mine! Oh! Oh! Oh! In my heart, travel is a friend of mine. Oh! Oh! Jolly! Jolly! Yah! Oh whoa, whoa! Jolly! Jolly! Yah! Ohhh, travel is a friend of mine! Whoa, whoa, whoa!'

I don't think he'll be making the cut for the next Chinese X Factor, but at least he's got a few lyrics going. Luckily, the cabins on either side of his seem to be empty. I hate to think what the sozzled Russian, long since departed, would have made of it. I expect a few sparks might have flown.

The change of bogies also came with a switch of dining carriage; I never did get to say goodbye to the calculator-controller, his wife and Igor. I go to take a look. A new dining carriage is a very big deal on the Trans-Siberian. This one has a simple interior with booths in which there are worn red seats, tables with white cloths and vases of red plastic roses. Two guards near the galley drink beer from bottles concealed from view beneath the table – perhaps to avoid detection by a superintendent. I order 'diced chicken with green pepper' from the 'ME NU' – plus a couple of beers.

The chef and the guards enter into an animated conversation. They appear to be arguing quite vehemently, but just as the disagreement is reaching its seeming crisis point, one or the other shrugs indifferently as if to say, *Whatever. This is just my point of view.* Silence ensues and then a similar heated debate rises and falls. I suppose you've got to find a way to kill time on a long train trip.

We pass paddy fields and pull into towns with familiar-looking bullet trains on the other platforms; I'm a bit of an old hand when it comes to Chinese trains now.

I'm also at a loose end. Not knowing what to do with myself, as it's impossible to read *War and Peace* after a couple of beers, I order a bottle of Great Wall of China red wine. This is partly out of curiosity and also because I fancy 'having a few' after the long journey.

Great Wall of China red wine is just about the worst wine I have ever tasted, although it gets steadily better after the first glass. The chef and the guards look my way approvingly as I make my way through the best part of the bottle. 'Great stuff, great stuff,' I'm muttering to myself as I make my way back to my cabin, after contemplating buying a souvenir bottle (but not being quite that far gone).

We arrive at Beijing station at 05:31. I feel rough.

On the platform a Chinese trainspotter is taking pictures of our train and seems in an excited mood. I'm not so lively, but this is the first chance I have had to speak to a real, live Chinese trainspotter.

I go over and ask him if he likes trains. It's pretty obvious he does, but I need to break the ice.

'I have a lot of train pictures,' he replies.

I enquire whether there are many Chinese trainspotters.

'Oh yes, very many,' he says.

His name is Yun Cheng and he is from Shanxi province, he tells me. 'Just a very little number of Chinese like trains as I do. But China has many people, so there are many train fans in China:

400,000. There are websites. Do you mind if I show you some pictures?'

Yun Cheng proceeds to flick through photographs of trains that he has stored on his phone.

'Do you want to know about Chinese railway?' he asks.

'Yes,' I reply.

'This is 25-G coach. This is 25-T coach. This is 18 coach, East Germany,' Yun Cheng says, pointing at my train. I have little idea what he's talking about. The locomotive belongs to China Railway, I learn, and dates from 2015. It's brand new and runs on electricity.

Another train enters the station. Yun Cheng's ears seem to prick up. 'The ZI57 express from Taizhou to Beijing!' he says. 'The ZI57 express from Taizhou!'

He rushes off to see the ZI57 express from Taizhou, his camera bag bouncing crazily as he goes – just as double-anorak's had back in Crewe on the dash to platform one to see the number-37 freight locomotives. Trainspotters: they're the same all over the world.

I leave him to it and head up a ramp to Beijing railway station, thinking how strange it is that I was here just a few months ago.

The travel writer Eric Newby described the Trans-Siberian Railway as 'the big red train ride' and it is just that. Big, long, with red carriages, and hard to get your head round. Somehow I've reached the capital of China from Europe *without leaving the ground*.

It is an odd sensation. Yet this might one day be small beer for trains.

A scheme has been mooted to link Moscow with Alaska by rail, via the remote city of Yakutsk and a tunnel beneath the Bering Strait. This would in theory open up the possibility of travelling by train from London to New York, a truly mammoth journey of around 13,000 miles taking a fortnight. Engineers have considered the viability of a 65-mile East-meets-West tunnel between Big Diomede and Little Diomede Islands beneath the famous stretch of sea. This is twice the length of the Channel Tunnel and would not prove technically challenging, engineers say. In 2011, delegates at a conference in Yakutsk met to discuss the potential project, which some estimated would cost £60 billion with a completion date of 2030. Keen to bolster the local economy, a leading politician in Russia's north-east gave the tunnel his blessing. Times, of course, have changed somewhat since then. Deteriorating relations between the White House and the Kremlin make the idea, which Nicholas II dreamed of as long ago as 1905, seem fanciful. But what a train journey that would have been – and perhaps still could be...

For me, however, another big country, with another big ride, awaits.

Oh yes, and I never did quite finish *War and Peace*.

8 | AUSTRALIA: MUTINY ON THE *INDIAN PACIFIC*

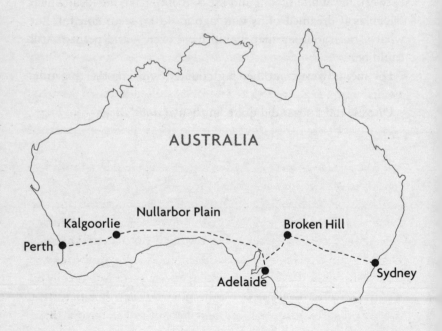

AUSTRALIA

Perth • - - - Kalgoorlie • - - - Nullarbor Plain - - - - - - - - Broken Hill • - - - • Sydney

Adelaide

IT'S A SUN-DRENCHED morning at East Perth terminal and the *Indian Pacific* gleams brightly beyond the long, cool shadows of the station. Two dozen stainless steel carriages stretch along the slowly bending, boomerang-shaped platform. Light plays on ridges of steel and the indented old panels of the cross-continental train.

Little rectangles of metal riveted by doorways explain that our coaches date from the late 1960s and early 1970s. They were built in New South Wales by Commonwealth Engineering – which, it is explained, received a licence for the sleek bullet-like design from Budd, a metal fabricating company based in Philadelphia. The oldest carriage I can find is from 1967.

I've long ago learnt to seek out such details. Checking them out has almost become second nature. How old is this train? Where does it come from? How fast can this thing go? These, and other such queries, are the nuts and bolts of rail enthusiasm – and as easy as it may be to mock having an interest in these 'train facts', as I might have in the past, they do somehow add to the sense of journey.

Call me a trainspotter, if you like, though I don't think I've reached that stage *quite* yet.

Luckily, John Brinkley, one of three train managers for this *Indian Pacific* service – so named as it travels from the Indian Ocean to the Pacific Ocean – is on hand to answer questions. He's a rotund man with a twinkle in his eyes, and looks as though he could have been a decent rugby prop forward in his day. He's welcoming guests on the platform and pointing them towards their correct carriages, and class of travel, for our three-night journey to Sydney. We are departing on a Sunday at 11:55, arriving on the east coast in four days' time, where we will pull into Sydney Central station on Wednesday at 11:07.

Those are the basics, but Brinkley goes on to say that the locomotive is an NR-19 with 4,000 horsepower, a top speed of

115 kmph and an average speed of 89 kmph. The journey will take about 65 hours with five scheduled stops, during which water and supplies are to be taken on and brief local tours are arranged for passengers. As well as the 24 carriages and locomotive, there are two 'power vans' (to give the loco a boost when required), a luggage van, and three motor-rail trailers carrying cars at the back. This train has three classes: platinum (extremely well appointed, with double beds and a swanky dining carriage with a free cocktail bar), gold (sleeper cabins and a lounge with free booze, plus free meals in a smart dining carriage), and red (the lowest class, effectively 'economy', with reclining seats and a cafe where you have to pay). I am travelling in gold for two nights followed by a night in red. The train is precisely 567 metres long and weighs 1,087.3 tonnes. Brinkley tells me that the carriages have a 'ribbed, late art deco' style.

It's not often that you find train managers who are quite so well informed. I ask Brinkley if the free drink on board in gold and platinum ever leads to any trouble. Brinkley raises an eyebrow. 'Yes, we'll call police to remove guests, if they're boisterous or threatening,' he says. 'Intoxication. Stuff in their cabins. That happens.' By 'stuff', I take it he means private stashes of liquor. Smoking is banned, although once, Brinkley says, 'a gentleman even lit up in front of me.' He pauses as if to suggest that was a very stupid idea indeed – which it was. 'The police took him away.' He pauses again, holding back his punch line for effect. 'You could say he was a smoker to the end.'

Brinkley tells me that the train hit a camel on the way from Sydney to Perth a couple of days ago: 'Damage to the loco – we had to repair an air pipe. We blow silent animal whistles and the horn, but it still happens. Kangaroos keep out of the way, generally. Kangaroos are pretty smart.' I'm keen to see one, I say. 'Your best bet is around dusk, mate,' replies Brinkley, who tells me he worked for the Royal Australian Navy for 22 years before joining Great Southern Rail, which runs the *Indian Pacific*, 16 years ago.

He points me in the direction of gold class, tells me to 'enjoy the journey, mate' and begins talking to another passenger, who I gather is an off-duty train driver from Sydney on his *fifth* trip on the *Indian Pacific*. 'Each journey is completely different: the feel of the carriages on the track,' says Troy, when I get a chance to ask him. 'Being a driver, I can tell: each train is unique in itself.'

'In what way?'

'It's just the feel, mate; I can't explain. Then there's the country: oh wow, the expanse! It's the only way to see Australia: down by the tracks. You just don't get that at 30,000 feet, mate.'

And off he skips, like true train lovers all over the world, to take a picture of the shiny loco at the front.

'He's going to say he met all these stupid Aussies'
Perth to Kalgoorlie

Booze, fags, camels, kangaroos, top speeds and the 'feel of the track' covered, I board the *Indian Pacific* in a gold-class carriage fitted with single cabins. A corridor snakes along the middle, allowing each cabin an L-shape with a clever stainless-steel pull-down sink in a corner.

The 'hospitality attendant' for the carriage, Ryan, who is on his third journey in his new job, tells me there is no Wi-Fi. 'It's good to get away from all that,' he says. Which I suppose it is.

I settle into one of the two comfortable blue seats facing one another in my cabin. These are to be converted into a bed later by Ryan during 'bed service' while we are at dinner.

An Australian woman in one of the single cabins has a complaint. 'I feel a little claustrophobic. Can I upgrade?' she asks, sounding panicky.

Ryan: 'I'm afraid the train is fully booked.'

The lady: 'It's just the pictures on the website were different.'

A conversation ensues with 'on the website it was different' being repeated several times, to no avail. Ryan rides it out. The cabins *are* quite small, though they are a cut above most, if not as spacious as those on the Istanbul–Tehran train. I'm quite content.

We still haven't moved off. I put my feet up and read a map, provided by the pull-out table, which says that *Aboriginal people who encountered the early steam train at Ooldea considered it to be a great white snake, carrying wicked spirits*. And who could blame them, after many millennia without large metallic objects billowing trails of steam in their remote land. The first rail link between east and west, I read, was opened in 1917 (requiring several changes of train). Part of the impetus behind the construction of the line was, according to a loudspeaker message as we pull away, to allow the movement of troops. Over many years there had been a 'fear of Russian invasion', although the strength of that fear had ebbed and flowed depending on world events. Nervousness about Russian ships calling in with guns at Sydney and Melbourne dated back as far as the Crimean War, when the British outpost of Australia might have been vulnerable to attack by sea. Fortifications were bolstered in most major ports. It wasn't just the Japanese who were twitchy about Russian imperialism back in the nineteenth and early twentieth centuries.

I go to seek out Ryan to ask about lunch and find him by a cabin where a giant man – another prop-forward type – is crammed on one of the blue seats, looking disgruntled. His name is Dave and he's an Aussie retiree who used to work in the civil service in Canberra. He wears a toad-like expression that seems to suggest: *I'm going to have to sleep in* this *for three nights*. He does not appear amused.

Ryan points Dave and me in the direction of the dining carriage. We weave along narrow corridors as the *Indian Pacific* chugs through the eastern edge of the capital of Western Australia, with its Thai restaurants, vintage-clothes shops and houses with solar panels. Walls facing the rails are covered in graffiti that begins charmingly, if a little bossily, *LOVE YOUR CHILDREN MORE THAN YOU*, continues with an unlikely, but well-minded *WE MUST OUTLAW WAR*, and moves on to the rather less charitable and blunt *HATE YOUR EX*. Cluster-bomb clouds are scattered in a royal-blue sky. Gum trees with peeling bark and drooping limbs line the track. We clatter across a green metal bridge.

No messing about, Dave and I go for a (free) beer in the lounge. We order Crown Lagers – 'Australia's finest' – and sit in the most prominent seats by the bar. We've beaten everyone else to it and are rather pleased with ourselves. Dave can only just fit in the burgundy leather chair and he leans forward, telling me about Chinese investors who are buying property in Sydney, pushing up house prices, and taking over 'all the coal mines in Hunter Valley'.

Others join us, but we are soon called to the elegant dining carriage, where a waiter seats Dave and me opposite an elderly couple named Joe and June. We're in wine-red booths, which are separated by frosted-glass partitions cut with a swirly pattern. Walls are clad in tan-coloured wood and there are shiny brass fittings. Joe (bald and with a tendency to poke a finger when making a point) and June (in a navy cardigan and tinted prescription glasses) are retired, too. He's a former carpenter and she was 'one of the first front-of-house barmaids in Adelaide, drove taxis, sold real estate, and did the jobs to fit in with children; you didn't have childcare in those days, you married young and you just got on with things; life was difficult but it was good, you didn't have to do training, you learnt on the job'.

All of this is communicated almost immediately. June also tells me that she's 'never been overseas; there's nowhere I want to go'. Joe, meanwhile, says, 'You're going to get beaten again: very badly.' He's talking about cricket. England and the Aussies are about to play in a crunch Ashes series.

Large (free) glasses of wine are poured. 'Artisan bread rolls' are consumed – these are deemed the starter – followed by a main course of jewfish served with 'bok choi and coconut rice'.

Joe to Dave: 'Do you like the fish?'

Dave to Joe: 'Not really.'

Joe to Dave: 'No flavour.'

Dave to Joe: 'Pretty bland.'

I quite like it after all the tasty but a tad repetitive *borscht* on the Trans-Siberian a couple of weeks back; I'm on a veritable charge of trips now. The final course consists of either strawberry panna cotta with 'strawberry coulis and fairy floss' (cotton candy), or cheddar cheese with glazed figs, strawberries and almonds. After hunks of dark-brown bread and chunks of meat on the outskirts of Omsk, panna cotta, glazed figs and bok choi seem positively exotic.

Dave tells us that he loves trains and has been from Singapore to Bangkok on the *Eastern and Oriental Express* in Pullman class. He, Joe and June are all train fans, they say. Then Dave hauls himself up. 'I'm going to bide my leave, I'm just about cut in half here,' he says. The table is pushing into his substantial midriff. This is the only meal Dave eats in the dining carriage. The rest are served to him, and two others who join him for the same reason, at one of the drinking lounge's larger sofa-booths that understanding waiters especially set up with cutlery and crockery. I don't think it's the first time such emergency measures have had to be taken.

Dave departs, stage left (in the direction of the bar).

June tells me about a recent trip she and Joe took on *The Ghan*, the train from Adelaide in the south of Australia via Alice Springs – the nearest station to the famous monolithic rock formation of

Uluru (or Ayer's Rock) – to Darwin on the north coast. *Ghan* is a shortening of *The Afghan Express* and is named after Afghan camel crews who helped explore Australia's interior during the nineteenth century. I had been tempted to take *The Ghan*, which has been running on standard gauge between Alice Springs and Darwin since 2004; previously it only went from Adelaide to Alice Springs on an unreliable service (with the tracks disused after the new Ghan began). But something about travelling across the entire breadth of the continent on the *Indian Pacific* appealed to me. Besides, *The Ghan* seems to crop up repeatedly in travel magazines. I wanted to go on a less obvious journey... and meet Australians, not holidaymakers in search of a big red rock.

This strategy seems to be more than working.

'Flying is boring,' says June, though she is not impressed by the sleeping arrangements on the *Indian Pacific*. 'We had to book two single cabins as we couldn't climb on to a bunk. They're not catering properly for the elderly generation and we're the ones spending and travelling.' She takes a sip of wine.

And just as I'm thinking it's a bit rich that Australians complain about 'whingeing Poms', she puts my thoughts in order. Joe has gone to the toilet. She leans forward and whispers, 'This is our last trip. My husband is dying of lung cancer.'

I say that I'm sorry to hear this, forgetting all about 'whingeing Aussies'. It's a fair comment, I suppose, that the bunk cabins are not especially comfortable for the elderly, who make up the mainstay of those travelling in gold class, at least on my journey. Joe and June are having to pay extra for the two single cabins and are not even together on their 'last trip'.

Joe returns and looks thoughtful. 'It's like the moon,' says Joe. 'No trees.' He's gazing out of the window at the now wide-open landscape. Shrubs and rust-red soil disappear into infinity under the deep blue sky. 'Nullarbor: no trees. Like the moon. You've got to see the Nullarbor before you die.'

We have not yet reached the much-feted Nullarbor Plain, which is further east and is where we will traverse the world's longest straight stretch of railway track: 297 miles of it. Already though, the scenery is wild and rugged: the harshest and least forgiving-looking of any on these rides. There's not a kangaroo, nor any other sign of life, in sight.

At the bar I order another (free) Crown Lager. Dave is back in Position A. Space is made available for Joe and June. A gold-class group has gathered post lunch in the gold-class lounge, drinking gold-class booze: Shane, a former mechanical engineer, who appropriately once worked in a gold mine; his wife Diane, a former city draughtswoman (responsible for parts of Canberra); a Kiwi couple who have been to see the distinctive red-rock formations on holiday in the north of Western Australia ('the Bungle Bungle Range is amazing'); and a mammoth man named James, who is even bigger than Dave and cannot fit in the burgundy leather chairs, so he sticks to a sofa. James hardly says anything.

Our discussion covers a gamut of topics.

The sale of a house in Australia for $57 million. Dave: 'You could go to a lot of Rugby World Cups for that.'

Gin. Joe (ordering another one): 'I only drink gin on trains. Whisky gets to you after a while. Rum is too sweet.'

Kalgoorlie, our next stop. Dave: 'It's got all the same mod cons as Perth, it's just further from the beach.'

Billabongs. Shane (pointing out of the window): 'That there is a billabong, Tom. We also call that a pond.'

The Western Australian wheat belt. Dave. 'A lot of the world is fed from that wheat belt. A lot goes overseas.'

Sheep farms. Dave: 'Rawlinna station is bigger than Lebanon and it's owned by a single family.'

Cattle farms. Shane: 'There's one in the Northern Territory that's bigger than England: 1 million acres, 10,000 cattle and they can't make a profit. It's too far away. It would cost $1,000 an hour to round them up. Then put 'em in trucks. Then transport them. They don't bother rounding them in. They don't cut their balls. They just let 'em run free with no fences. They call it eco tourism.'

Joe reminisces about an old job at Tennant Creek gold mine in the Northern Territory: 'I worked at a cookhouse. I was helping build it. I was the chippie, the carpenter. The guy who ran it was drunk for one week out of every two. I never seen anything like it. They would only pay him every two weeks coz he drank so much when he got his pay. He drank it all. In Tennant Creek it was like that. If you didn't turn up with twelve beers if you went to see people, they didn't want to know you.'

He sips his G & T.

The others are listening, nursing their drinks. I'm not sure whether they know Joe is on his last trip. It's as though the rhythm of the train on the track and Joe's deep mellifluous intonation has lulled the group, as though we're sitting round a campfire listening to old stories.

'Tying up wheat bags. That was another one,' Joe says, not explaining where he had this job. 'Ten bob a bag. That was a lot in those days. Yes! It was tough back then.' As if to prove how tough, he adds, 'I saw a cat attack a dog: the only time I ever did see such a thing.'

The symbol of the *Indian Pacific* is inspiring: a wedge-tailed eagle in flight, painted yolk-yellow on the side of our train (and printed on menus, tickets and souvenirs in the little gift shop in the bar). It's an uplifting logo suggestive of the *Indian Pacific* soaring across this vast nation and its baking red-earth hinterland. The service began in 1970, following the completion of an east–west standard gauge track. While it had been possible to cross the vast nation by train before, this was a lengthy, tiresome passage, partly because there were so many different gauges. When developing each part of Australia in the nineteenth century, local governments decided which size of track was best suited to their needs. Victoria, being then a wealthy, densely populated colony, opted for 5 feet 3 inches (the Irish gauge), with viaducts and bridges and a grand scheme. New South Wales went for the more modest standard gauge of 4 feet 8½ inches, while Queensland, South Australia, Western Australia and Tasmania opted for a narrow gauge of 3 feet 6 inches, which suited little railway lines zipping off to isolated communities; narrow gauge was cheaper and quicker to lay than heavier-duty lines. The result was a hotchpotch of tracks across Australia that required all sorts of hopping on and off.

So much embarking and disembarking invoked the ire of a certain American novelist on a world tour in the 1890s. Before reaching Ceylon and India, Mark Twain stopped off in Australia in September 1895 during his long journey to give lectures and collect material for *Following the Equator* so he could pay off debts. On arrival on a steamer from Vancouver, Twain was asked by reporters of his views on Australia, and he surprised some by remarking: 'I don't know. I'm ready to adopt any that seem handy.' The writer, at the time one of the most famous men on the planet, later got into his stride. Having been introduced to leading politicians, he wrote: 'Australia is the modern heaven – it is bossed absolutely by the workingman.' But there was one thing that really annoyed him: switching trains.

When he reached Albury in New South Wales, he was made to move on to another steam service in Wodonga in Victoria: 'Now comes a singular thing: the oddest thing, the strangest thing, the most baffling and unaccountable marvel that Australasia can show. At the frontier between New South Wales and Victoria our multitude of passengers were routed out of their snug beds by lantern-light in the morning in the biting cold of a high altitude to change cars on a road that has no break in it from Sydney to Melbourne! Think of the paralysis of intellect that gave that idea birth; imagine the boulder it emerged from on some petrified legislator's shoulders.'

Twain was perhaps being a little grumpy. The tracks were a historical legacy from the pragmatic early days of trains, before the Australian federation of 1901 and more organised national coordination. Yet his tetchiness did have a basis. All the different tracks were a nuisance. So the opening of the *Indian Pacific* line had symbolic import. The continent had been tamed. Or as the Australian poet Henry Lawson once wrote, referring to the first Australian railways: 'The mighty bush with iron rails' has been 'tethered to the world.'

The *Indian Pacific* provides plenty of time for reflection. The empty, open landscape seems to invite fanciful thoughts. The scenery becomes drier and drier, flatter and flatter. Gum trees with flinty, dainty branches rise wispily from orange-red soil. Grain silos with peeling paint loom upwards, with no one about: are they still being used? Thin, scraggly sheep look half starving: do they belong to anyone? The sky has become a canopy of gold, red and indigo clouds framed by perfect blue. On the horizon I can see the curve of the Earth... or maybe that's just my imagination.

Beyond Merredin, with its Oasis Motel and row of pick-up trucks parked outside, we come to sidings that are home to the locos and carriages of CBH Group, the country's biggest grain exporter. The silos must be in working order, after all. A water tower advertises Kalgoorlie Beer. Old electricity and telegraph poles stand with twisted wooden fittings and wires hanging down. Rickety barbed-wire fences divide fields. A farmer with his head down, ignoring the train, inspects a crop. Jet-black crows peck in ditches. Light fades in a fusion of peach and purple as darkness descends, clouds parking quietly for the night above the tiny town of Carrabin. Silos stand in silhouette. Long shadows stretch beyond the train, catching the shape of the wheels. Billabongs reflect the stillness of the sky.

This is what trains in Australia provide: a glimpse of life on the ground that you just don't get on planes. I watch and doze, listening to the 'Chardonnay/Manhattan' jazz-and-blues music channel on my cabin's sound system. Classical music – Beethoven, Strauss – soon seeps from next door. Pop music rises from another wall. The aural jumble is slightly maddening, but not so bad. I turn off 'Chardonnay/Manhattan' and watch the dark world outside. It's funny to think of us in our pods in our silver train, slinking eastwards.

Such reveries do not last long. I go over to the lounge a quarter of an hour before my allotted time for dinner; passengers are given slots to avoid queues. The drinking crew are still in Position A, but the mood seems to have shifted in my absence.

'Stopped for bad play, did you? But Dickie Bird said you could start up again?' says Dave, mentioning the former English cricket umpire. He's not asking; the questions are rhetorical, and meant for all the others about him to hear.

Thinking he's just indulging in 'Aussie banter', I say something along the lines of 'Right you are, mate.' And I go up to the bar to get a drink.

A couple of steps past him, almost at the bar, I hear him say loudly for all others to hear: 'And what are *we* going to write about *you*?'

I'd been open with him earlier about my train rides. This was obviously, as I'm about to discover, a big mistake. With my back still turned to the lounge, as I wait for my drink, I hear someone comment: 'He's going to say he met all these stupid Aussies!'

I return with a (free) Crown Lager to sit down on the edge of a sofa, waiting for my dinner slot. As I do so, I realise I'm open prey. Dave turns to me and tells me about someone he had heard of who shrink-wrapped a steam train to protect it from rust, as he did not have enough cash to put it in a garage. 'You can write that in your little book!' he says, loudly once again, after telling his tale.

'Er, thanks, Dave,' I say, turning to a new neighbour and hoping Dave will cool down.

I introduce myself and ask my neighbour's name.

It's Sal, whose first, archly delivered, words are: 'Oh, I've heard all about you!'

This is not said in a good way. I have seen Sal making his way between swaying carriages during the day. He has a tan and wears ripped jeans. He seems reluctant to talk, although he tells me he prefers cruise ships to trains as they have more space. Then he stops abruptly, stares at me with disdain, and looks away.

Time seems to tick slowly. There's nowhere to hide in the gold-class lounge of the *Indian Pacific*. Dave glares at me. He's almost growling beneath his breath as he does so. Joe drinks a G & T and says nothing. By asking a few questions earlier, I seem to have turned into public enemy number one. All the other seats are taken and dinner has yet to be called. Anyway, I would lose face by moving from where I'm sitting now.

I turn to another neighbour. Her name is Angela; she has a bulbous red nose and seems hostile, too. Her form of antagonism is, however, subtly different from the others. I have made the further error of carrying a small notebook. She pointedly looks at this and begins to tell me a long-winded life story involving drives between Sydney and the outback and close collisions with various animals. As she rambles on, she eyeballs my notebook and I feel obliged to take down her convoluted tales that seem to hinge upon the importance of 'seeing the mountains' in life. Jotting notes seems the only way to keep her happy. This approach, however, also has an advantage: I can simply nod and say 'oh yes, really' occasionally while waiting for dinner. This goes on for what seems like a long time. I can feel the searing eyes of Dave. How have I found myself in this position?

A shrill woman with a shock of blue-grey hair interrupts us. I have neither talked to her nor taken her in yet. She seems to know all about me as well. She looks at me and asks, 'Are you freelance? Are you doing this for yourself?' This is not said in a good way, either. Fortunately, she is called away for dinner before I can respond.

Sal turns on me. 'I was born in…' he says. And he stops in mid sentence and stares at my notebook as though I should write down what he is about to say. He's got a smart-alec expression. He's obviously completely taking the ****. Things are spiralling out of control here. I turn on him and, in a voice no one else can hear, tell him to back off in no uncertain terms. He is speechless, livid with indignation.

Pleased with this, I go to the restaurant, dreading the meal ahead in case I draw one of my new enemies as a dining companion. Fortunately, I'm put with a charming couple, and we chat genially about trains for a while. All is relaxed once again. That is, until Angela makes a beeline for our table, sits next to me and continues her long-winded life story, with asides on her children's lives, too. On and on she goes. The polite couple begins to notice that I've had enough of her (I think – in fact, I know – I may be guilty of raising eyebrows, and other involuntary facial expressions). Although the beef fillet with red-wine jus and potato galette is excellent, it's an awful meal. After dessert, Angela, finally letting her guard down, asks my name and says that she is going to 'get my resource officer to pick up on that'. I have no idea what she means by this (and I wonder if she does herself). She is, I have worked out by now, what might commonly be termed 'a bit of a wind-up merchant'.

So begins the mutiny (against me) in gold class on the *Indian Pacific*. I get the sense that Australians may be a little touchy about Pommie reporters. That all I want to do is enjoy the ride and indulge in a little 'train talk' does not, to them, seem possible. I must have some more sinister English agenda.

Never mind. We stop at Kalgoorlie (population: 31,000) in the dead of night. A brief coach tour has been arranged at 22:45.

It's a bizarre scenario. Those of us who wish to – some of the Australians don't bother as they've seen Kalgoorlie already – file on to coaches and listen to the story of the town's 1893 gold rush told by a blonde guide who arrived at the remote mining city a dozen years ago but stayed as 'red dust gets in your veins'.

Evocative turn-of-the-twentieth-century wooden buildings give the centre of town a frontier feel. The streets are wide so camel trains could perform turns, we are told. Camels, apparently, risk dislocating their shoulders if made to step backwards. We are told that 'skimpies', or barmaids, in the town might expect to make $500 a night in tips from the many miners working in local gold mines. We are shown a white picket fence where gold was first discovered, a short distance from a working mine with a 1,200-metre 'super-shaft'. Kalgoorlie is a well-to-do town and, as if to prove this, the guide tells us that the local Woolworths brings in $1.2 million a week: 'The biggest takings of any Woolworths in Australia.'

We are also driven to 'infamous Hay Street', where various brothels are to be found. Takings in these brothels are down, says the guide, as many of the prostitutes in town now 'work out of motels using mobile phones'. This practice is, she says, 'less hygienic', for some reason or other. Daytime tours of one of the brothels are available for $20. 'It's not dirty or smutty; it's interesting, the history of prostitution. They show you rooms. The oldest pro is sixty-seven. You go, girl!' says the guide. A session with a pro in a room might set you back '$350 and upwards', the guide happily informs us. 'We were going by in a coach one time and a young lad was just coming out. He clicked his heels and ran away, poor lad,' she says.

Lord of the Flies on the Nullarbor
Kalgoorlie to Adelaide

You do get a fleeting flavour of towns along the way on the *Indian Pacific*. After Kalgoorlie, we visit the 'ghost town of Cook' the next morning, where we are allowed off the train for half an hour.

I manage to avoid gold-class hostilities at breakfast and enjoy strolling about Cook (population: four), where we have been told to keep out of old buildings as they could be dangerous. The town is in South Australia in the middle of the desolate Nullarbor Plain. It came into being with the railway in 1917 and was an important medical and supply centre for the region and the passing trains until 1997, when new railway owners downscaled its importance. A weather-worn sign says: IF YOU'RE CROOK, COME TO COOK. QUEEN CITY OF THE NULLARBOR. *Crook* is Australian slang for 'ill'. The handful of residents now appears to consist of caretakers for the *Indian Pacific*.

I wander round red-dust yards, inspecting the old wooden buildings, a basketball court with broken hoops, a tennis court with a ruined net, and a sign advertising the long-closed Cook Golf Club, where 'sand green fees' were once $2. I also talk to a cattle, sheep and arable farmer from one of the other gold-class carriages; gold class is split in two with the impassable platinum-class carriages in the middle. Being cut off from my now poisoned gold class, he knows nothing of my notoriety. He tells me he finds the train relaxing and goes on four-day trips every now and then. He's teetotal and says, 'A lot of people are actually just here for the drink.'

Sam, another gold-class man from the other side of the train (it's all a bit *Lord of the Flies* on the *Indian Pacific*), is inspecting the front of the blue and yellow locomotive, which has no fewer than five horns. He is full of admiration.

'There's something about trains, mate,' he says. 'I don't know what it is. People come to Australia and they hop on a plane to Alice Springs – they have no idea how big the country is. I like that a train has its own track: its own bit of land. It has its own area and it goes its own way. I just like that.'

He pauses, says 'excuse me', walks to one side, pauses for a few seconds and returns. 'Just letting out some of the good stuff,' he comments, on his return.

I do not enquire into Sam's exact meaning here.

Sam tells me he's a rugby fan and that he supports the Associates Rugby Union Club based in Swanbourne, Western Australia. He is short and squat with a bald pate and bushy eyebrows: more of a scrum half than the many ex prop forwards on my side of the train. Sam asks if I would like to hear a song. I say I would. And so he begins: 'Rule Britannia! Marmalade and jam! Five Chinese crackers up your arsehole! Bang! Bang! Bang! Bang! Bang! Ra-di-adi-ah-da! Ra-di-adi-ah-da! Ra-di-adi-ah-da!! Up Soaks!'

Only in Australia. His cries echo across the Nullarbor Plain. Sam's team is about to play today, so he felt like giving them a distant cheer.

We move on under a mottled sky. The land is rocky but flat. A black line seems to mark the horizon, where the orange plains studded with dried-out shrubs meet the end of the world. We pass a little airstrip by a town called Barton. White-painted tyres mark a dirt runway.

I read a few poems about railways from a brilliant collection I've brought with me entitled *Train Songs* – Edward Thomas, Seamus Heaney, Philip Larkin, T. S. Eliot and Thomas Hardy are all there. It's interesting that almost every contributor selected for the book is male: is there something about trains that appeals particularly to the male mind? Perhaps – or, let's face it and be honest, definitely – though many women I've met on my travels so far have been train lovers, too. Emily Dickinson, Elizabeth Bishop and Wendy Cope are among the few female poets included in *Train Songs*.

An extract from Cope's 'Strugnell's Sonnets' catches my eye. The poem wittily describes the effect on others of reading poetry on a train: how if 'all seats are taken' you can leave your 'fellow-passengers severely shaken' by pulling out a slim volume of verse. This, says Cope, is proof that 'to recluses… poetry has its uses'. I intend to take *Train Songs* to the gold-class dining carriage later.

Tarcoola comes. Tarcoola goes. In 1893, there was a gold rush in Tarcoola (population: 38). My cabin map says the town is named after a racehorse that won the Melbourne Cup that year. I have a lazy afternoon, in the company of *War and Peace*; on its second trans-continental train, my copy has begun to take on such a tattered look that most second-hand bookshops would surely turn it down. The many miles of the Nullarbor tick by. I listen to a bit of 'Chardonnay/Manhattan' jazz, my channel of choice during daydreaming on the *Indian Pacific*. Every now and then I go to make a cup of tea in the little kitchen at the end of the carriage. Hardly anyone is about. I expect Position A is more than well occupied in the lounge.

I skip lunch in the dining carriage as it's so peaceful in my cabin, opting instead for a few snacks I brought with me. I listen to more 'Chardonnay/Manhattan' jazz. I read. I snooze. This is how long train journeys should be.

When dinner is announced, I go over tactically late so I can avoid various 'characters'. This of course involves running the gauntlet of the gold-class lounge, but this gauntlet cannot be avoided if I want to eat a hot meal. I slip by quietly enough at first, missing the attention of the three diners who have selected to eat in the lounge because it's more comfortable. Then I come to the shrill woman with the shock of blue-grey hair. 'I hope you have taken all their emails so you can send them free copies,' she says, her voice like nails on a chalkboard.

Her body language could be summed up in one word: hostile. She appears to have been sitting in wait for me and seems to be relishing this encounter in some sort of perverse way. Her tone suggests that she is somehow doing a public good: tackling a miscreant, the bad apple in gold class. I think that by 'taken all their emails', she is referring to the people I have talked to on the train. Is she, and are they, under the impression that I'm some sort of Stephen King-rich novelist heading straight to the bank with a multimillion-dollar book–film rights deal after milking their memories one afternoon on a train? Is this what it's all about – do they want a slice of an imaginary Steven Spielberg deal?

'Oh yes, of course,' I reply.

This seems to make her blood boil. What is it with this woman with a shock of blue-grey hair? What have I done to her? She regards me with eyes heavy with make-up and loathing. I don't think I'm particularly good for her health; various indicators of well-being are skyrocketing in the wrong direction. I slip by, thinking: *what next?*

Having negotiated the gold-class lounge with only one hateful conversation, I approach the dining carriage – another social minefield, as I found last night. There is, however, at least an element of freedom: the choice of where to sit. I dine with Joe and June, who chat away cheerfully about what we saw today. We have a very nice meal.

The *Indian Pacific* may cover long sections of outback where not a lot goes on, yet there's plenty of action. The early morning delivers Adelaide, where we once again board coaches for a short tour. The guide on my coach intends to take us to Mount Lofty. He refers to Mount Lofty in reverential tones as though it's some sort of promised land, although he also tells us that we 'won't see a view' when we get there as it's cloudy. *Oh well*, we think as we drive off, listening to how Adelaide became a free settlement in 1836 (i.e. it wasn't settled by convicts). The city now has a population of 1.3 million out of South Australia's population of 1.67 million. Vineyards, fruit groves, sheep and cattle provide employment in the interior of the state, but unemployment is a growing problem in the capital: 'Ford and Toyota are closing: component parts. Another 20,000 are losing jobs. Pretty difficult times ahead.'

We are shown the flying-saucer-like Adelaide Oval sports stadium, opened by the Rolling Stones. Within its grounds, we get a glimpse of a statue of Sir Donald Bradman, who played for South Australia for many years and is considered the best-ever Test cricket batsman. The guide then points out houses worth $1.2 million, explains that a round of golf costs $28 – 'so it's quite affordable to play golf' – and waxes lyrical about a series of mansions on a hill but 'won't comment on their value as I'm not sure what they are worth right now'. These have enormous verandas with fancy lacework and are marked off by whitewashed picket fences. The guide tells us to look to the right to see some 'smaller type houses', and says you can pick up somewhere in the suburbs for between $320,000–500,000: 'That pricing is available.' It's as though he's assessed us and thinks the suburbs are probably better suited to our pockets. I begin to wonder if he's a moonlighting estate agent.

Adelaide seems clean, green and well-to-do – a tempting place to come and live, indeed. We drive to a car park on Mount Lofty, where the guide tells us that the person who needs to show us in has not arrived as it is before 8 a.m.: 'If you want to use the restrooms do get out, but there's no point in leaving the coach otherwise.' The mountain appears to be closed. A couple of people use the restrooms.

And that, for us, is the magnificent Mount Lofty. We drive back to the station in 15 minutes of silence.

'We're on time!' says the guide, sounding extremely relieved when we arrive. He must have been worried we'd miss the train.

Adelaide Parklands terminal is notable for its extensive gift shop selling silver spoons, packs of cards, jigsaws, train whistles, computer mouse mats, aprons, golf balls, polo shirts, beer glasses and – my favourite – battery-powered beer-bottle coolers that make train sounds when lifted... all stamped with the *Indian Pacific* wedge-tipped eagle logo. I go to buy one of the train-noise beer holders as life would not, I feel, be complete without one.

As I wait in the queue, someone bumps into my backpack. 'Oh sorry,' says the shrill woman with the shock of blue-grey hair. Then she realises it's me. 'Oh, it's you. It's your bag. I'm not sorry.' And she moves away. She is with her husband, who trails a couple of steps behind and who never speaks a word that I hear during the entire journey from Perth to Sydney.

Gunzels, transvestites and metrosexuals
Adelaide to Sydney, via Broken Hill

This is the last I am to see of my gold-class friends. At Adelaide, I am downgrading to red class. My main bag is put in the luggage van as there is no storage room where I am going. Red class is separated from my former gold-class section by platinum class. There is no way that the woman with blue-grey hair can get to me; the fine-dining platinum-class elite with their double beds and high-end cocktail lounge blocks her passage.

I settle into my red and purple red-class seat with a sense of relief. Backpackers and senior citizens make up our number in the solitary red-class carriage. We are here to travel from A to B without three-course meals, cabins playing light jazz, and one-upmanship in the free Sauvignon Blanc and Crown Lager lounge. I am sitting next to a twenty-something guy wearing a loose-fitting grey tracksuit and reading a book on an iPad. He flicks a glance and nods to acknowledge his new neighbour and – formalities over – returns to his book. The seats are not massive but they're at least the business-class size of those on a plane, though they do not fully recline.

The train jolts forth. John Wicks, the duty manager, stands before us, in his fifties with an Elvis quiff. 'Your world ends at that door,' he says, after introducing himself. He's pointing to the far end of the carriage. We are not, I gather, to venture elsewhere on the train.

We are told how to lock the toilet door so as 'not to share a toilet moment with forty-seven other people'; the red-class carriage fits 48 and the toilet is in a prominent position at the front. We are also to 'use it as a toilet only: does everyone agree?' There is no answer. 'Excellent. Beautiful,' he says.

In the adjoining Matilda cafe-bar carriage, Wicks says, it is 'not kosher to sit there without purchasing something'. He puts in a good word for his cooked breakfasts. 'I've had phone calls from Gordon Ramsay and Jamie Oliver saying, "I heard about your breakfasts." I said, "No. I want the twenty bucks an hour that Great Southern Rail is paying me."'

With this, he wraps up his spiel and we are left in peace. We are travelling northwards back up the line from whence we came, and are to turn east at Crystal Brook on the final leg to Sydney. Adelaide has been, effectively, a detour. A stop-off is planned at Broken Hill in the early evening, where there is to be another coach tour. I go to the apple-green cafe-bar carriage, known officially as Matilda's Restaurant, though I can't see any sign of a Matilda and 'restaurant' may be stretching it a bit.

We are still in the outskirts of Adelaide. Heaps of cargo containers, streams with dumped shopping trolleys, warehouses covered with graffiti and scaffolding yards gradually fade away. Verdant countryside opens up. I order a coffee so I'm 'kosher' and before long get talking to Wicks, who tells me he used to work as a stand-up comedian.

'Eye contact, it's very important,' he says, explaining his approach to his welcoming speech.

I ask him if red class can get unruly.

'There has been trouble in the past,' he says. 'I pride myself on the fact that I don't chuck people off. Eye contact. And let them vent. That's what's important.'

'You've never chucked anyone off *ever*?'

Wicks thinks for a moment and then relates a story of a man he found shooting up heroin in the toilet: 'He said, "Look, I take my drugs, man." I said, "Look, I've got kids in there." We were at Manguri and the police from Coober Pedy came to take him.'

I ask him about Australian trainspotters. 'Do such people exist?'

'We call them train gunzels. A gunzel is a person who is really stuck on one thing. In Sydney you get guys on the platforms. This carriage here is the CDF924 – that's the number for Matilda's Restaurant. The guys on the platform will say, "Oh, I haven't seen that for a while." There's one station, Midland, near Perth, where you will always see them. In fourteen years working here, always at least two of them.'

'Have you ever had gunzels on board?'

'Oh yeah. I had a guy who went up to Alice Springs and Darwin. He'd sit there and take pictures and notes on every train we crossed and every station. Then he came back and did it all again.'

Wicks leaves. Remaining kosher, I buy a chicken wrap. Long emerald fields open up. An old-timer near me says, 'There's a wind down the coast.' I have no idea how he can tell.

I see a couple of kangaroos in the far distance. They look like fox-coloured traffic cones. Beyond a wind farm with 43.2-metre blades – as we are informed by a speaker announcement – we turn at Crystal Brook. The train begins to rise through arid rolling landscape populated by dirty sheep. An old-timer joins the other old-timer and they begin to drink Carlton beers. A neighbour claims she saw a wedge-tailed eagle; in which case I did too, as I saw the same bird. Another speaker announcement begins and someone rambles on sentimentally about the outback: 'Distance, space, time... until you actually get out there and experience it...

when I get out there I can feel my emotions change.' Not long afterwards, we roll into Broken Hill.

Broken Hill is a mining town famous for its lead and zinc deposits: the Broken Hill Proprietary Company, as it once was, merged in 2001 with another company to form BHP Billiton, the world's biggest mining company. Light is fading rapidly, it's almost 6 p.m., and I cannot face another coach tour in the dark – or the possibility of mixing with gold-class foes. So I decide, in true Australian style, to go walkabout.

The mining town is eerie in the early evening. Empty streets are lined with ghostly, late-nineteenth-century, red-brick buildings with corrugated roofs and ornate veranda-balconies. I look into a deserted bar connected to the – sadly closed – Night Train nightclub. It would have been excellent to have had a drink at the Night Train nightclub. I take in the ornate stuccoed facade of the 1905 town hall; the first proper development in the area around Broken Hill began in 1883 when silver was discovered in nearby Silverton. I walk on, along Argent Street, past the Barrier Social Democratic Club (where folk are queuing for its Tuesday Steak Night amid madly-flashing pokie fruit machines), and come to the target of my stroll: the Palace Hotel. This big corner hotel, dating from 1889, has a unusual history as it featured heavily in the 1994 film *The Adventures of Priscilla, Queen of the Desert*, which is all about the unlikely subject of drag queens in the outback. Not entirely sure what's coming next, I enter and discover a tall reception with bright murals depicting bucolic scenes, mounted stuffed birds and cabinets displaying leopard print high heels. Further inside is a pool table, a bar and no sign of drag queens. I order a beer and a barmaid says that *Priscilla* is one of the biggest-grossing Australian films of all time: 'The film is iconic. It was successful because it's got heart, a very human heart. It's about more than queens in the outback. It's a human story that was very timely, especially so soon after AIDS.' A pamphlet on the bar advertises a Broken Heel Festival to be held at the hotel later in the year. Its motto? 'Life in the outback is never a drag.'

All quite unexpected, as is the fact that Broken Hill lays claim to being the scene of the 'only enemy attack on Australian soil in the First World War'. According to a tourist booklet I pick up at the Palace Hotel, a train bound for nearby Silverton was 'fired upon by an ice-cream cart flying the Turkish flag'. This was shortly before Anzac troops joined the fight against the Turks at Gallipoli.

Our train rolls on through the night, rising into hills. I manage to sleep well enough in red class, waking to see a tangerine sky. Brown cows munch grass in dew-covered fields. I enjoy a Gordon-Ramsay-quality Great Australian Breakfast, sitting near a wild-looking Asian man wearing camouflage-style clothes and holding a plastic knife and fork upside down as chopsticks to eat his bacon and eggs. Lithgow and Bathurst flash by and we ascend through the spectacular Blue Mountains to Katoomba, where we are 3,336 feet above sea level. The Asian man starts making awful spitting sounds. We descend from the mountains.

A tattooed man behind me tells his tattooed girlfriend/female companion that 'neo-masculinity is revealing the true nature of women... with the rise of metrosexuals, women who have been sleeping with bad boys are looking for other options... new metrosexual men are manipulating their techniques to attract women: sophisticated techniques... nice guys have no luck, women are all on the game and they get money easy – they've got more money than guys... blokes have to work hard for a living...' And so on and so on, nonsensically, as we enter the capital of New South Wales.

'Sydney: what a dump,' says the tattooed man.

'Along the railway track it doesn't look so good,' his tattooed girlfriend/companion replies. She has not previously got a word in edgeways.

We pass graffiti-covered walls and a platform with a long double-decker commuter train, and pull in to Sydney Central station. It is 11:20. Not bad, just 13 minutes late. We've travelled quite a way – and the *Indian Pacific* has been quite a ride. I fetch my bag from the luggage van and slip into the streets of Sydney.

I have a plane to catch to another famous harbour city, where I'm about to take the third of my trio of transcontinental trains.

One final point: despite several predictions to the contrary made by fellow passengers on the *Indian Pacific*, the English cricket team went on to beat Australia in the Ashes of 2015. The BBC headline put it this way: *ENGLAND HAMMER AUSTRALIA TO REGAIN THE URN*. After the defeat, the Australian cricket captain Michael Clarke announced his retirement from Test cricket and said, 'it's not for want of trying, but the boys have been beaten by a better side'.

I'm sure the Position A crew will be pleased to be reminded of that.

9 | AMERICA: TRAINS, PLANES AND AUTOMOBILES (MAINLY TRAINS)

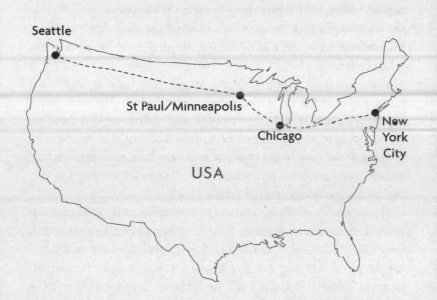

IF YOU PUT 'excited train guy, New York' into the YouTube search box, you're soon treated to an insight into what trains mean to (some) Americans. In the States, people with an excessive interest in trains – the equivalent of Britain's trainspotters or Australia's gunzels – are known as 'foamers'. This is because, it is said, they foam at the mouth when they see a particularly wonderful or interesting train.

The subtitle of the YouTube film is: 'Crazy foamer in North Creek at the Saratoga and North Creek Railway'. The film has had more than 3.4 million views at the time of watching. This, I notice, is considerably more than President Obama's latest State of the Union address in which the American head of state lays out his vision for his final two years in office. More than double the number, in fact. In case this marvellous train lover's clip is ever wiped from the online world, however, I'll describe what happens here.

In short, a train arrives – but it is not just any train. It is a special train, and Excited Train Guy is soon in raptures. The train has a bulbous, upturned nose and orange and yellow streaks running along the side of the otherwise brown body of the locomotive. Excited Train Guy begins his commentary in a tone that sounds excited yet somehow restrained: 'Oh, I've been waiting for this moment for months and it's finally here!'

This period of cool observation does not last long. Bells ring out from the locomotive. Excited Train Guy begins to get very excited, very quickly indeed. The train rolls forwards beneath an oyster-grey sky. 'I'm FINALLY going to get a heritage unit on camera!' he says. 'YEAH! ALL RIGHT!' he bellows. 'Look at that: a 1953 EA! WOOO-HOOO! Oh yeah, listen to that bell! Yeah, listen to that bell! Ah, take a look at that!'

The locomotive blows its horn, sending out a deep resonating sound. Excited Train Guy: 'OH MY GOD! WHOOOOO! LISTEN TO THAT HORN!' The horn blows again. 'OH MY

GOD! SHE'S BEAUTIFUL! SHE IS BEAUTIFUL! YEAH! ALL RIGHT! OH UH OH...'

A blue, yellow and grey locomotive with *Saratoga and North Creek* written on its side is at the rear of the short train. It's just come into view. Excited Train Guy is temporarily lost for words as he assesses the new loco. 'Oh no, it's a BL2 too!' More horns blow. 'Oh, the SNC 52! OH MY GOD!' Quieter now, as though in awe: 'Oh, we're going to watch this – oh! This is special! This is special! Oh! Oh, that horn gives me the chills! And the chills have nothing whatsoever to do with how cold it is here!' As he says this, his camera pans round, following the train, catching a glimpse of another foamer who is also recording the moment. Excited Train Guy: 'AH! OH! That doesn't stop a foamer, especially when it comes to heritage equipment!' He is referring to the cold, which clearly means nothing to a foamer when an SNC 52 is passing by. 'Ah, this is fantastic! OH! Oh, my goodness! Look at that: blue and grey! Oh! Coupled to the – oh! – Iowa Pacific! Number 518! WHOOO HOOO!'

This cry is so loud that the other foamer appears to look round to take in Excited Train Guy. The horn blows again. 'AHHH-HAAA! WOOO! Listen to that horn! Oh, that's fantastic! Oh my gosh! Look at that! All right. Ah! Oh!' He seems to be catching his breath here, and he quietly wonders what a couple of words written on the side of the blue, yellow and grey loco mean. He's not sure. 'Oh well,' he says, as though you cannot have it all in life: some mysteries will always remain. He perks up. 'Ah! This is just awesome! I have been waiting for this for months! Look at that: Illinois Central livery, right here in North Creek! Ah! That is AWESOME!' More bells. 'Aaahh! Wooo! Oh yeah! Can't believe I got this!' More bells, once again. 'Oh yeah! Ah! Heee-ahh!'

The footage cuts out.

It is a remarkable, infectiously joyous film – and the 4,600-plus comments from YouTube viewers pick up on Excited Train Guy's celebratory vibe: *I feel so happy for the guy, good on him!... This guy's excitement is contagious. I'm smiling and feeling happy even though I don't care about trains at all... I'm genuinely happy for this guy and that something this innocent can make him so happy... This guy is my hero!... Woohooo!*

Trains in America mean a lot (perhaps a little more to some than to others). The conquering of the West and the bringing together of the world's wealthiest and most powerful nation relied on the country's railroads, which literally connected America from sea to shining sea in the mid nineteenth century. The completion of the first transcontinental railway at Promontory Summit in Utah on 10 May 1869 was a major moment – and media event – celebrated by the hammering of a 'golden spike' in the final sleeper. News of the symbolic act was sent immediately by telegraph across the country in a one-word message: *Done*. All of a sudden, the Wild West was not quite so wild any more. Dreams of 'going west' to seek fortunes and a new life – thoughts of which had been stirred during the heady gold-rush days of 1849 – took on a greater sense of reality.

Railroads prospered for many years to come, helping to determine where cities and towns grew as America blossomed. Tracks soon formed an impressive web across the vast nation and the luckiest passengers enjoyed getting about in plush carriages designed by New York State-born George Pullman (1831–1897), who was at the forefront of developing comfortable sleepers and snazzy dining cars. Trains were not only highly practical; they were fashionable too. Railroads continued to boom at the turn of the twentieth century and well into the 1930s, although by then things had begun to change. The introduction of affordable cars for the middle classes, famously beginning with the Ford Model T in 1908, provided trains with their first serious competition. This newfangled way of getting about proved immensely popular. In the 1920s, state highways sprang up, followed not so long after by lengthy interstate roads. Train use began to tail off slowly, and just as it did, another challenger to the railroads came along. By the 1940s, propeller planes linked many cities, becoming the passage of choice among those who wanted to get about quickly and who could afford the fares. When jet aircraft with cheaper tickets arrived in the late 1950s, trains – as a means of travelling across the vast distances of the US – took a major hit. Hopping on planes suddenly made a lot of sense. Airlines such as Pan Am and Trans World Airlines took off, literally. Passengers and freight could zoom above the clouds, while trains chugged along below, waiting at sidings and generally looking extremely old-fashioned by comparison.

Trains were feeling the strain. Lines were losing money and could not keep up. The government had to step in. The result, in 1971, was the formation of Amtrak, which took over most intercity passenger lines. This federal-backed service has not, however, turned around the fortunes of US trains. Amtrak Railroad's current debt is about $1.3 billion and in its latest financial results, the organisation boasts that its 'federally funded operating loss of approximately $227 million was the lowest level since 1973'. Amtrak appears to be proud of a $227 million deficit – which is, admittedly, half what it was in 2007, so some progress appears to have been made.

Yet despite all this, the historical role of trains in America – so important during the golden era of frontiers and fortune-making of the nineteenth century – hangs in the background of the country's remaining passenger lines. For this reason, and because some simply enjoy trains, many Americans still love rail travel. Excited Train Guy in North Creek is not alone.

I decide to go from east to west, travelling in the direction of the nineteenth-century dreamers, starting in New York City. Trains to be taken: two from John F. Kennedy International Airport to Manhattan (where I am to stay a night), a subway ride to Brooklyn and back, one overnight train from New York's Penn station to Chicago (on the *Lake Shore Limited* service), another from Chicago to Minneapolis (on the *Empire Builder* service) to spend a day or two learning about a key figure in the history of American trains, followed by another *Empire Builder* train from Minneapolis to Seattle. Total distance to be covered: 3,180 miles.

'Hey, man, why you takin' a picture of me?'
AirTrain, the subway, New York Transit Museum and Grand
Central Terminal

Getting from JFK International Airport to the right part of Manhattan by train requires catching the AirTrain and then the blue E line on the subway to the heart of the Big Apple.

A busy, unremarkable AirTrain speeds along and drops me at Jamaica station, where I wait on a platform watching tattooed folk with headphones sauntering past, bouncing to the beat of their music. A bald man wearing a Che Guevara T-shirt sings a Latino song. Skinny guys, who may or may not be gang members, hop by in hooded tops and pristine Nike trainers.

I take the E line subway in a carriage with plastic lilac seats, sitting beside a man whom I assume is a painter and decorator as his jeans are splattered in paint and turps. Nobody makes eye contact. There are no 'mind the gap' announcements. Anyway the gap is much smaller on the New York Metro than it is back home; plus New Yorkers, I can already sense, do not need to be bothered with such obvious messages. They seem too hard-boiled for that.

Soul music awaits at Lexington Avenue and 53rd Street station. A three-piece band with a drummer, guitarist and lead singer is playing a tuneful song entitled 'Let's Just Kiss and Say Goodbye'. I stop to listen as the battered stainless-steel train departs, with

Stars and Stripes painted on each carriage. The lead singer croons on about his 'darlin'', who he's been meeting in secret and with whom he's been doing 'wrong' – presumably conducting an illicit affair. They decide to part, to kiss and say goodbye. His smooth soulful lyrics drift along the busy platform. A crowd has formed and a few are tapping feet, closing their eyes before the next train comes. It's the best train music so far on these many and varied journeys; certainly a cut above the patriotic Russian tunes on the run into Moscow. When he finishes, I ask the lead singer about the song. It's by a group called the Manhattans, appropriately enough. I thank him and drop two bucks in a guitar case.

'Yeah, man,' he says.

My hotel, the Roger Smith, is in Midtown, close to Grand Central station. I picked it for this proximity as I'm intending to engage in a little light New York City train research in the morning before taking the *Empire Builder* to Chicago.

This 'research' can be broken into two parts. The first involves a visit to the New York Transit Museum, I still remember what Charlie said in Kosovo about museums being important to 'rail knowledge'. So after an early night, I head to Grand Central, where I eat breakfast in the cavernous basement food hall; an appropriate start to a 'train day', I feel. I can recommend the porridge plus the mango and banana smoothies from a circular food stall that seems to go by the name of Dishes.

From Dishes, I walk to Grand Central's subway station. At the ticket machine, a man whom I initially take to be a station employee helps me press the right buttons for a ticket to Brooklyn. Having done so – the machine was incredibly simple – he says, 'You got a little to help, man?'

I give him a dollar.

'Awl-right,' he says.

On the train to Brooklyn I sit next to a twenty-something man wearing a massive grey T-shirt; it must be XXXXXL-sized. He has wrapped his arms inside this T-shirt in order to keep warm. I have never seen anyone do this before. His head rests against a partition by the door. He's fast asleep, and cuts an odd figure. The journey is otherwise uneventful.

We arrive at Borough Hall station, with elegant old mosaic signs giving the station name. Outside, I listen to a deranged black man, whose trousers are almost falling off, crying: 'I'LL MURDER YOU BLACK SISTERS! BLACK BITCHES, MAN!' Nobody walking by seems to bat an eyelid.

Trestle-table stalls offer cheap fedoras and DVDs. A skinny man clutching a cane is asleep on a subway vent. His trainers are by his side, their tongues lifted out so his shoes can ventilate. A towel is wrapped round his neck and his head rests on the edge of a black bin liner containing his possessions; a rudimentary alarm system, it seems, should anyone try to make off with his bag.

The New York Transit Museum is in a basement connected to an old, disused subway station in which heritage carriages and locos are stored. It's a funny sort of place – tucked away, with few visitors when I go. I examine exhibits on the early days of New York's subway; ground was broken on the first line in March 1900 and services began in 1904. Displays tell me that many of the early tunnels were created using a 'cut and cover' technique: a big trench was dug, the tunnel installed, and the earth refilled. This method came before more sophisticated 'deep rock mining' and 'underwater tunnelling'. There is a section on the history of turnstiles and tokens on the New York subway, with multiple examples of each from over the years. Here you can learn all about the groundbreaking Round End Kompak Model of 1946, with its metal plates to prevent vandalism, as well as the innovative Automatic Fare Card turnstile of 1992, which was created with slanted sides to 'reduce leverage for leapers, while the narrow passageway inhibits people from crawling under the arms'.

Beyond are (many) information panels on the building of bridges. Brooklyn Bridge, which opened in 1883, is the star of this section. On the day after its formal opening, 150,000 people walked across the bridge, while it hit the headlines a year later when 'circus impresario P. T. Barnum led a herd of 21 elephants across'. It's also intriguing to learn that the vast structure across the East River was made before the invention of power tools, so it was 'effectively built by hand'.

I check out the shiny carriages and locos in the old subway station, which would no doubt be of great interest to Excited Train Guy, and as I walk along the platform I suddenly realise something: although the history of turnstiles and tokens on the New York Metro may not exactly be for *everyone* (being brutally honest), I'm quite enjoying the New York Transit Museum. The setting is strangely fascinating, allowing you to slip into the lives of the passengers back when these creaky trains spun beneath the skyscrapers of Manhattan. Old adverts for Campbell's tomato soup and Veribest corned beef have been preserved in carriages, as have messages from the US Food Administration during the Second World War: *FOOD WILL WIN THE WAR. WE OBSERVE MEATLESS DAYS, WHEATLESS DAYS, PORKLESS DAYS.* After the war, oversized passengers apparently became an issue as they were contributing to cramped carriages thanks to a rich diet during years of full employment. A *New York Times* editorial commented: 'With more and stouter people about it is only a matter of time before the [subway] car must explode.' Vintage station signs warn that spitting is unlawful and that *carrying lighted cigars, cigarettes or pipes on the cars, stations or station stairways* is not permitted. Visitors must also refrain from resting on their canes on escalator steps, while 'meddlers' are warned that tampering with escalators could result in a prison sentence.

The New York Transit Museum is both for aficionados and the casual train lover – which is, I suppose, how I categorise myself by now, having perhaps quietly moved up a category from 'someone who likes looking out of the window'. There's something satisfyingly rewarding in making the pilgrimage. Just a handful of others are around during my hour-long visit (including a couple of definite foamers).

I return to Grand Central for part two of my New York City train inquiries. I've signed up for a Municipal Art Society tour of the station. I booked in advance ($20) and Christine is waiting, as promised, by the entrance to platform 29. This is on the main concourse, with its magnificently high ceiling painted peacock blue and decorated with symbols of the zodiac, way up above the passengers weaving across the pink Tennessee-marble floor. I know the colour is peacock blue and the floor is pink Tennessee-marble as Christine, a slight figure dressed in green and black, with New Balance trainers and peace-symbol earrings, tells our small group so. Christine has grey hair in a neat bun, glasses and an inexhaustible knowledge of Grand Central, which we are soon scooting around, learning that the platforms can handle 700 trains daily, while the subway copes with 250,000 passengers. It's estimated that half a million people walk across the main concourse each day. More than 21 million tourists are believed to come to gawp at the station every year, making it the tenth most popular tourist attraction on the planet, according to *Travel + Leisure* magazine – whose word I'll take on the matter.

Alert soldiers with weapons defend key corners of this world-famous attraction as Christine informs us that Grand Central is technically a 'terminal not a station' and that it is a 'marriage of technology and aesthetics' as well as a 'monument to movement', the brainchild of the entrepreneurial Cornelius Vanderbilt in the 1860s.

'Vanderbilt was a poor farm boy from Staten Island,' says Christine. 'He had a job on a ferry, but then he borrowed some money for his own ferry from Staten Island to Manhattan. The journey would take two hours in those days.'

Step by step his ferry business grew, with steamboats soon introduced, before Vanderbilt – who had rapidly developed into a hard-nosed businessman – seized the opportunity to take control of a train line that ran from Harlem to 26th Street, where it met a horse-drawn service to the tip of Manhattan. At around the same time he bought the 'wasteland' where Grand Central now is. 'Everyone thought: "You're nuts. New York City is all downtown."' says Christine of Vanderbilt's decision. This move, however, helped reinforce Vanderbilt's position as one of the richest men in the country. Grand Central opened in 1871 and Vanderbilt lived a few years to see its potential realised (he died in 1877). An acorns and oaks motif, later introduced in his honour, now runs throughout the station: a nod to Vanderbilt's rags-to-riches story.

We stroll past the special waiting room for guests of the glitzy Biltmore Hotel, learn that the facade is made of granite built over a steel cage, that the station was rebuilt in its current Beaux Arts form in 1913 when electric tracks were introduced (this was a response to a terrible steam locomotive accident in 1902), and that the symbols of the zodiac on the ceiling are back to front as the painters made a mistake when copying a drawing from sketches while peering down from their ladders. We take in the 50-foot statue of Vanderbilt close to a decorative station facade topped by Mercury, the Roman god of travel, financial gain and thievery. 'Though no one mentions the thievery,' says Christine, having just done so. In the days of Vanderbilt's empire-building, a certain amount of cunning – if not outright theft – was required, with some public officials doing pretty well, by all accounts, out of applications for licences and planning permission.

We return inside to see the famous oyster bar (setting for many a shot from *Mad Men*, the television series about the Midtown advertising boom in the 1960s), and the four-faced opal clock in the centre of the concourse, near a giant Stars and Stripes that has hung from the terminal's 125-foot ceiling since 11 September 2001. We also learn that a tennis court exists up on a top floor at the front of the station – which seems rather hard to believe.

But the big story about Grand Central is: *it's still here*. Despite protests from the likes of Jacqueline Kennedy Onassis and criticism from *The New York Times*, the city's original Penn Station – another glorious, if not quite so splendid, structure not so far away in Manhattan – was demolished in 1963. 'The "air rights" above it had been sold, so the station came down. This was a shock to everyone,' says Christine. Penn Station's neoclassical columns and birdcage-like, sky-lit concourses were replaced by a functional-but-dull underground station beneath Madison Square Garden, an indoor sports and entertainment arena. 'This was,' says Christine, 'a watershed moment.' Following Penn Station's demolition, all old buildings in New York appeared to be under threat. Yet Grand Central survived owing to campaigns made by the likes of Onassis and many others. Penn Station had become an architectural martyr: its destruction such a dire mistake, realised in retrospect, that further major blunders were avoided. In 1976, Grand Central was classified as a National Historic Landmark, thus providing protection from greedy developers. Given that the station played a central role in popularising the Midtown of Manhattan, encouraging entrepreneurs to build the likes of the Chrysler Building and the Empire State Building, this seems only right. The 'travesty' of what happened to Penn Station, says Christine, remains in New Yorkers' minds.

After going to see the unusual, one-court Vanderbilt Tennis Club (which does indeed exist and where games cost $210 an hour), I return to the Roger Smith Hotel, pick up my bags and catch a cab to the 'new' Penn Station. I'm dropped by a brute of a concrete and black-glass tower block that stands next to Madison Square Garden. Beneath the ugly tower is a sign for the platforms.

I pause on the pavement to look about. As I do so, a tramp sidles up. 'Can y'spare me a little change, brother?'

He holds a piece of cardboard on which he's scrawled: LOST EVERYTHING BUT MY FAITH IN GOD. DOWN ON MY LUCK. HUNGRY.

Hanging around looking like a tourist can be an expensive business in New York City. I give him a dollar.

'Thank you, brother. God bless you and have a good weekend,' he says.

Then I go inside and take a couple of pictures of a concourse with US cities flashing on a departure board. As I do so, I'm interrupted.

'Hey, man! Hey, man!' A bedraggled guy wearing an untucked camouflage top and old shoes hobbles up to me. He looks furious and is pointing at my face. 'Why you takin' a picture of me without my permission!' he yells. 'MAN, YOU TAKIN' A PICTURE!'

His face is a couple of feet from mine now. He has chestnut eyes with pinpoint pupils. He does not seem capable of blinking. I tell him I didn't mean to, I was just taking a picture of the station. A taller man with ruffled sandy hair, who looks as though he might sleep rough on one of the subway vents, joins the bedraggled guy. *This is not my greatest station moment*, I'm thinking.

The bedraggled man is agitated and bouncing on his toes. I've stepped away but he's veering towards me – not letting me get out of his pouncing zone – pointing at me as though appealing to the sandy-haired newcomer.

'I'M TALKIN' TO HIM,' he yells.

The taller guy says, 'You ain't no more, 'less you want the cops to come.'

The bedraggled guy contemplates this and starts saying: 'TAKIN' MY PICTURE! I'M TALKIN' TO HIM!'

The sandy-haired guy holds him back and whispers in his ear. My enemy's chestnut eyes burn in my direction.

As they do, I take my leave, resisting the urge to turn and take another snap for fear of becoming an item in the late edition of the *New York Post*: *BRITISH FOAMER IN PENN STATION BUST-UP*. Subhead: *TRAIN TOURIST SAYS: 'ALL I WANTED TO DO WAS GET A PICTURE OF THE DEPARTURE BOARD.'* For one thing, this might not look so great if it popped up on Google searches. For another, I'm not sure my travel insurance covers fights with pissed-off US veterans at Penn Station.

'Amtrak is run on a dime'
New York City to Chicago on *Lake Shore Limited*

Platform seven of Penn Station feels like a dungeon. Dim lights flicker in a gloomy enclosure, where our sleek *Lake Shore Limited* train awaits. Down a narrow platform crammed with passengers, I find carriage 12, where the sleeper cabin is the same size as on the *Indian Pacific*. The attendant's name is Kevin. He seems friendly but harassed.

We pull away. A horn echoes. We rise slowly into the afternoon sunlight. Glimpses of brown, flowing Hudson flit by between tower blocks. Razor wire runs along a wall by a factory. *BEAST*, says graffiti by a rusting fence. Then the scenery opens, the river in full view. Thick forest covers the far bank. Vines hang from tall, straight trees near the track. Cyclists spin along a dirt trail. Two old-timers rest on tatty swivel chairs that look as though they've been rescued from a skip. They're fishing on a leaf-strewn bank. A pot sits on a rock, awaiting their catch. Are the old fellows fishing for dinner? It looks that way. On their funny swivel chairs, they make an arresting sight.

It's startling how quickly the big smoke – one of the biggest smokes of all – disappears when you leave NYC by train. Not so long ago I was in a traffic jam in a yellow cab, soon to be threatened by a veteran with a dislike of cameras. Now I'm in *Huckleberry Finn* land with little uninhabited islands and shafts of soft orange sunlight playing on russet and lime-green trees. Currents ripple on the river. Metal-framed bridges soar high. A bullet-bodied bird sails beyond a rust-red sugar refinery. The forest resumes. Silos arise. The trees come back. A dog walker sticks his fingers in his ears to keep out the train's horns – a little melodramatically, if you ask me. We cross a viaduct studded with rivets. The river winds onwards beyond a marsh of lilac-tipped reeds.

We pass Irvington, former home of Washington *Rip Van Winkle* Irving. His house is visible near the station, it is said, though I cannot make it out. Croton-Harmon is next, then Peekskill and Garrison. The latter seems to be the station for West Point Academy across the river: red-brick buildings with battlements, sprawling on a hill. Former alumni include Presidents Grant and Eisenhower, and Robert E. Lee and Douglas MacArthur, says the handy *Lake Shore Limited Route Guide*. This is provided free in the cabin and is the best such pamphlet yet.

We stop at Poughkeepsie, chosen by the Vanderbilts and the Astors for weekend retreats. This is also where Samuel Morse, the inventor of the telegraph and Morse code, once lived. Thank you, *Lake Shore Limited Route Guide*. From my window I can see an Irish pub, a fishing jetty, and not much else.

'Albany's comin' up. Albany's comin' up,' says Kevin over a speaker. And so it does. Passengers leap out at the Amtrak station for the capital of New York State, going for a quick smoke on a platform close to a sign warning: *IMPAIRED DRIVERS TAKE LIVES*. Perhaps this message is necessary as the city's bars have a 'last call for alcohol' at 4 a.m.; later than elsewhere in the US. Thank you once again, *Lake Shore Limited Route Guide*.

In the dining carriage ('All meals are included in your scheme,' says Kevin) I sit at a blue-leather booth facing a man in another booth with blue hair and *SKUNKS* written across his enormous T-shirt. He's even bigger than the largest of the gold-class Aussies. We stare at one another expressionlessly for a second or two. If we were wild beasts, I'd be on the one hand concerned that he was considering eating me, while on the other I'd be more than certain I could outrun any attack.

I'm joined by Stan, a plumber, and Bette, who works in computing. They're from Oxford in England and are on a two-week train trip from New York to Chicago and Washington DC. Bette wears a pearl necklace and a cardigan. Stan has a grey polo neck, a crew cut and a gravelly voice. They like the 'adventure' of trains as 'they're much more exciting than planes' says Bette.

'On a plane you might say "hello" but that's it. Not like this,' growls Stan.

I ask a few questions about their journey and Bette says, 'You sound like the immigration department.'

I try to stop being nosy (I don't want another *Indian Pacific*-style mutiny on my hands). We eat our Amtrak Signature Steaks, served with a peppercorn sauce and a baked potato with sour cream and vegetables. This comes to 945 calories, says the menu, which lists the calorie count of every dish. Seven out of ten, is Stan and Bette's verdict, though I think they're being pretty generous (the steak is as tough as an old shoe). Then we discuss the crazy little toilets in our cabins.

'There should at least be a dividing curtain,' says Bette. The toilets are, we all agree, ridiculously prominent in the cabins. Bette's concluding thoughts on the too cosy set-up are: 'It's not something to try if you've only been with a girlfriend for six months.'

They return to their cabin and I go to the cafe bar, where the attendant asks me, 'Whaddya want?' She has lazy eyes but is also, somehow, super sharp at the same time. I take her to be a New Yorker, though I don't enquire. I request a Sierra Nevada Regional Craft Ale. She looks at me with an expression that says: *Yes, I guessed as much – you'd have to have the fancy beer.* The alternatives are Special ($4.50), Domestic ($5.50) and Import ($6.50). My Regional Craft is $7. She fetches a bottle and levers off the cap using an old crack in the ceiling above the booth. She catches the cap as it flicks off, almost without looking.

It is dark now; shadowy outlines of buildings and trees slide by. Regional craft beer in hand, I sit at a table in the dining carriage. There are two other passengers: a young tattooed woman eating a microwaved pizza and a large man consuming a hot dog. These feats are conducted swiftly. They depart. I am alone. This cafe bar is shared with those who are not in sleeper class. These passengers are in the equivalent of the *Indian Pacific*'s red class, with seats not beds. I walk along a couple of darkened carriages to see how the other half lives. People are sprawled with legs in aisles. Films flicker on iPads. A man wrapped in a blanket holds a little dog; I hadn't expected pets on board. I use the toilet, which is a disaster zone (I shall say no more).

I return to the cafe and order another regional craft beer. The lazy-eyed woman performs the same trick.

Then I meet the conductor. She is softly spoken with hair swept to one side, hoop earrings, a gap in her front teeth and bags under her eyes. It looks as though she works hard at her job. A notepad with location references sits on her table in the dining carriage. The conductor makes marks as we move. Radio messages from the driver call out from a walkie-talkie into which she occasionally mutters messages such as '2031 West. 2031 West.' From her, I learn the following: there are 11 carriages on this train of which three are sleepers, two are for dining and six are seat-only. So the 'other half' is, in fact, the other two thirds. A total of 263 passengers are on board. There are two General Electric locomotives pulling the train.

The conductor tells me a story about a collision with a car when she was working a shift: 'There's a blind spot near Syracuse. A lady thought she could get through a crossing before a barrier came down. We had three engines up front. The car was smacked up pretty good. It got caught between two engines. She got out OK though. She was very shaky.' A blind spot, she says, is where the tracks curve to the extent that the way ahead is partially obscured.

I sit with the conductor, drinking my regional craft beer. She picks out and eats an occasional single tortilla chip from a little plastic bag. She tells me that she used to be a flight attendant and that she has 'been around and seen it all'. She worked for her airline for 12 years: 'I did everything but fly those planes.'

We are joined by another conductor, who has a crew cut, a blue peaked cap and keys jangling on a belt. He worked for the US Air Force for 30 years, 10 months and 9 days, he says. He took on the Amtrak job after retirement from the air force to earn extra cash as 'I have children in college'. He looks upon my regional craft beer with approval and tells me he likes 'Dogfish Head: it's got a picture of a fish on the bottle'. He also enjoys Guinness, Kilkenny and German beers: 'None of them is bad.'

The three of us fall into silence for a while. It's close to midnight. An elderly woman in black sits at a table across from us and begins to read *The Good Soldier* by Ford Madox Ford. After a while she puts down her book and introduces herself. Many years ago she worked for the *Chicago American* newspaper, but 'went into computers' when the paper folded in 1974. She's heading for a reunion of ex *Chicago American* employees (the paper had several names over the years including *Chicago Today* at the end, I learn). She gives me her thoughts on trains in America: 'I love train travel, but it's not the same as it was. You used to be able to go from any little town to any little town, several times a day. Then in the 1960s, the government abandoned railroads for highways. Since then we've had Amtrak: just a few routes.'

Our train is already an hour behind schedule, the conductors tell us.

'That's one of the troubles: the freight trains have priority,' says the woman in black. 'No long-distance Amtrak train is on time. Often it's not late by minutes – it's by hours. There's no political will to do anything about it. Hardly anyone takes the train. Everyone drives or flies. It's faster to fly. You have more autonomy if you drive.'

She goes misty-eyed, recalling the days before the government abandoned railways. 'Gambling and playing poker. College kids, we were. Couldn't drink – well, we weren't meant to. Florida to Mississippi, on to Louisiana – that's where we'd pay the bill.' By settling up in a state where the legal drinking age was lower, the college kids seem to have got around the drinking laws. 'The trains were hopping with servicemen – all along the Gulf Coast, military installations.'

The woman in black pauses. She has thoughtful, expressive, pale-blue eyes. The mistiness has gone, replaced by a spark. It's clear from the way she talks that those days of poker, drinks and servicemen were vibrant and alive to her: not like the dusky, empty dining carriage with me, her and the two conductors now. 'Trains are not American at all,' she says, seeming to refer to their current status in the country, not their historical import. 'Nobody really takes them. Except for commuter trains, they're a backwater. Amtrak is chronically in financial straits.'

I ask her if she is in a sleeper. She's not. She's in one of the seating carriages. 'Don't worry about me: I can sleep on a bed of nails,' she says. 'The class divide,' she adds, looking towards the seating carriages. She sighs and closes *The Good Soldier* with a snap. Her sigh seems to suggest: that's just the way it is, and the way it always will be. The woman in black says goodnight, picks up her book and disappears in the direction of the 'other two thirds'.

When a freight train passes at night on Amtrak, it feels as though the air is being sucked from the cabin, reminding me of the Trans-Siberian Railway. I sleep well enough, lying on one side; there's little room to move. In the morning, I wake and pull down the blind to see fields of glorious golden crops. I take a shower at the end of the carriage, though the water runs out when I'm still covered in soap. I manage to splash enough on to remove the suds. Then I explain what happened to Kevin. 'Oh, they'll fill it up in Toledo anyway,' he replies. Kevin looks exhausted. Amtrak employees seem to have long hours. He tells me that we switched locomotives from electric to diesel-electric at Albany. We are two hours late, he adds, currently in Ohio, somewhere between Elyria and Sandusky. The latter was part of the 'Underground Railroad that helped slaves escape to freedom before the Civil War'. Thank you, *Lake Shore Limited Route Guide*.

At breakfast, I meet Larry.

'Hi, I'm Larry,' he says, as he sits down opposite me at one of the booths. American trains really are incredibly sociable. He is in his seventies, with thin, neatly combed grey hair, blue eyes and a navy waterproof jacket. He lives in East Lansing, Michigan. We order Railroad French Toast and Larry hands me his card: *H. Lawrence Swartz, PhD, Chairman & CEO, America by Rail… the best way to see America!* I am, by chance, eating breakfast with the founder of the 'number-one group travel company with Amtrak'.

Larry considers our meeting to be serendipity, which I suppose it is as he's a fount of knowledge about US trains. His company, begun in 1983 and now run day-to-day by his son, takes 3,000 mainly senior citizens and 'some enthusiasts' on escorted rail holidays each year; tours to the national parks in the West are his biggest sellers, as increasingly are 'rail-and-sail' packages transporting those who are afraid of flying from the interior of America to ports to catch cruise ships. Repeat business is strong, with one in five customers booking his train trips again. Larry got the idea for America by Rail in his forties. During his childhood he had been taken by rail with his mother to military camps around the US, where his father was posted during the Second World War. The memory of those early days sparked a moment of realisation one crisp morning when he was travelling on a train in Ontario: 'I was in tears. I knew then: I just love trains. Trains are wonderful. On a train, people can talk: they're going somewhere but they're not going anywhere. They have the time.'

I ask Larry if he agrees with the woman in black about the decline of US trains. Larry does. He too believes Amtrak is financially stretched. He feels it is badly underfunded: 'The travel dollar in the United States: 60–65 per cent of all government money goes on highways; thirty per cent on airports; two per cent on Amtrak. Trains were the Wild West and the old way of travel, but we don't need them any more: that's the federal way of thinking.'

Larry refers to one success story: trains are now the number-one way of travelling between Washington DC and NYC. This is despite a tragic recent derailment on the line in which eight people died and 200 were injured.

'Let me tell you something, Tom,' Larry says, all of a sudden. Larry feels that our meeting is such a coincidence (I have mentioned *Ticket to Ride*) that he wants to tell me a personal story. Or maybe he just always opens up to strangers. 'My favourite part of the female anatomy is the eyes,' he says.

'Could you say that again?' I ask.

'My favourite part of the female anatomy is the eyes.'

'Oh,' I say.

Larry explains: 'Years ago I was in a college choir when I met Nancy. But then I took the proverbial long walk for fifty-one years.' Larry is talking about his marriage to another woman, I gradually surmise. 'There was a college reunion, when I met Nancy again, but I was with my wife. I thought Nancy looked very good, but I was with my wife: I never thought I'd see her again. Then my wife sadly died.' This was in 2009. Sometime after that, his memory was jogged: 'One Friday in July, the good Lord said to me: "Remember Nancy Norris." I wrote her a seven-page letter. Six months later we were married.'

He had, it seems, remembered Nancy's eyes.

We eat our Railroad French Toast (180 calories). Switching subject, I ask Larry – one of North America's most knowledgeable train men – what his favourite train journey is. He tells me it's from Vancouver to Toronto on *The Canadian* service (sadly I am not managing to fit this one in). He goes on the train each year with Nancy, and he invites me to join them on their next trip. Larry also likes the 1930s carriages built by Budd of Philadelphia that are used on America's *California Zephyr* trains – the same company behind the *Indian Pacific*'s carriages in Australia.

We finish our Railroad French Toast. Larry says he's a bit disappointed the blankets in some cabins had not been unwrapped and laid out by the carriage attendants who make the beds at night. He notices things like this and tells me he's going to have a word with the train manager about this and a few 'other matters'. We finish our twice-refilled cups of coffee and get up to return to our cabins. 'Amtrak, Tom,' Larry says, as a parting comment. 'Amtrak is run on a dime.'

He pauses, looks down the dining carriage and adds quietly: 'On a dime, Tom. It's too bad really.'

Toledo comes. We stop. Smokers alight. Water supplies are replenished as passengers come, passengers go. We roll west across bridges, passing container carriages, buttercup crops, picket fences, Stars and Stripes, cornflower skies, wind turbines, hawks, golf clubs, horses, water towers, dogs on trailer steps, long thin roads, turkey vultures, baseball fields, *WATCH FOR TRAINS* signs, Confederate flags, bankruptcy ads, the small town of Bryan, the even smaller town of Waterloo.

'South Bend is comin' up,' says Kevin over the speaker. A neighbour tells me she slept on a table at a station in New Jersey for 14 hours as another train, a couple of days ago, was late. Amtrak is going to 'get a talking-to'. 'I'm putting you in my travel journal,' she says, though we haven't talked all that much.

We chug on: Alka-Seltzer depots, tractors on trailers, a Shooters bar, Gary in Indiana (Michael Jackson's home town), storm clouds, steel plants, rusting trucks, Chinese containers, Whole Foods Markets, Pet Smart Grooming Pets Hotel, windows of a metro train glowing green in a tunnel... Chicago.

'Everybawdy ay-else goddit'
Chicago to St Paul

Let's just get this out straight away: Chicago is, for me, a disaster.

Lake Shore Limited pulls into Union station a couple of hours late, but there's still plenty of time till my next train, the *Empire Builder* to St Paul, Minnesota. Union station is modern and nondescript with soulless waiting lounges and a dull food hall. Outside, paving stones lead to a muddy green river surrounded by smoked-glass skyscrapers, where an Amish family wearing straw hats, bonnets and purple aprons stand by a railing. The men have long beards but no moustaches. They seem to be discussing an important matter. I feign interest in a boat and eavesdrop.

'Shall we go to Burger King?' asks one bearded man without a moustache to another.

'I don't like Burger King,' says the other bearded man without a moustache.

'Ruth likes Burger King,' the first man replies.

'What about Pizza Hut?'

'I don't like Pizza Hut,' says the first bearded man without a moustache.

'Ruth really likes Pizza Hut,' says the second.

And so on. Here I am, hoping for insight into an important non-mainstream American culture – and all I get is this.

Inside I eat a sandwich and go to a waiting lounge before realising via an announcement that I'm eligible, as a sleeper customer, to go to another, better lounge. Never turn down the chance of a fancier lounge! This must be one of the first rules of twenty-first-century travel. I go to my new lounge, which is pleasingly plusher, with cushioned armchairs, a free-to-use computer and free soft drinks and coffee. I sit opposite a man in shorts whose calves are squashed against his armchair so that each is about 12 inches across; I do not exaggerate. Announcements are made for the *Texas Eagle* and the *California Zephyr* services. Neighbours discuss President Putin: 'He's mafia. KGB.'

An announcement is made that my number-seven *Empire Builder* train to St Paul is delayed by half an hour. I relax and read a book. Then another announcement is made, ten minutes later, that the seven-two-seven train is about to depart. I keep on reading. A last call is made for the seven-two-seven train. I keep on reading. After about 20 minutes I go to see how my train is faring with its half-hour delay. The number-seven train to St Paul is no longer on the departures board. I have an immediate sinking feeling.

'I cawled the seven-two-seven three times. Three times I cawled the seven-two-seven,' says a large man by the counter – who says 'seven-two-seven' very fast.

'But I'm not on the seven-two-seven train. I'm on the seven train.'

'Dat is the seven-two-seven train,' he replies. 'SEVEN and the twenty-seven. Dat's two train numbers for one train: one goes to

Seattle – the seven. One goes to Portland – the twenty-seven. Dat's the seven-two-seven.'

'Oh,' I say. 'But I thought my train was delayed half an hour.'

'The seven-two-seven got brought forward from the yard.'

'Oh,' I say. Pause. 'Where I come from, if a train is delayed, it does not usually become un-delayed.'

The large man takes me in for a moment. 'Everybawdy ay-else goddit,' he says. He raises an eyebrow.

'Oh,' I say.

Pause.

The long and the short of this quickly becomes clear: I will have to wait a day for the next train. But I am due to meet a contact who has kindly arranged to meet me at St Paul and take me out at 9 p.m., when the train arrives. Much organisation has gone into this meeting. We are to go to a restaurant and afterwards to a famous music venue. It's all part of an intricately planned two-day visit (with some important train history thrown in, naturally).

'Are there any alternatives?'

'Well, yey-as,' says the man, who appears to have decided that I'm not a troublemaker, just an English idiot. 'Yey-as.'

Within 15 minutes, thanks to my new Amtrak friend, I am booked on a flight to Minneapolis–St Paul International Airport. The cost is $69 on Southwest Airlines; almost exactly what the train ticket cost. I catch a $25 cab to the airport and an hour later I board my plane. I arrive at Minneapolis airport four hours before the *Empire Builder* is due. I feel disappointed with myself for being so dumb, and frustrated by the strange announcements.

Yet I have learnt two lessons.

The first: listen very carefully to Amtrak employees with strong Chicagoan accents.

The second: in America trains really are an endangered species. Planes in the States are like buses. They get you there quicker and, often, cheaper. No wonder Amtrak is in the doldrums.

'We call this the Badlands'
St Paul and Minneapolis, then the *Empire Builder* to Seattle

Cheryl Offerman, my contact from the Minneapolis Convention and Visitors Association, meets me at the airport, from where we go to a steakhouse and then to the First Avenue club, where the local musician Prince recorded parts of his famous *Purple Rain* album in the 1980s. We have a very good night out, with Cheryl's take on my mix-up being: 'Tom, I know that with Amtrak, anything is possible.'

The trains do seem to have a bit of a reputation.

I'm staying in downtown Minneapolis, which has a rigid grid system of streets and is beside a section of the Mississippi river that's home to St Anthony Falls, the highest waterfall, with a 23-metre drop, in the northern stretch of the Big Muddy. St Anthony is the reason Minneapolis thrived. The falls provided the energy required for the mills that made the city and the region the world leader in flour production from 1890 to 1940. Of course, ships on the Mississippi were an important form of transportation for the goods, produced by companies such as Pillsbury and Gold Medal, but railways were key to opening up markets too, first in the east and then the west.

By far the most important local railwayman was James J. Hill, whose nickname was the *Empire Builder*, after which the trains from Chicago to the west coast are named. He lived in a big red-sandstone house on a hill in St Paul, the 'twin city' to Minneapolis, just across the Mississippi and not far from where the novelist F. Scott Fitzgerald was brought up. Cheryl and I go to take a look.

Like Vanderbilt back in New York, Hill was self-made. At the age of 16, blind in one eye after an accident with a bow and arrow, he emigrated to the US from Ontario, Canada, to seek his fortune, arriving in Minneapolis aged 18. He did not hang about, first working on a steamboat line before shifting to trains, realising that valuable local resources such as iron ore, copper, timber and wheat could make him a millionaire if he played his cards right. He took control of a poorly run, unprofitable line, turned it around and went on to construct an important bridge across the Mississippi as well as tracks all the way to the west coast. The final spike was struck in 1893, completing the northern line across America. But unlike each of the other transcontinental railways, including the one that passed by Promontory Summit in Utah, Hill's Great Northern Railway did not go bust. This is partly because Hill sensibly made deals with the workers to avoid long, costly strikes. By the time of his death in 1916, he was one of the richest men in the country, worth more than $2 billion in today's money, some estimate – which would be more than enough to sort out Amtrak's current financial woes.

His St Paul house, now a museum, is a testament to the great riches of the glory days of the railways, with its electric lights, boiler room, grand dining room, piped organ, fine-art gallery, en-suite bathrooms, billiards room, library and sophisticated security system of caged doors and alarms (his wealth made him a major target for burglars). Hill had become a tycoon of the first order, yet he is not as prominently known as the flashier Vanderbilts and the Rockefellers on the east coast. Nevertheless, probably because of Fitzgerald's childhood proximity, the writer mentions Hill in his masterpiece, *The Great Gatsby*, in which the St Paul trains mogul is held up as a shining example of American success. When Gatsby dies, his father says that Gatsby might have gone on to be a 'great man' like Hill and contributed to building up the nation, if he had lived.

Excited Rail Guys, and anyone crossing the north of the US by train, should take the time to drop by.

St Paul's Union Depot is deserted. It's a beautiful building with a grand hall featuring a high, arched ceiling, Ionic columns and friezes depicting trains. At its peak in the 1920s, almost 300 trains stopped by daily. Now it's a shadow of its heyday, with a few commuter services and the occasional *Empire Builder* train; Amtrak began using the station a couple of years back.

From the almost empty concourse, I enter a waiting chamber at 22:10, being *very careful indeed* not to misunderstand what's going on.

A flamboyant but poker-faced guard says, 'I behove you to make your way to Platform C.' Outside of characters in Shakespearean or other early English plays, perhaps, I cannot recall anyone using the word 'behove' in speech before.

A neighbour says, 'They're calling the seven train, but I'm on the twenty-seven. I don't know about this seven train.'

I and a few others put him straight.

We board and I find my sleeper berth, which is smaller than all the others so far: less than 1 foot's floor space when the bed is down. It's on the lower deck of the double-decker train (my first).

Curious about this new two-level monster, I make a pilgrimage to the bar/lounge carriage, where I buy the fanciest possible beer from a smarmy barman. The bar is on the lower level, but there is seating on the top deck, where I locate a little blue swivel chair. This lounge has wide, curving 'observation windows'. It's a fabulous place. I sit back and watch orange sodium light from street lamps dancing on the surface of the Mississippi. The train creaks away and rolls beneath a bridge. Then we judder to a halt.

A bald guy in a heavy lumberjack shirt sitting on a sofa across the way says, 'I hate it when this **** happens.'

I nod wisely, as though I hate this **** as well.

We are waiting for the 'dropping-off of two extra cars', the bald guy believes – whatever that may signify.

'Oh yeah, I hate it when this **** happens,' he repeats.

I nod once again.

The bald guy, I notice, hardly ever takes his eyes off the Mississippi river. I fall into the same habit. There's something hypnotic about the light on the water.

A kerfuffle breaks out in the bar down below. Because we have stopped there is no electricity in the carriage. This means the cash register does not work. This also means that customers, of which there are quite a few, cannot be served drinks. Voices are being raised and a few customers are returning upstairs, shaking their heads and muttering about Amtrak.

'I really hate this ****,' says the bald guy, who really seems to mean it.

My neighbour says he's in one of the seating carriages but plans to rest overnight on the sofa. He bagged his spot earlier in the evening. During the night he says he intends to help himself to the conductors' coffee station below by the bar. 'They caught me doing that once,' he says. He's heading for Spokane, Washington. He seems a canny sort.

We move. The bald guy and I stare out at the river. The gaudy lit-up skyscrapers of Minneapolis loom into view, then we're into the countryside and an ink-black beyond.

'Fifty miles an hour now,' says the bald guy, who seems to be able to calculate the speed from many years on the railways. 'Doing fifty, pickin' up speed.'

It's a very long way across Minnesota through the states of North Dakota, Montana and (a little bit of) Idaho to Washington. I especially love this part of the journey because of its famed 'big sky' scenery. We are travelling through parts of the US few tourists visit, roughly along the route of the famous 1804 Lewis and Clark Expedition, commissioned by President Jefferson to find a passage to the west coast. It's a land of wide plains and small towns, grain silos (also known as 'elevators'), cornfields, truck stops, lumberyards, farms with white picket fences and shiny black cattle.

The train pauses at Minot, North Dakota, which was put on the map by the Great Northern Line and was nicknamed 'Little Chicago' during Prohibition due to the Mafia's local liquor-smuggling operations.

I jump off and buy a copy of the *Trading Post* and *Minot Daily News* from a 75¢ vending machine. *FEDS WANT MORE PRAIRIE DOGS ON NORTH DAKOTA GRASSLANDS*, splashes the *Daily News*. Prairie dogs (squirrel-like rodents) provide food for black-footed ferrets, and the numbers of black-footed ferrets need to be bolstered, say the Feds. Ranchers, however, do not like black-footed ferrets as they damage pastureland. It all sounds controversial. Elsewhere, another story reports on a member of the Standing Rock Sioux tribe who has been jailed for 18 years for stabbing a Bureau of Indian Affairs superintendent. Meanwhile, the *Trading Post* runs a feature on the second annual Soggy Doggy Day at a local school, during which dogs are allowed to play in its swimming pool.

A fog descends. Long trains with oil-tanker containers sit at sidings. We rumble on alongside a creek. In the lounge, there's a flicker of cards. A ginger man wearing a cap, who's been on the phone telling his mother that he does not want his partner to retire as he does not want to have to support her (his partner seems intent on retirement), looks out of the window and says to me, 'We call this the Badlands.'

He goes on to say that in Portland, where he's heading, 'some people just drink beer and smoke pot: you can get your brain smoked out'. It would, however, be a big mistake to get caught smoking pot in 'North or South Dakota, Iowa, Kansas, north Texas or parts of west Minnesota', he says, as though providing a traveller's tip. The possession even of rolling papers could lead to jail in these places 'especially if you are a person of colour – the cops might roll their eyes at you if you are white, but not if you are a person of colour'. The ginger man tells me the name of a town where 'if you are not from there, you just keep going – don't stop there'. This is said in the manner of more travel advice. Furthermore, the ginger man does not approve of fracking: 'It's really bad – earthquakes, water going bad, they pump chemicals into the ground.'

We have a rambling discussion about fracking, and then we pull into the station at Wolf Point, Montana, where I go for a platform stroll. As I do, an indignant woman approaches.

'He doesn't know anything about it,' she hisses. She'd overheard the ginger man talking to me earlier. 'My husband does. He's in oil.'

Her husband, a bald man, steps forward.

'We've been doing it over sixty years,' he says. He's talking about fracking. 'There's no problem. Everyone was rolling their eyes in the carriage listening to that guy. He has his right to an opinion but what the heck.'

At lunch I sit with a black family from Detroit. They're going on holiday to Seattle and like travelling by train. Daniel is a retired government employee and Allie is a retired care worker. Their son Brandon is with them, who works for Xerox. Daniel's father was in the US Marine Corps during the Second World War and was awarded a Congressional Gold Medal. The Marine Corps was, Allie says, the 'last part of the US military that was integrated' – with black soldiers mixed in with white soldiers.

Our conversation hops about. Daniel bemoans the decline in Detroit's car manufacturing. 'You ever see a robot buy a car?'

'No,' I reply.

'That's right. Did you ever see a robot buy a car? Uh, uh, uh. *People* buy cars.'

Allie talks about the sad state of Detroit's once beautiful Michigan Central station, which closed when Amtrak stopped going there in 1988. Now it's a ruin. 'That 1920s train depot is a symbol of Detroit's blight: not putting new windows in. It's been stripped down. They found a body in it one time.'

We finish our chicken and mash meals. Sights in Seattle are recommended. Then Daniel looks out of the window and sighs.

'Yes, this is the life,' he says, after a while. We are rolling through prairie-land. 'This is easy. This is living. This is great.'

Which kind of sums things up for me, too.

I go to my cabin and watch clouds piling high in the sky as the sun fades. We come to the Rockies, at the point where Lewis and Clark crossed all those years ago. Darkness falls.

I go to sleep early and in the morning we are moving through the Cascade Mountains, passing apple orchards, rivers and a town called Leavenworth that is said to look like a Bavarian village.

A glorious expanse of water opens up: the Puget Sound, an inlet of the Pacific Ocean, with Mount Rainier rising splendidly in the distance. We have reached the other side: from sea to shining sea. Cargo ships and US Navy frigates sit by marinas. Fishermen cast rods on jetties. Walkers lead dogs by the shore.

Then we wind past CenturyLink Field, home of the Seattle Mariners, and stop at Seattle's King Street station. This is another superb American train station, dating from 1906 and ordered by James J. Hill; a red-brick Italianate affair with a tower modelled on the Campanile of St Mark's Square in Venice. I sit for a while marvelling at the intricate cornicing, mosaic floor and original ceiling lamps. It's cool and calm and can't have changed much in a century. I love it.

Railroads do still mean a lot to America, and hopping on board this northern route across ten states – New York, Pennsylvania, Ohio, Indiana, Illinois, Minnesota, North Dakota, Montana, Idaho and Washington – brings that home. It would have been 11 states, of course, had I not missed the seven-two-seven that *everybawdy ay-else* got. I bypassed Wisconsin thanks to my impromptu flight; though I learnt what challenges Amtrak faces when airfares are *so* low. Trains do seem old-fashioned in America these days and 'run on a dime', as Larry said. But that's also part of their slightly chaotic charm.

Now I'm going on a much shorter hop, and the journey begins at my front door.

10 | BORDEAUX, FRANCE: FAST TRAIN COMING

ST PANCRAS STATION, 7 a.m. I've been here many times before. A few years back I wrote a travel book about the high-speed train revolution sweeping Europe entitled *Tales from the Fast Trains: Europe at 186 mph* during which I went on a series of jaunts from St Pancras, mainly with my girlfriend. The journeys catapulted me as far as Girona in Spain (great cathedral; loved the tapas; pleasingly eccentric Dalí museum), Marseilles (tasty *bouillabaisse*; interesting old streets by the port), Cologne (for a frankly debauched beer-drinking weekend), Lille (saw the First World War sites; watched a rock concert) and ridiculously romantic Bruges (a sure-fire winner on the bedroom front, as the tabloids might put it – and I just have).

Europe seemed almost to be shrinking as high-speed tracks spread across the continent. This has continued apace since, with Paris to Barcelona now a super-speedy 6 hours and 25 minutes.

So I know St Pancras and its marvellous hotel designed by George Gilbert Scott (first guests: 1876), as well as its magnificent and enormous William Barlow train shed, opened in 1868 and inspiration for Grand Central's very own such shed. I have read the words at the base of the statue of John Betjeman, Britain's (rather more portly) equivalent to Jackie Onassis, who campaigned to save St Pancras from demolition in the 1960s: 'Deep blue above us fades to whiteness where / A misty sea-line meets the wash of air'. Yes, it seems to capture the setting perfectly (even though the lines were written about Cornwall in the poem 'Cornish Cliffs'). I have passed so many times through the tunnel towards Kent that I've begun to recognise the graffiti. There's my old friend *TOXIC CUT*, and there's the more uplifting *HOPE*. Glad to see the authorities haven't rubbed you out after all these years.

In short, I have become very accustomed to the old place.

Yet why is it I still get a buzz every time I visit?

I'm travelling to Bordeaux with an old university friend and we have chosen our destination on the basis of a certain local produce: its wine. While we both agree that this is an excellent enough reason to visit, we are informed that there are also many cultural sights to be seen in this western French city. Danny was my partner in crime in Cologne when we visited many of the city's biggest dives in what seems, looking back, to have been some sort of attempt to break the weekend world record for consumption of Kölsch beers, while also devouring our fair share of Wiener schnitzels, wild-boar sausages and goulash. In between, we appear to have bothered to take in a gallery or cathedral or two.

We have, however, grown up quite a bit since then, we have told ourselves. Danny even has three kids (although he did already have two of them in the Cologne days) and I now have nephews and nieces. It is 20 years – OK, plus a bit – since the British educational system spewed us into the world of employment. We are still in jobs; responsible, sensible adults heading off for a cultural weekend, with a couple of glasses of *bon vin rouge* in the evening over which to ruminate on our day's aesthetic pursuits.

This is what we have been saying, at least, in the run-up to Bordeaux.

On a 'serious trains note', though, I have a background plan. Yes we're intending to have a great weekend away, but a visit to Bordeaux will also, I hope, reveal something about how important railways can be to a destination almost 200 years since the first passenger train between Liverpool and Manchester transformed Britain's industrial north and set the ball rolling for big changes across the globe.

That is what *I've* been saying to myself, at least, in the run-up to Bordeaux. I'm hoping that the 'one or two' *bons vins rouges* don't get, too much, in the way.

'I love old stations: bringing order to chaos'
London St Pancras to Gare du Nord, the Paris Métro, and
Gare Montparnasse to Bordeaux

'Zee doorz will be clozin' zuun,' says a muffled announcement. Danny and I are running slightly late. We have business-lounge passes and have been drinking complimentary coffees and eating complimentary croissants while reading complimentary papers at stools by a slate table. Danny has tucked *Le Monde* beneath his arm. 'Posing value,' he says. Then he looks around and comments: 'It is only when you see the moneyed elite up close that you realise how unattractive they really are.' He is prone to such pronouncements, said for exaggeration to get conversation going. There are plenty of very good-looking, very wealthy people about. We argue about the matter for a while, slurping further complimentary cappuccinos and munching second rounds of complimentary croissants.

On board we have a four-seat table to ourselves. It comes with purple leather armrests and headrests, plus a table lamp. We are close to seat number 61, but the legendary train guru Mark Smith, also known as The Man in Seat 61 (whose first-rate website ought to be any reader's first port of call when it comes to the practicalities of arranging a train trip), is not there. Smith chose the name for his train-booking and reference website on the basis of this being his favourite premier-class seat on Eurostar. Today his spot is taken by a woman reading a book.

Familiar warehouses, tower blocks and *TOXIC CUT* lead to a tunnel as we are offered 'perfect start to the day' breakfasts with recipes by the French two-Michelin-star chef Raymond Blanc. These are either an English breakfast with a spinach and tomato flan or smoked salmon with cream cheese, red onion and capers. Which don't sound especially two-Michelin-star, perhaps... though we put them away happily enough, washed down with more coffee, as the train zips through Kent, passes a white horse on a chalk hill and plunges into the black echo of the Channel Tunnel (opened: 1994).

We are through to the other side at 10:27, skirting fences with rolls of barbed wire to protect the tunnel from illegal immigrants hoping to sneak through. The sky is grey. The fields have been ploughed in corduroy grooves. I settle back and read a paper that reflects on the recent bicentenary of the Battle of Waterloo, quoting the 'Official Bulletin' of *The Times* of 22 June 1815: 'Glory to Wellington, to our gallant Soldiers, and to our brave Allies! Bonaparte's reputation has been wrecked, and his last grand stake has been lost in this tremendous conflict.' Stirring stuff as we enter the Little Corporal's old stomping ground. Meanwhile the *Daily Mail* runs a report under the headline *PM: UK MUSLIMS HELPING JIHADISTS* that seems uncannily pertinent to this part of the journey. The British prime minister is reported to be about to give a speech condemning 'Islamic State and its medieval outlook', saying that it is 'one of the biggest threats our world has faced... There are young people, boys and girls, leaving often loving, well-to-do homes, good schools and bright prospects travelling thousands of miles from home to strap explosives to their chests and blow themselves up and kill innocent people. To live in a place where marriage is legal at nine and where women's role is to serve the jihadists, to be part of a so-called state whose fanatics are plotting and encouraging acts of despicable terrorism in the countries from which they have come.'

Fresh out of the tunnel – beyond the barbed-wire coils – it seems more than strange that anyone would be willing to head *out* of the UK to go to a dusty jihadist stronghold in a faraway land, while so many others are desperate to come the other way.

We speed on through muddy fields and wind farms, reading our various complimentary papers. The grim tower blocks of the Paris *banlieue* soon arise. We enter a tunnel that leads to a wall covered with graffiti and more towers, before arriving in Gare du Nord, bang on time at 12:57.

'I love old stations – another age. Bringing order to chaos,' says Danny, launching into a mini thesis on the topic as we weave between green steel columns to the M4 Paris Métro line, buy tickets to Gare Montparnasse and stand in a carriage next to a group of college-aged American students, one of whom is complaining about French cuisine: 'I don't like fish food. Why is there so much fish food?'

This culinary conversation continues to Montparnasse, whereupon we wait in a nondescript modern concourse until our platform flashes up and we board our SNCF (Société Nationale des Chemins de fer Français) TGV (Train à Grande Vitesse) to Bordeaux. We have another four-seat table, first class, except that this time we are facing an elderly French couple.

The tall elderly Frenchman in front of me, who appears to wear some kind of corset, promptly falls asleep with his legs stretched out so there's hardly anywhere to put my feet. I roll my eyes and manoeuvre into a church pew style sitting position. Danny helpfully tells me, 'Don't be too harsh. You'll be old and doddery one day.' All very well for him to say: he has plenty of room as the elderly man's wife, opposite, is tiny. And off we go through suburbs, past wind farms, golden cornfields, copses and bales of rolled hay. Chateaux with fairytale towers come into view, needle-shaped church steeples, dragonflies above a sultry river, towns of bungalows, medieval stone bridges and then vineyards – many, many vineyards. We appear to be heading in the correct direction.

We pass a golf course. 'I will never play golf or ski,' says Danny.

We hurtle onwards eating *club jambon et fromage* sandwiches delivered by an attendant. My knees have gone numb from my unusual sitting position. We cross a bridge beyond a derelict plot, and the train comes to a halt.

We have arrived in Bordeaux, where, much to Danny's amazement, I go to the front of the train to check the locomotive, which appears to be a number 307 TGV.

These trains, at a push, can reach 574.4 kmph (357.16 mph) – a record set in April 2007 between Meuse and Champagne-Ardenne stations. This is the fastest a conventional train has ever gone and you can watch a rather startling YouTube film of the event. This clip has had almost 5 million views, outdoing even the Excited Train Guy's stats, and I say 'rather startling' as it just doesn't seem right for a regular-looking train to be going *quite that fast*.

Big Night Out – *big city dreams*
Bordeaux

There is a story behind the choice of Bordeaux for this weekend. While the current journey from Paris to the famous wine city is a reasonably zippy 3 hours 19 minutes, this will be reduced to just 2 hours in 2017. It is all part of a major scheme known as the Ligne à Grande Vitesse Sud-Europe-Atlantique, involving the laying of a new high-speed track between Tours and Bordeaux – one of four such *grands projets* now under construction. France has always been good at high-speed trains, launching its first such line in Europe in 1983, the Ligne à Grande Vitesse Sud-Est between Paris and Lyon, with speeds of 186 mph. This Lyon service was Europe's first truly fast long-distance train.

The slicing of travel time between Paris and Bordeaux is much anticipated as it is expected to contribute in a big way to a rejuvenation of a city that, 20 years ago, was not in the best of states. Its port area was by all accounts dark, dreary, rundown and home to 'a seedy underworld', according to a group named Bordeaux Expats, consisting of Britons living in the region. Pollution, traffic gridlock and ramshackle buildings were the order of the day. Since then, however, a magnificent new bridge across the river Garonne has been built, which opened in 2013, connecting banks near the port; a network of trams has been introduced to reduce road congestion; and development of the port and its docks has begun, with yuppie apartments springing up and a multimillion-euro futuristic wine museum about to open – which looks like some sort of UFO, or perhaps a squeeze of toothpaste, depending on which angle of observation you take.

The brainchild behind much of this is Alain Juppé, a former French prime minister who is now the city's mayor. Yet underpinning it all is the new train line, which many believe will see people commuting to Paris – with its overcrowded suburbs, and expensive property prices and rents, and tricky public transport – while bringing up families in leafy Bordeaux, taking advantage of its relatively cheap, spacious apartments. This is Bordeaux's train dream.

Danny and I take a taxi from the Gare de Bordeaux-Saint-Jean. It's a distinguished station dating from 1898, with grand archways and a fine railway clock. This clock is 'defended' by a lion-like figure with a grotesque, devilish grin – looking a little as though the beast has had one too many.

Our route takes us past a row of shops and La Plage nightclub. 'That looks promisingly seedy,' says Danny, oblivious to Bordeaux's new clean-cut image.

Beyond kids playing basketball, a square with a grand fountain and the Charles Dickens Pub, we reach our hotel, The Yndō, a new, small, arty place on a side road, where we have two rooms with doors with crazy locks that require positioning an electronic key and then twisting the handle in a certain precise manner. These locks are tricky enough to start with but are likely to prove nigh-on impossible upon our return later, as we are about to embark on the city's new Urban Wine Tour, another part of the local government's plans to make Bordeaux a place you'll want to visit.

While waiting in the lobby for Danny to return from his room (perhaps he's locked himself in), I ask the hotel's owner, Agnes, a charming woman who I can tell has already detected a certain Keystone Cops element in her new guests, what the unusual hotel name means: 'Neer-thing! Neer-thing! It is zee way of life: softness, tenderness, smile, calm. It eez a very contemporary way of life.'

I nod as though I understand what she's going on about. Danny returns.

We strike out into the early evening along cobblestone, labyrinthine streets.

Our first stop on the Urban Wine Tour (which seems to consist of a few recommendations of bars on a simple map you can print off the internet) is Brasserie Bordelaise, a dusty-bottled place with rough walls painted white and simple wood tables, near the fine medieval church of Saint Rémi. We take in our surroundings and order wine and various hams and cheeses, soon getting talking to the owner's wife Stessi, who says, 'When we get the new train, Bordeaux will be on zee up! A lot of Parisians will come! They will install their families! That is why today, if you buy a house, you know the value grows. The trains will change our lives, for sure.'

Stessi joins us at our table. It's that kind of brasserie: friendly and with happily flowing drinks. 'Oh, I very much like trains,' she says, as she calls for a glass of red for herself and continues singing the city's praises. 'Oh yes, it's going on zee up for sure. It's a lot cleaner and safer here now.'

We toast Bordeaux – and drink more red wine. Stessi orders a dish of oysters, on the house. The oysters arrive and we slurp them down, accompanied by an additional glass of white. 'They come from an hour away, all are fresh!' says Stessi, referring to the oysters, not the white. She proceeds to show us a webpage on an iPad listing 620 wines. About 80 per cent of Bordeaux wine is red, we learn. The most expensive bottle here is 2,800 euros.

French taxes are discussed: 'Zee French pay too much taxes,' says Stessi. 'Too much! Seventy-five per cent taxes. Then zere is ten per cent on zee food, twenty per cent on zee alcohol. Since President Hollande it has changed: now we pay even more taxes!'

Gérard Depardieu crops up: 'He's is in Russia now.' The prolific French actor was granted Russian citizenship a couple of years back. 'He was complaining about too much taxes, so he left.'

We order more red wine.

Stessi reminds us that Bordeaux is on zee up.

Danny asks Stessi what she thinks of Dominique Strauss-Kahn, the French former head of the International Monetary Fund, whose career hit a rocky patch after allegations of sexual assault made by a New York hotel chambermaid.

Stessi looks into her wine glass. 'Oh!' she says. The very mention of 'DSK' seems to provoke a shock. 'I am ashamed!' she says. 'He is brilliant. But his family life: not so good.' She pauses. 'We prefer things to be done behind closed doors – rather than knowing zee private lives.'

We raise a glass to French discretion... and drink more red wine.

Danny and I say goodbye to Stessi and shuffle onwards to the next wine-tour stop, round the corner: Aux Quatre Coins du Vin. Here, we discover, you buy cards with euros stored in them and then slot the cards in a machine to sample some of the best wine Bordeaux has to offer in either 'tasting size' glasses, half glasses or full glasses. We are assisted in this endeavour by Christelle, who is in her twenties and seemingly amused by the two already slightly shambolic Englishmen who have just spent an hour or more with the wonderful Stessi.

'A taste of black truffle. 2005: a very good year!' says Christelle. 'A Bordeaux Superior – that's a type of appellation.'

Danny and I nod in a manner we hope appears knowledgeable, even though it is quite clear that we know close to nothing at all. We roll the liquid in the glass (copying Christelle) before downing our tasting-size wines. It's *très bien* indeed. We press another button at Christelle's behest, sampling a fine red with a taste of 'black fruit, liquorice and cassis' from Château Franc-Mayne, followed by a delicious glass of Château Clinet.

'Very strong, smoked and round in the mouth,' says Christelle. We murmur our approval.

Danny compliments Christelle on her language skills and she says, 'I learn speak English in seven years.'

Then we move on. We witness a street brawl. Two gangs wearing sports clothing seem to be attacking each other near a convenience store. One set of guys wearing sports clothing appears to be on the retreat, but a member of their gang has been caught by the other gang wearing sporting clothing and is getting a battering: kicks to the body on the ground. Even from a distance of 50 yards, it makes us wince. Windows and shutters have flown open on the narrow street and people are yelling down. The fight quickly breaks up and the gang members scatter.

We stop at a bar named La Ligne Rouge, which is down near the river Garonne, for another glass of red on the official wine tour. The owner tells us that Bordeaux is like 'a beautiful sleeping woman'. A local who overhears our conversation strongly advises us against going to La Plage nightclub: 'Who tell you to go to this place?' Apparently, a couple of tourists might stand out a little among the tough Friday-night crowd. Instead, he informs us, although we had not enquired, that 'all the prostitutes are in the south' of Bordeaux. We appear to have reached a stage of the evening in which we look as though we are interested in 'all the prostitutes in the south'. Which cannot, on reflection, be all that good.

We stop for an ill-advised final pint at the Sherlock Holmes Pub near the hotel. This has Victorian-style booths and signs advertising a quiz night.

'They're trying to be a pub here, to be fair,' comments Danny, 'except the beer's very expensive and all the lads over there have half-pint glasses whereas in the UK you'd be embarrassed to have half pints.'

On this profound note, so ends our Big Night Out in Bordeaux.

We do see some of the non-alcohol-related local attractions of Bordeaux, including a modern art museum and the cathedral, but the highlight of our trip is a tour in an open-topped vintage 2CV car named Desiree, owned by Martine Macheras, an outgoing former English-language teacher who set up her tour-guide business a couple of years ago. 'It has been hard to start with, but now tourists are coming,' she says, echoing the upbeat mood that we've encountered throughout the city.

The next morning, feeling slightly less than *très bien* after last night, we are soon puttering along in the bumblebee-coloured car, examining the remains of a Roman amphitheatre, passing a park next to a square where Mayor Alain Juppé has an apartment, and pausing to see the statues of the philosophers Montesquieu and Montaigne in the wide-open Esplanade des Quinconces.

Martine drives on, skirting a recently re-landscaped area of parkland with a large fountain that's known as the 'water mirror' due to its reflections, and passing a statue of Louis-Urbain-Aubert de Tourny, who oversaw much of the eighteenth-century design of the elegant buildings that remain in Bordeaux. We visit the shell of the soon-to-open wine museum in the rejuvenated docks, cross the stunning Jacques Chaban-Delmas bridge and pull in to the Darwin Centre.

This is the perfect place to understand the new side of Bordeaux that's growing up in anticipation of the faster trains from Paris. Set in a former military barracks dating from the 1850s, the Darwin Centre consists of a laid-back restaurant and bar, with a 'wellness centre' offering yoga classes, a food market, open-plan offices for online start-up companies and a down-to-earth atmosphere.

We sit in a big atrium, drink hair-of-the-dog organic Darwin beers (motto: 'where is your fresh vibe?') and eat organic burgers.

'It would be silly not to try an organic beer,' says Danny, who is still looking a little green from the Urban Wine Tour.

'Everything is organic!' says Philippe Barre, the centre's founder, overhearing him as he comes over to say hello. Barre is excited by Bordeaux's future and pleased that the local authorities did not allow the grand old barracks to be destroyed to make way for apartment blocks, as had been planned. He shows us the smart offices, now used by 140 companies and an art gallery. He explains that 'this is international urbanism' and that he has connections with similar set-ups in San Francisco, Berlin and Lisbon. 'We exchange ideas... We have to change our ways of doing cities,' says Barre.

There are now 500 people employed at the Darwin Centre, many formerly unemployed. More or less everything at the centre is made from recycled materials. 'We believe that it is not the more intelligent who survive: it's the people who adapt. That's what we have tried to do: adapt. We don't believe in technology for technology's sake. It should be used for humans,' says Barre. He goes on to explain that before the old buildings were used as barracks, they were where France built many of the trains used in the wars against the Prussians in the nineteenth century: 'This was a strategic place to do that, away from the action.'

Barre has had to break local bureaucratic planning rules to get his centre up and running but it has the backing of the mayor and the future looks rosy. 'Before, this was a neighbourhood that was sleeping, there was nothing very much,' says Barre. 'Now look.'

It's a positive message in a vibrant corner of a city where the future seems pinned to the new trains coming soon. Danny and I have another organic beer in the courtyard among Bordeaux's new movers and shakers, then return to the city centre thanks to a lift from Barre, who's going that way and tells us: 'I love trains. In Europe, I only travel by train or cars. Even if I go to Morocco, I go by train. I love it. It's real travel. It's quite expensive, but when you mix trains with cars it can be economical, and if you travel by night, you don't waste any time.'

Train lovers: they're everywhere.

Two Liverpudlians from Lourdes
Bordeaux to London St Pancras

After a repeat night out with a few variations of bar venue, we return to London via Gare de Bordeaux-Saint-Jean. Danny is drinking bottles of water and seeming less keen on travelling by train. 'I suppose you can't put it in your book but it would have been better if we'd flown back,' he comments.

I ignore this.

Two Liverpudlians sitting near us are returning from Lourdes, where they have gone to take the holy water I get talking to them. One of them has had a 'twisted bowel operation' and can't fly for 18 months. The problem with Lourdes, they say, is that there are a lot of hills and it is 'hard on the legs'.

And so, via the Paris Métro and a bit of waiting around, we return home, somewhat subdued by two days out on the town. At St Pancras, the Daft Punk song 'Get Lucky', featuring Pharrell Williams, is playing over Eurostar's sound system as we eventually pull in after our 62-hour getaway in Bordeaux. And it is only the next day that we realise we have been very lucky indeed.

The following morning, French ferry workers on a wildcat strike cause massive disruptions by setting fire to barricades by the Channel Tunnel. All Eurostar trains are cancelled. Thousands have to seek last-minute hotels in London and Paris, and the backlog of passengers takes days to clear.

C'est la vie unfortunately – once or twice a year something of the sort seems to happen. *CHAOS AS BLAZING TYRES BLOCK CHUNNEL*, screams the *Express*. *HOLIDAY PLANS GO UP IN SMOKE*, says the *Mirror*. Meanwhile *The Sun* takes a different tack: *THE BEAST OF CALAIS: THE WEALTHY FRENCH LEFTIE WHO IS RUINING BRITISH SUMMER HOLIDAYS*. The article goes on to describe the 'bearded' Syndicat du Maritime Nord union leader as a 'shell-suit-wearing socialist with a £1.5 million property empire and a taste for posh cars' who earns £6,000 a month from being a landlord on top of his union work. The report reveals that he has a 'beauty therapist wife' (seemingly regarded by *The Sun* as unsuitable wife material for a union leader) and that the 'wealthy French leftie' owns a Peugeot 508, though he apparently once possessed an Audi (hardly a fleet of Ferraris or a garageful of Bentleys).

I look back over our couple of (overindulgent) days away, trying to think 'trains', not red wine and nights on the town. What is striking is how often, without prompting, people kept coming back to the new railway in conversations: the speedier link to Paris being seen as some sort of magic key to rich new possibilities. Nobody we met disagreed with that. A boom time could be round the corner, everyone seemed to agree. Bordeaux, as Stessi reminded us so often, appears to be well and truly *on zee up*, and likely to rise even further very soon.

Already there is the investment by the old port, plus the trams, bridge and Darwin Centre schemes. Parallels, I suppose, could be drawn with the railway mania of the nineteenth century, when railways lifted places from obscurity in the then modern world (though that might be over-egging it just a bit).

Yet new lines definitely do still make a difference: or why else would anyone be building them? Across Europe it's the same – from Zaragoza and Valencia in Spain, to Łódź and Poznań in Poland, to Würzburg, Nuremberg and Stuttgart in Germany – as well as within France itself, with more fast tracks opening up the likes of Vaires-sur-Marne, Vendenheim (near Strasbourg), Rennes, Le Mans, Toulouse, Orléans and Caen. The decades to come will see new lines open by the dozen and the shape of Europe change for travellers as connections become easier.

The high-speed train revolution on the Continent has only just begun.

11

CHINA; NORTH KOREA; ITALY TO POLAND; PERU; SPAIN; SWITZERLAND TO ITALY; POLAND, KALININGRAD AND LITHUANIA: TRAINS, TRAINS, TRAINS

OVER THE YEARS I have been on a fair few trains in faraway places. Like souvenirs or stamps on my passport, I've picked up train memories that have lodged in my mind more firmly than other aspects of travel such as planes, boats or staying at hotels. I can't say why that is. I'm not a train obsessive, no matter how this book may seem. and I never will be, though I can see nothing wrong in being one. I've just come to the conclusion that trains almost always make for a more interesting way of getting about. Why is that? Well, from mutinies in Australian gold class to the secrets of rail enthusiasm in Kosovo, health tips from the Dalai Lama's cardiologist in India and debates on the pros and cons of fracking in America's Badlands, I've begun to realise that there is a random factor that makes a rail journey quite unlike any other form of travel. You're never quite sure what will happen next.

Trains seem to rattle out stories, as though the motion of the track acts to shake up thoughts and loosen tongues. There's a world outside the window and a whole separate world within.

Here are some snapshots from before I started *Ticket to Ride*.

'Happy troubles' and no mobile phones
Beijing, China, to Pyongyang, North Korea (2008)

I'm on a shiny green train from Beijing to the capital of North Korea, sharing a cabin with a man in a grey suit with a red Workers' Party badge on his lapel. He seems unsettled by my presence. He has placed a jar of blueberry jam on the cabin's small table, and beneath the table the red cap of a bottle of spirits pokes out of a bag. My companion's eyes briefly acknowledge mine, before flitting nervously away. This is as close as we are to come to communication. Seeing as he does not appear to want to say hello, I decide to call him 'Albert' – the first name that pops into my head.

Albert makes a fuss about storing his case. He ventures onto the platform to smoke a cigarette, watching me through the window. Another man in a grey suit pauses by the door to look in at me. He has big, brown, deadpan eyes. He moves away, and so does the train, through the dusty Beijing haze. Albert returns and, without looking my way, wordlessly and methodically collects his blueberry jam, bottle and luggage – and goes to the next-door cabin, where I hear him jabbering to other passengers. Maybe he doesn't want to be seen with a westerner: in cahoots with the 'enemy', hatching revolutionary plots on the 17:25 from Beijing.

Another neighbour, a rotund man with a squint, has a box of beer delivered to his cabin. These North Koreans seem to know how to party on a train. Albert and the men next door already have drinks on the go. These are accompanied by a feast laid out on pink plastic dishes. I walk slowly down the corridor with its blue carpet and grimy curtains, checking on the state of the various festivities, feeling a bit left out. At the end of the carriage I find the toilet, which consists of a hole in the floor. Between carriages, small men with oily hair and white shirts are smoking. There's always one or two of them there.

Beyond Beijing, heading east, the sky reappears out of the fug of city pollution, turning lavender in the twilight. I eat noodles using hot water from an urn and drink 'Tony's firewater'. My guide in Beijing, named Tony, gave me a little bottle of spirits: 'It will help you sleep well.' A flick and shuffle of cards comes from Albert's cabin. Laughter breaks out down the hall. The rotund man's cans open with a click and a fizz. The parties are now well under way, though I have yet to receive an invite. I close my cabin door. The seats have a burgundy-green-and-white checked pattern. An oval mirror hangs on the door by an empty magazine rack. I fall asleep quickly, enjoying the reassuring judder of the track.

Morning sun casts yellow beams on jagged hills. The train enters a tunnel. We exit and come to trees with delicate white blossoms, lakes and a valley with terracotta-roofed houses. We stop and Chinese immigration officials check my passport. Outside is a concrete town, with the Yalu Hotel in the foreground. A roundabout is decorated with fake plastic deer. We are shunted about a bit. Silence reigns in the other cabins. Two hours pass. Then we cross a long bridge into North Korea, where I can see a rusty, empty funfair near the riverbank: is this for show so the Chinese imagine everyone in the Democratic People's Republic of Korea is having a grand old time? From a distance, although not up close, it must look that way.

We stop near the funfair by concrete steps to an immigration building. My passport is taken by a man in green. There's a long wait, so I close the cabin door, lie down and snooze. I wake to find two officers sitting cross-legged opposite me, watching intently.

One wears a rough, green military uniform with a cut-off collar. He has a broad, moon-like face and an inscrutable expression. The other has flinty eyes and a slick grey suit. They wear red circular badges featuring the face of North Korea's founding father, the Supreme Leader Kim Il-Sung, who helped defeat the Japanese and set up the country in the 1940s (he passed away in 1994). Their shoes are neatly placed on the floor.

The moon-faced man asks, 'How do you do?'

'I'm doing fine, thanks,' I reply.

The man in grey asks, 'Do you have a mobile phone?'

I say I do.

He asks for it and seems pleased I have one. He takes the Nokia, examines the casing, places the offending item in a brown envelope, seals the ends with tape, stamps a red mark over the seal and says, 'Do not use mobile phones in North Korea.' He hands me the envelope.

I am requested to open my bags.

The man with the moon-like face asks, 'May we smoke?'

I shrug.

They light up Marlboros.

Through the smoke, they peer at my possessions.

'What is this?' snaps the grey suit. It's a book by T. S. Eliot.

'Poetry,' I say.

He looks suspiciously at the cover. The other officer flicks through my guidebook to North Korea, examining the pictures and grunting.

'And this?' It's a thriller by Lee Child.

'Ah, crime action thriller,' says the man in the slick grey suit, as though this is absolutely OK with him.

I also have a copy of William Makepeace Thackeray's *Vanity Fair*; I expect I'll have plenty of time to read during my nine-day tour of North Korea.

'So you like the classics. *Van-it-ee Fair*. Is reading your hobby?' I reply that it is.

'So you are a tourist?'

I'm travelling under the guise of working for a tour operator to help them hone their itinerary, though I'm intending to write about the experience for a paper. To save complication, I just say, 'Yes.'

'Are you married?' asks the grey suit.

I say I'm not.

He draws on his cigarette, exhales and replies, 'A single man may live like a king but die like a dog.'

With that, they hand over my passport.

'Happy troubles,' the moon-faced man says. At least, this is how it sounds.

'Sorry?' I reply.

'Happy troubles,' he repeats – and I realise he is saying 'happy travels'.

They depart. I am in. My visa is in order. I have received free life-counselling from a North Korean border guard. I am a tourist in North Korea – probably the most secretive country on the planet.

The train rolls on to Pyongyang, the capital; from Beijing to Pyongyang is about 600 miles. Oxen pull carts across barren, dried-out dirt fields. Figures in blue outfits cycle by. There are no vehicles, apart from the occasional official van. Kim Il Sung smiles from advertising hoardings. Children at stations seem shocked to see a whitey (me). Great concrete towers emerge. Women pause from seemingly doing nothing and turn to salute the train. I am visited by two officers in green uniforms who sit opposite, smoke cigarettes and stare. They go away after a while. More empty brown landscape opens up.

We enter a long tunnel and emerge by a tall, partially finished building shaped like a Ku Klux Klan hat. The train squeals to a halt in a long, gloomy station with ballroom music playing over speakers. Hundreds of passengers disembark, almost all wearing suits. Albert looks blankly in my direction and follows the crowd.

I step off the train onto the smooth concrete platform.

'Hello, are you a tourist?' asks a man who, like everyone else, is in a suit with a badge of Kim Il-Sung. This is a bit of a *Dr Livingstone, I presume?* moment. I am clearly, among all the North Koreans, the most obvious holidaymaker. And so I meet my guide and 'observer' (who rarely lets me out of his sight in the days to follow).

There are, he says, about 50 diplomats at any one time in Pyongyang, as well as maybe 40 tourists. So I suppose I'm foreigner number 91 in the communist state (population: about 25 million). We drive in a Toyota Land Cruiser past more posters of Kim in the direction of a tall, shiny hotel, where I eat dinner alone in an extravagant ballroom with pink and pastel-blue walls.

We board our train to Glory
The Pyongyang Metro, North Korea (2008)

The Pyongyang Metro opened in 1973 and is deep, about 100 metres beneath the surface of the capital. Long, neon-lit escalators descend whitewashed tubes to grand, spotless platforms approached by stone steps with fancy marble balustrades. Pink and green chandeliers hang from the ceiling. Mosaics depict Kim Il-Sung smiling heartily as happy workers follow in his wake holding little red books. In the mosaics, everyone's teeth are pristinely white and they have good posture and broad shoulders, though there is a tendency to lean ever so slightly forwards, as if pushing the nation onwards to fine new feats of communist endeavour.

I go down into the metro with two guides. One guide is not enough, I have discovered. Guides work in pairs – maybe to keep an eye on each other in case one feels the urge to tell any home truths. 'We are going from Renaissance to Glory. There are seventeen stations, covering 35 kilometres and the temperature is 11–14°C,' says the small female guide, who must only just be 5 feet and has a scurrying walking style and a ramrod gait. Renaissance and Glory are station names. The guide is good on figures. I ask how much a metro fare costs in North Korea and she tells me that it's 5 won. This, if I have it correctly worked out, is about 1p.

Operatic music plays and people stare; all quite normal in Pyongyang. It's not crowded, and the station is wide with a high ceiling and a short platform. A train, with pistachio-green and cherry-red stripes, arrives at the opposite platform. I ask the diminutive female guide, who is more talkative than the thin man who met me at Pyongyang station, what one of the murals means. She replies, 'The success of the workers, farmers, factories and universities.' The North Korean economy appears to be booming.

We board our train to Glory. We sit at green plastic seats lined along a red linoleum floor. At the end of each carriage framed portraits of Kim Il-Sung and his son Kim Jong Il, the reigning supreme leader, hang on wood-effect walls. Neither smiles and both wear navy-blue jackets with the top buttons fastened. Kim Jong Il looks jowly and sports his trademark bouffant haircut.

My guide translates a sign, which says that walking is banned. I ask what would happen if I broke this rule. She looks at me as though I am crazy. 'An attendant would ring a bell,' she says. 'They would lecture you.'

I sit still. The passengers nearby are stony-faced and inscrutable. 'Some people are shocked at how westerners look,' the guide says. We talk for a while. She tells me she is not allowed to use the internet or email. She has two children aged five and eight. She studied English for five years and has been a translator/guide for eight. She surprises me by saying that she has been to Bulgaria, Russia, China, Lebanon and Jordan, where she floated in the Dead Sea.

At Glory we exit and take a long escalator that emerges by a square with a fountain of marble maidens and a bronze of Kim Il-Sung. His right arm is held aloft, saluting the fine achievements of the Democratic People's Republic of Korea – though in his long raincoat and comfortable slacks he looks a little like an accountant hailing a bus.

Overground or underground in North Korea – at every turn and on every train – a supreme leader is never far away.

'Pike-perch with stuffed peppers'
Italy to Poland on the *Venice Simplon-Orient-Express* (2010)

All down the line there are hundreds of them: Polish trainspotters. They're out in force; perhaps never before seen in such numbers. The *Orient Express* from Venice is passing through. Word has got out among Eastern Europe's railway nuts.

We boarded by the Grand Canal and have travelled during the night through the Alps into the Czech Republic and Poland, where our first stop is to be in Kraków, after which the train is to continue westwards to Dresden and Calais. It's a trip of a lifetime on an inaugural *Orient Express* route.

The trainspotters of Trzebinia wave and snap away at the fine old navy-blue 1920s and 1930s art deco carriages. Most look like part-timers, out on day trips especially to see our unusual train, but others – well, you can just tell they have been on these platforms when lesser game has passed. The shoulder cases, the long lenses, the scraggly hair, the sandals and socks, the inability to put down the camera and simply watch. As we head north-east, it is the same at most stations. There is a feeling of celebration, almost of liberation, as though the train is being cheered on: is this how troops feel on entering a freed land?

Maybe a little, without the plush furnishings and fine cuisine. Our train is very posh indeed. It is configured thus: three dining carriages (waiters with gold buttons and bow ties; tinkling piano at dinner); six beautifully maintained sleeping carriages; and a loco. The carriage we are in dates from 1929, with mahogany-panelled cabins designed by René Prou, considered a master in this area of expertise. A sign says that the carriage was 'used as a brothel in Limoges, 1940–1945'. My companion, who has taken to little-black-dress-and-pearls for dinner as though to the *Orient Express* born, has a chuckle when I tell her this. We're dressed in our finery, heading into the depths of Eastern Europe in an old knocking shop.

Our cabin has a tiny sink in a mirrored corner cabinet. The mahogany is inset with patterns depicting tulips, foxgloves and sprigs of bracken. Purple flowers poke out of a thin silver vase. An olive-green sofa to one side converts into a bunk (this task is performed by a steward while dinner is served). A small fan hangs from the ceiling, though there's no air conditioning. Pete and Genevieve in the next-door cabin, an electrical engineer and a doctor's receptionist from Basingstoke who are celebrating an anniversary, have thoughts about the latter. 'A lady down the hall said that this train is cheaper than a divorce,' says Genevieve, who is finding the close confines hot and stuffy. It *is* a bit tight. There's also no shower room. 'This is authentic,' explains the super-smooth train manager Bruno, a single bead of sweat working down his brow.

You can't help feeling for Bruno: there are a lot of well-to-do passengers who expect affairs to be conducted just so. At one dinner I overhear him in conversation with an American woman of a certain age and wealth, who snaps: 'You're back. Oh, you're here again, are you? I would like a non-alcoholic drink. One without grapefruit juice. I can't drink grapefruit because of my pills. And no sugar, please.'

'Of course, madam,' says Bruno. A non-alcoholic, non-grapefruit, non-sugar drink is fetched.

Beyond more Polish rail enthusiasts at Czechowice-Dziedzice, we cross fields of wildflowers and nettles. We are eating a lunch of 'pike-perch with stuffed peppers' in our red-lacquer dining carriage – decorated with a motif of deer, sheep and trees – and being attended to by three waiters as we pass Oświęcim. This is the train station for Auschwitz: a grim, grey, low-level building next to a long platform.

Coffee and chocolates are about to be served, but suddenly I just can't eat a thing.

Press trip in the Andes
Cusco to Aguas Calientes, for Machu Picchu, Peru, on the
Hiram Bingham (2005)

The man from the Press Association is unwell. He is suffering from altitude sickness and has been treated with oxygen from a canister. That was back in Cusco (elevation: 3,400 metres); now we're on the train to Aguas Calientes at 2,000 metres to visit the ancient Inca site of Machu Picchu, so he ought to feel better, though he still looks wretched: groaning with his head in his hands. We are in the observation car of the *Hiram Bingham*, an *Orient Express* train, listening to an acoustic guitarist accompanied by a man with a recorder playing a Peruvian tune.

A few of us are feeling queasy, although the reporter from the *Oxford Mail* and the journalist from *Masonic Quarterly Magazine* seem just fine. The previous evening we dined on guinea pig in Cusco. Guinea pig is a local delicacy, we were assured by our guide, who earlier that day had taken us to see the creatures scurrying across a village yard. Out came our dishes, each guinea pig with its legs perched on a sweet potato, wearing a half-tomato 'cap' with a decorative mint sprig. The animals' mouths were propped open by slices of carrot in what disconcertingly seemed like *hey-how-you-doing?* smiles.

The reporter from the *Oxford Mail* had tucked straight in, using hands, not knife and fork, as instructed by our guide: this is the Peruvian way. Her plate was soon bones. The man from the Press Association had turned from white to pale blue. 'I do not want to eat a blinkin' rat,' he stuttered. Doing so would be, he said, going way beyond the terms of his contract. He really was having a rough time. Meanwhile, the woman from *Masonic Quarterly Magazine* had stomped out of the restaurant without touching her plate. 'All of you, you're all monsters!' she said, as she went to eat elsewhere. After she had gone, I tried a few bites: it was awful, with a metallic, fizz-on-the-tongue taste. I wished I had joined her.

So we had gathered at Poroy station near Cusco this morning and boarded the *Hiram Bingham*, after watching a performance of dancers in red and pink outfits. Now we're in the observation car amid brass fittings and walnut panels listening to Peruvian folk songs and drinking champagne. At least, I am, along with the woman from *Masonic Quarterly Magazine*, the reporter from the *Oxford Mail*, a writer from *The Lady*, and the British representative of the tour operator Cox & Kings (the man from the Press Association has declined the bubbly). Cox & Kings has arranged everything on our behalf, including the guinea-pig extravaganza, in return for coverage in our various publications. This is how a press trip works – and we are on one. The representative of Cox & Kings is calm, and needs to be; under the stresses of international travel, some of the journos are beginning to crack up.

From the windows of the 1920s Pullman observation car, we watch as the Andes soar above, great slippery stone slopes plunging to the valley floor. The train twists along a jade river. On curves we can see the locomotive and carriages bending ahead. From an outside deck at the back, the track disappears through a heat haze towards Cusco. Women in red cardigans and straw hats herd sheep or sell bananas and citrus fruit at little stalls, though we never pause to take a look; there are no scheduled stops.

The *Hiram Bingham* is named after the Honolulu-born explorer who was, in 1911, the first outsider to come across the ancient Inca site of Machu Picchu.

The journey takes four hours, and brunch is included in a dining carriage with white tablecloths. As we eat (no guinea pig today), we look out and can see dots on the Inca Trail path; human ellipses plodding along with backpacks. The average hike over 50 miles from Cusco to Machu Picchu takes about five days, staying in simple lodges along the way.

On our press trip it's not like that. We arrive. The bottles of champagne are put away. A band and dancing troupe starts up. The man from the Press Association, who has been slumped in a chair drinking soda in a corner, grimaces and blinks upwards. 'Are we there yet?'

One of the wonders of the world awaits.

'¿Qué es esto?'
Barcelona to Zaragoza, Spain (2013)

I don't think I've ever seen a security guard's eyes open quite so wide.

I'm at Barcelona's França station, about to catch a train to Zaragoza, 1 hour 40 minutes away by AVE high-speed train. Barcelona marks the rough halfway point of a 1,000-mile journey around Spain's heartland that began in Seville and continued to the sleepy little city of Albacete, principally known for its traditional knife-making industry, followed by a stopover in Tarragona, a charming port with a fine Roman amphitheatre.

So far I have been travelling on Alvia trains, with a top speed of 156 mph. They're no slouches, but from Barcelona to Zaragoza and onwards to Madrid I'm to take even faster AVE trains, the most modern in Spain. These have a top speed of 194 mph and when they get going, as I'm about to discover, they feel as though they're floating on air. Spain has very good high-speed trains: perhaps the best in Europe.

During two hours in Barcelona, I have seen the famous La Rambla pedestrian street with its knick-knack shops, florists, poseurs and food stalls. I've taken in Antoni Gaudí's Casa Milà, a highly peculiar house that looks like melted wax, while eavesdropping on a guide pointing upwards and telling her tourists: 'Can you see the waves? Can you see the seaweed?'

Then I returned to França station, collected my bags from a locker and reached the security checkpoint for my AVE train. For the Alvia trains there had been no such X-ray machines, so I am surprised to see them, though I think nothing of it. I place my luggage on a conveyor belt and step through the X-ray frame for passengers.

On the other side I wait for my bags. But there is a delay.

After a while a guard with a moustache says to me, 'Eh! Eh!' He has collected my larger bag and put it to one side.

I go over, thinking, *What is it this time? Too much toothpaste?*

'Eh!' he says again, and points at the offending item: my bag. 'Open, *por favor*! *Por favor!*'

Here we go again, I'm thinking. *Too much shaving gel. Did I leave a bottle of wine in there? Anyway, nowhere says liquids are banned. What is this?*

I open my bag and suddenly it dawns on me.

At the top, glistening – almost sparkling – in the station's neon-strip lighting, are two sets of traditional Spanish steak knives bought as Christmas presents in Albacete. Next to these are three packages in bubble wrap.

The security man picks up one of the boxes of knives, which look like a set of daggers a blindfolded magician might hurl at an assistant pinned to a board. He feels their substantial weight. I've gone for the quality ones, with nice solid handles. Then he points at the packages in bubble wrap, though I can sense he seems satisfied that there has already been a massive breach of weapons regulations.

'¿Qué es esto?' he asks. Then he says, his voice rising in pitch, 'What? What eees deees?'

I open the packages to reveal three large, super-sharp Albacete carving knives. I'd really gone to town with the Christmas presents back in the traditional knife-making capital of Spain.

The security guard hardly knows where to look: I am in possession of a small cache of blades. It's not as though I've forgotten about a penknife attached to a key ring. If this were a drink-driving test, I'd be escorted to the nearest cell to sleep it off for 24 hours. The guard makes as though he is about to confiscate the lot.

'They are gifts for my parents!' I plead. 'Gifts! Christmas gifts! Presents for loved ones!'

I'm not sure he understands a word of my blabbering. I also realise I'm doing a pretty good impression of Basil Fawlty.

He does, however, waver. He seems to have deduced that, although I may be a lunatic, I'm not on a mission to launch a mad steak-knife attack. My guidebooks and general tourist clobber do not fit the usual suspicious suspect's profile. Likewise my begging about Christmas presents and mention of my father's birthday – laying it on a bit thick there, I admit – probably do not conform to the usual responses of an al-Qaeda operative when put under pressure.

He picks up the offending items. The look in his eyes says: *The rules, the rules: I cannot let these through.* Then he glances about (no colleagues are watching), drops the knives in the bag and hooks a thumb towards the train. Without looking back, he returns to his X-ray monitor.

I zip up the bag and go – like my traditional Spanish knives – sharpish.

The best train in Europe
Pontresina, Switzerland, to Tirano, Italy, on the
Bernina Express (2011)

Alpine winter-sports holidays do not have to involve throwing yourself down a mountainside, hoping your insurance covers whatever potentially life-threatening injuries you pick up during a week in which you have repeatedly shelled out 30 euros a day for spaghetti bolognaise lunches that appear to have been cooked by a 13-year-old on work experience, served at tables jammed with continental types disdainful of both your poor on-slope acumen and your rubbish mountain dress sense.

No, they can be better than that. You do, however, need to readjust your definition of 'sport' to include 'taking a train'. If you are happy to do this, it's a cinch.

And so I find myself on what I consider the best train in Europe. The *Bernina Express* runs for 90 miles between Switzerland and Italy, passing through 55 tunnels and crossing 155 bridges. At one point the railway, completed in 1904, reaches 2,253 metres (7,391 feet), making this the highest railway 'crossing' in Europe: the tracks traverse the mountaintops of Switzerland and pass into Italy. There is a higher train in Europe, also in Switzerland – the Jungfrau Railway, which touches 3,454 metres – but most of this is in a tunnel, so it's quite boring really.

The *Bernina Express* is not at all boring. I board at Pontresina, close to the posh Swiss ski resort of St Moritz, to take a 27-mile stretch across the high point and into Italy. A few Swiss skiers are in my carriage. They are lugging their foolish mountain equipment, while I am travelling pleasantly light, without cumbersome ski boots or any other nonsense. It is good to watch them struggle with their poles, and an added delight to realise they have got on the train in the incorrect direction for St Moritz. They disembark at the next stop to wait for a return service. For a while, I watch them with disdain for their poor train acumen and rubbish train knowledge. Ah, the small pleasures in life.

The *Bernina Express*, I should say here, is a tomato-red train that travels on a metre-wide track. The track is a recognised UNESCO World Heritage Site, and this, I believe, means that it is protected for ever – which is a wonderful thing. After the skiers have realised the error of their ways, we continue peacefully into the Swiss mountains. The windows are shaped to offer panoramic views of the peaks, curving upwards around the edge of the train's roof and thoughtfully tinted to keep out the high-altitude glare. The ridges above are clear on this sunny day, offering a diamond sparkle above slopes thick with pines.

A coffee trolley comes with a jolly toy antelope-type creature attached to the front. The male attendant wears a blue apron with a flowery pattern on its collar as well as an expensive TAG Swiss watch (everyone in Switzerland seems to be rich, even the train-trolley staff). He informs me, rather un-cheerfully given his garb, that the creature is an ibex, not an antelope. Stupid of me to have made such a mistake. However, I buy a coffee and take his grumpiness merely to be a local Swiss quirk that's all part of the mountain experience.

Cross-country skiers follow us for a while on paths alongside the track. I watch their hypnotic movement as we rise gently. Little black squirrels scurry in the snow and hawks soar above the pines. We pause at a station named Morteratsch. This is at the foot of a long ski run considered famous in these parts, though what a lot of exertion when you could be drinking coffee on a train with panoramic windows and trolleys with toy ibex. Further stations appear with names such as Diavolezza and Lagalb. The latter is at 2,099 metres; Pontresina was at 1,774 metres. We have gone a fair way up.

The landscape now is white, white, white. Beside the road beyond Lagalb, giant nets hold back great heaps of powder. We pass a valley in which people are being dragged on skis attached to sails close to a frozen lake. This pursuit is known as 'kite skiing', I am later informed. Further on, we reach the highest point of our ride at the station of Ospizio. Then we dip into a tunnel that opens onto a skyscape of wispy clouds. From cliffs alongside the track, icicles dangle in frozen torrents, glinting in shades of blue.

Ears pop as we drop amid pines, and a river snakes below. At a place named Poschiavo, there's a hillside graveyard behind tall grey walls, as well as a Co-op supermarket. Then we come to the Brusio spiral viaduct, completed in 1908, coiling round on itself, the track rolling in a C-shape beneath one of the tall brick archways. The gradient here is one in seven.

Vineyards with skeletal vines, a higgledy-piggledy farm and enormous stacks of logs lead to Tirano at 429 metres, where a sign at the lemon-yellow station says: *ITALIA*. It has been a two-hour journey. I look around the sleepy town, eat a tasty little four-euro pizza at Buffet della Stazione, then catch the *Bernina Express* back to Pontresina.

What great 'sport' – and no broken bones.

'This is Tom. He likes trains'
Gdańsk to Malbork, Poland; Svetlogorsk to Kaliningrad, Russia; Klaipėda to Plungė, Lithuania (2015)

I'm on a journey from Gdańsk in the north of Poland to see the Russian enclave of Kaliningrad and then travel onwards to Vilnius in Lithuania, from where I am flying home. No train trips are planned, I'll just stress that here: none at all.

We are to drive to Kaliningrad, where I intend to nose about for a bit in Russia's peculiar Baltic Sea port, 200 miles from Russia's mainland, bordered by Poland to the south and Lithuania to the north. From Kaliningrad we are to drive to Lithuania's capital. A Lithuanian ground agent is sorting out the logistics of the whole trip.

I am travelling with John, a tour operator contact, who is conducting a recce of Kaliningrad. I am tagging along. On the flight over to Gdańsk I tell John about my recent train journeys and a light flickers across his face, though he merely nods and soon afterwards nonchalantly changes the subject.

The next day, however, John's manner has changed. As soon as we meet Herkus, our Lithuanian 'fixer', he quickly informs him, 'This is Tom. He likes trains!' On my behalf, the itinerary is immediately scrambled. And so we find ourselves, just a couple of hours later, at Gdańsk's Gothic red-brick station – all turrets, spires and zigzag roofs – about to catch a train to Malbork.

'Why Malbork?' I ask.

'It's got a castle! Something like that,' says John, sounding distracted as we locate our platform near three Polish trainspotters, and await one of Poland's new high-speed trains.

A shiny, silver-blue, bullet-nosed locomotive soon arrives. John's eyes open wide. He is temporarily lost for words. 'Excellent! Excellent! Train!' he eventually mumbles, oblivious to all else around him. We board.

Our train hurtles past a series of damp red-brick buildings and an abandoned quarry. 'Wonderful! Wonderful!' John says, his eyes misting over. He is dressed in a fleece and chinos. His hair is ruffled as though he's been scratching his head attempting to resolve a particularly tricky problem. Now, though, he seems at one with the world. We zip through a windswept, empty station at a place called Tczew. 'Oh, just wonderful!'

John consults the train's menu. Our carriage is smart and new with olive-green seats; the service began just a few months earlier. 'Look at this! Hot toddy! Just what you need after a day's skiing or for a cold,' he says, marvelling at the breadth of drinks on offer. We skirt a river next to a boggy marsh and arrive at Malbork station, another fine Gothic red-brick affair in a section of town with factories that's a long walk from the castle. 'And here's an industrial complex!' exclaims John. 'I'm so happy! So happy, I'm going to smoke a cigarette!' He hardly ever smokes. 'How wonderful to take in a place by train you only heard of last week in the middle of Eastern Europe.'

This is our first train experience based on 'This is Tom. He likes trains.'

The second is in Kaliningrad, the frankly weird enclave that was home to the eighteenth-century philosopher Immanuel Kant when it was known as Königsberg and was part of Germany. It was flattened during the Second World War, after which Stalin cannily negotiated for the land as part of the 1945 Potsdam Agreement.

'There is another train, Tom. Another train for you,' says John, at first sounding careful about introducing the topic. We are being taken round Kaliningrad's sights, which are not that many due to the war. On arrival the previous night, we had drunk fizzy lager and horseradish vodka at a thrash-metal music venue (the people of Kaliningrad have a thing for thrash-metal), and been shouted at in the street by lads in a car as we returned to the hotel. Their exact words were: 'Foreigners! Kill them!' Luckily, they did not attempt to carry out their threat. This night out has meant that we have been visiting the amber mines and Nazi bunkers of Kaliningrad with sore heads. However, when he mentions that he has 'another train' planned, John's whole demeanour lifts. His eyes take on an evangelical glint. 'Yes! Yes!' he says suddenly. 'Another train!'

John whispers to Olga, our local guide. We proceed to the seaside resort of Svetlogorsk. It is February and freezing. Hardly anyone is about. We take a look around, as though justifying going to Svetlogorsk in the first place, and then head straight for Svetlogorsk station, quite a collector's item for even the most diehard rail enthusiast. Olga is somewhat surprised that we have asked to come here.

A train with orange and green stripes awaits at the station. 'Train!' says John, rather obviously, but accurately. We board and Olga, who likes to take a philosophical perspective, looks around and comments, 'Yes, I suppose trains do create a different atmosphere. Like being in a cradle: the body behaves in a different way. I do like them.' We move off. John gazes out of the window, ogling the Soviet-era tower blocks. Not a lot else happens. We rattle along for an hour. John seems quietly content.

Part three of our train odyssey takes place in Lithuania.

Our Lithuanian fixer has flatly denied that trains are a possibility in his home country. 'When I said I'd like to take a short hop, Herkus told me there are no domestic trains, just international trains,' John confides in me. By now we are in the Lithuanian port of Klaipėda. John shakes his head, as though sad that a local fixer could be so out of touch with the Lithuanian train situation. Herkus has had to drive to pick us up from each of these train trips, so my guess is that he was being cunningly, and understandably, economical with the truth. Herkus drops us at

Klaipėda station, where we buy coffees. These are served in cups bearing the slogan: *COFFEE IS COMING BACK.*

You heard this first in Klaipėda.

Rain buckets down outside the main train station of Lithuania's main port. A small red and grey train pulls in. We scamper into a carriage. Then we move slowly away past walls with graffiti, men in orange jackets tending a digger, a series of derelict buildings and a field partially covered in slush. It appears to have been snowing. Beyond a heap of railway sleepers we come to the station of Plungė, where we disembark.

John smokes a cigarette as the train judders off Lord knows where. 'Ah, yes, yes!' he says, pacing towards the little station building, where a sign says that thousands of Lithuanians were sent to Siberia from Plungė between 1941–1952, during Stalin's Purges.

Herkus arrives after a while, appearing a touch road-weary, and John in some detail describes the journey by train from Klaipėda to Plungė.

'You counted the stations?' asks Herkus, raising an eyebrow.

'Yes, yes!' says John, lighting another cigarette. 'Excellent. A good one. I can tell Tom really liked it. Excellent. Really excellent.'

Herkus looks at us both, glances at the station, says nothing and drives us to the airport to fly home.

Tell a rail enthusiast you are interested in trains when you happen to be abroad together on a trip, and be prepared for... *all that comes next.*

INVERNESS TO KYLE OF LOCHALSH AND MALLAIG TO GLASGOW, SCOTLAND; KENT AND EAST SUSSEX, ENGLAND: **FOR THE LOVE OF TRAINS**

12

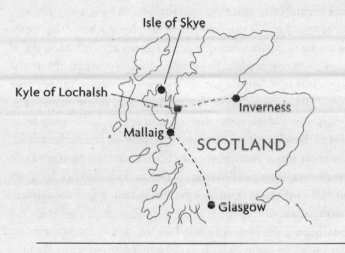

TRAINS TAKE YOU to many weird and wonderful places. I have now reached the 45-journey mark of these tales. I have covered 21 far-flung countries and many thousands of miles, but my final four rides are to be on home soil. If you don't count my adventure up in Crewe and my speedy journeys between St Pancras and the Channel Tunnel, I have been saving the 'home of trains' till last.

In this book, I have touched upon the importance of trains to Britain's industrial success during the crucial Victorian era. The British invented them and, for many years from Robert Stephenson's *Rocket* onwards, Britain was the world leader. Across the globe, the expertise of British engineers was called upon to construct many of the lines upon which I have travelled, from those in America's Midwest to India's tracks into the Himalayas, Australia's great Nullarbor run, and the first railways of China.

But *Ticket to Ride* is not, as you will have gathered by now, intended to be a history of trains and railways. Instead, it's a celebration of them, with references to the past when the early days seem especially important to the ride. There is simply too much 'train history' out there for me to cover comprehensively while describing the eclectic mix of journeys I have somehow accumulated. Besides, other authors have tackled the subject fully and admirably; I'm a particular fan of Britain's leading train buff and crystal-clear writer Christian Wolmar. His *Blood, Iron & Gold*, on how railways transformed the world, is an absorbing, wide-ranging read.

This has been a journey into the love of trains; an attempt to understand why so many people still have a soft spot for them from the average Joe looking out at the world from a carriage to the most committed hardcore gricer.

Now I'm about to depart on some of the loveliest trips of all. After hurtling to the far-flung corners of the globe, I've come full circle. I'm home. It's time to sit back, relax, reflect... and enjoy the final rides.

By lochs, burns and glens
Inverness to Kyle of Lochalsh, and Mallaig to Glasgow,
Scotland

At Inverness station, an engine rumbles as I wait for the train to the Kyle of Lochalsh. I've just been to the WHSmith where Sheila, the sales assistant, has told me: 'Everybody gets so excited. You can't help but get excited with them.'

Sheila is referring to the rail enthusiasts who come to this station to take the journey on which I am about to embark, a 70-mile trip across some of the most beautiful countryside in Britain. The Kyle Line, as it is known, opened in 1897 at great cost. An estimated £20,000 per mile was spent to cut through rock and to build bridges (29 altogether) to link Inverness on the east coast with the Kyle of Lochalsh on the west. It was an important connection as cattle could be loaded to be sent to market, reaching London from the west of Scotland in 21 hours. Previously it had taken six weeks to lead beasts by hoof along drove roads to reach trains going south.

The railway was almost closed during Dr Beeching's cuts in the 1960s, but the line survived this – and another scare in the 1970s – thanks partly to enthusiasts from Friends of the Kyle Line, who lobbied with passion and no small degree of cunning to save the track. I use the word 'cunning' as there was, at the time, a chance of oil discovery in deep waters off the west coast. Were this to happen, the railway would be extremely useful for transporting materials needed on oil-rig platforms. Campaigners played this up. Politicians, partly swayed by the prospect of riches, granted a reprieve.

There are many contenders for my favourite train journey in the UK, including Paddington to Penzance (especially down by the sea in Devon and crossing Isambard Brunel's bridge into Cornwall), Belfast to Derry in Northern Ireland (I love the meandering route to the north coast), and King's Cross to Edinburgh (with those fine views across the Tyne at Newcastle and on the turn into Berwick-upon-Tweed) – but the Kyle Line is my number-one ride.

You can pick up excellent little guides explaining what you see along the way from the WHSmith, which is just across the concourse from Bertie's Bar. Before going to the platform, I poke my head inside Bertie's, to find a solitary customer munching a sandwich with a dram of whisky on the side. He does not look up as I enter; the sandwich has his full attention. I can see no barman. An 'Alice's Wonderland' fruit machine flashes wildly. Time seems to have frozen in the 1980s or 1970s, or maybe earlier still. For a moment I just stand and look about. The only movement comes from the slow, steady chewing of the sandwich-eater. He has yet to touch his dram. He has yet to take his eyes off his food. It is a very strange setting. I give up on a drink of my own (still no barman) and leave him to it.

The train to the Kyle of Lochalsh is pretty peculiar, too, in a pleasant way. A handful of passengers joins the carriages, and I find a lilac seat with a jaunty pattern.

A conductor checks my ticket. 'OK, bud,' he says, before moving on to an elderly couple who have mislaid their tickets. 'Don't worry. You don't look like our usual fare dodgers,' he says. He disappears into the next carriage.

A whistle blows and the ScotRail train soon crosses a tea-coloured stream into undulating countryside, the land quickly turning gold and purple, khaki and mauve. Gorse and bracken cling to slopes by fields with chestnut horses. Piebald mountains tower above valleys. Lochs spread out before us, gloriously still and mirror-like. It's a sunny afternoon. Shards of light reflect off the water into the carriages of the train.

This is a blissful place.

We cut through pine-clad hills on a detour made necessary by a troublesome nineteenth-century laird who did not want tracks on his land. Here, on the steepest section, there was almost a disaster in 1897. A locomotive lost power at the top of the ascent and hurtled backwards down the line. It is hard to imagine how terrifying the experience must have been. Luckily, no one died.

We twist onwards beside a perfect loch. Gentle ripples and tiny eddies disturb the surface: salmon in the depths, perhaps. Grasslands open up with sheep huddled round feeding posts. Black cattle swish tails. A bird of prey swoops above a ravine. Then an estuary widens into view, with folds of fog in silvery grey above the choppy turquoise water.

This is one ride you never want to end. But beyond little stations named Dingwall, Garve, Stromeferry, Duncraig and Plockton, we pull into Kyle of Lochalsh, where we are greeted by a British Transport Police sign that says: *BEWARE GADGET GRABBERS' TACTICS*. Apparently there are three types of thieves on the loose: 'grabbers, snatchers and pluckers'. Each has their own devious way of relieving passengers of their smartphones and devices. It seems impossible that such characters could be lurking in such a gorgeous setting.

I catch a taxi past a tropical tree of some description (can it be a palm tree?) near the harbour master's office – somewhat unexpected so far north, though my eyes don't seem to be deceiving me. The female cab driver has a rail-enthusiast story. 'I had an elderly gent in here last summer. With his nephew, he was,' she begins. 'Picked him up and he was jumping about on the back seat like a little kid. I thought he'd just been made a grandad. I asked him what was up. He said, "We stopped by the Glenfinnan viaduct and took a photo." He told me this was otherwise known as the Harry Potter viaduct. I thought, *That's nice*. He was bouncing about as though he had ants in his pants – in his eighties, he was. There's a lot of them like that: trainspotters. I was quite happy that he was so excited.'

We cross a bridge onto the Isle of Skye, and draw up at my hotel. Then the driver surprises me. 'To be honest, trains are not my thing,' she says as we pull into the driveway. 'Not for me, really.'

And I give her a second look. It's the first time on these travels, I realise, that I've come across anyone who has said that. After criss-crossing the globe so many times, I seem finally to have found one: *someone who doesn't like trains*.

The Mallaig Railway runs from Mallaig to Fort William over precisely 41.75 miles. I know this as I bought a publication entitled *The Mallaig Railway* from Sheila at the WHSmith in Inverness. Around 25 miles from Mallaig, you arrive at the Glenfinnan viaduct of Harry Potter fame. This viaduct is 1,248 feet in length and 100 feet high, with 21 spans of 50 feet. It is constructed of concrete made of 'cement and crushed rock quarried from the cuttings through which the line passes at each end of the viaduct'. The viaduct opened in 1901, helping free up 'fish traffic' on the West Highland Line. Thank you, *The Mallaig Railway* booklet.

And it's a pretty big deal in train circles.

In the morning I catch a ferry from Skye to Mallaig and just make my train to Glasgow, which takes in the famous viaduct before plunging southwards to Fort William and beyond. The Skye–Mallaig ferry had been delayed, resulting in a dash across a car park and along the platform. A guard had watched my ungainly sprint, though when I said, 'Oh, thank you so much, just made it!' he had totally ignored me and blown a whistle.

So much for the 'hey, bud' of the last train.

But never mind: we're soon moving into golden hills, stopping briefly at Arisaig, the most westerly station in Britain, then weaving and rattling along the coast. Bright light rises from the sea on the edge of the North Atlantic Ocean as we pick up speed. Lochs, waterfalls and abandoned crofts soon lead to Glenfinnan, whereupon everyone peers out to glimpse the marvellous croquet-hoop arches. During the summer, the *Jacobite* steam train makes trips between Fort William and Mallaig – and this is the reason why.

It's not just a viaduct, it's a curving viaduct, twisting round so much you can see the train's loco and carriages ahead. I'm travelling in the off season. The journey on the ScotRail trains I am taking from Inverness to the Kyle of Lochalsh and then onwards from Mallaig to Glasgow cost the princely sum of £29. This is for a distance of 220 miles, which works out at 13p a mile. An adult return on the *Jacobite* itself is just £34. Trains can be pricey at times when compared to the cost of flights, but they can also be tremendously good value (and people often forget that).

From Harry Potter's viaduct, you can see Prince Charlie's Monument. This stone tower down by the seafront commemorates the raising of Bonnie Prince Charlie's flag at this location in August 1745 during the Jacobite Revolt. When this revolution did not quite work out – the prince's forces reached as far south as Derby, before retreating and being defeated by government troops at Culloden – Bonnie Prince Charlie (Prince Charles Edward Stuart) returned to these shores and fled, just eight months after arriving. So ended the Jacobite rebellion that gave its name to the steam train that now chugs past with coaches full of rail-enthusiast tourists.

From Glenfinnan we roll onwards to Fort William, where an announcement is made that the train is 'no smoking, including the use of electronic cigarettes'. I have a doze and wake at Rannoch, where fishermen get on and hikers get off. A passenger cries, 'Mavis, calm down!' near Ardlui. I look up and see that she is talking to her dog. At Garelochhead, more signs warn of the dangers of gadget grabbers. A sewage plant emerges near Dumbarton. On the outskirts of Dalmuir, I buy a can of Tennent's lager from the trolley and take in a council estate that looks like a prison. A warehouse with a corrugated roof lurks behind a spiked, metal fence. Litter-strewn banks line the tracks. A dozen or more magpies rest in a tree in Westerton, where a trainspotter takes snaps of our carriages. There's an Aldi supermarket. There's another estate, then another and another: tall, characterless blocks that remind me of housing in cities in remotest Siberia. It's all a far cry from the beauty of the Highlands and the quiet of the lochs on the line from Inverness.

We enter a tunnel and emerge with a squeal of wheels into Glasgow Queen Street station. My 13p-a-mile journey across Scotland is complete.

'I always take a note of a number'
Tenterden to Bodiam, and back, on the Kent and
East Sussex Railway, England

Plenty of train books wallow in the golden era of steam trains, looking back with starry eyes at the glory days when the *Royal Scot*, *Golden Arrow* and the like hurtled along. There are many excellent and enjoyable volumes that cover the nostalgia of steam, with all the old advertising posters, the shiny locos, and the class system of the carriages. To get an even greater nostalgia fix, you can also go to see the preserved locomotives at many wonderfully maintained train museums (my favourite is the excellent National Railway Museum in York, while the London Transport Museum is a joy). Then there are Britain's many 'heritage lines' with working steam locomotives, plus services running on main lines such as the *Jacobite* and the recently restored *Flying Scotsman*. So far, however, I have avoided such rides as so many others have been there before me. What more could I possibly add that has not already been written?

Instead, I've tried to capture the here and now of trains, what they are like to travel on today – the grouchy guards, the gadget-grabbing signs, the grim estates after mountains and lochs, to give a few Scottish examples – rather than put on a pair of rose-tinted glasses. Yes, describe some of the world's most beautiful routes, but try to tell it how it really is.

This said, I do want to take one lovely old steam train.

The Kent and East Sussex Railway opened in 1900, linking parts of the two counties that were isolated by the main-line railways. The line covers 10.5 miles between Tenterden in Kent and Bodiam in East Sussex. Its brief heyday lasted until the end of the First World War, when competition from bus companies and road hauliers who had bought surplus military vehicles put a squeeze on profits. So began a decline that led to its closure to regular passenger trains in 1954, although a few special trains were put on afterwards for hop pickers. Yet while that could have been that, rail enthusiasts stepped in. The line was saved and 20 years later it was reopened. Now the Kent and East Sussex Railway pitches itself as 'England's finest rural light railway'.

So, from the north of Scotland, I come to the south of England and the *Holman F. Stephens*, a bottle-green locomotive dating from 1952 and named after the line's original engineer and manager. It's a sunny day in Tenterden, Kent. I take a look at the loco in the station. A grey-haired man, with a flat cap and coal-blackened blue overalls, is attending to the train's furnace with a younger man in matching overalls. They seem pretty busy.

Instead of asking about their work, I go to the carriages and find a seat in a 1982 buffet car. There's a hiss and a rumble. The whistle blows and we chug into a countryside of fields lined with tumbledown hedgerows teeming with brambles and cow parsley. The wooden carriage has creaky red seats. Plumes of smoky steam pass the windows. Brakes squeal. I order a cup of tea from Debbie. Then I sit back and think about things for a bit.

Until now I've dared not tot up how far I've gone on all these trains around the globe. I know it's a very long way and has taken a very long time, but I have been saving the final sums. I have, I discover on counting, covered 22,304 miles over a total of just more than 21 days of journeys. To put this distance in perspective, the circumference of the Earth is 24,901 miles – just a couple of thousand miles more. This is an almost ridiculously long way to go on trains. Looking at it using another comparison, 22,304 miles is the equivalent of six journeys between London and New York or about four trips between London and Cape Town.

It's mind-boggling, really.

Then there's the time spent taking trains. While the total of 21 days sounds enough in its own right, when you take 505 hours and divide it by the average length of a working day (say, eight hours), this turns out to be 63 working days. Divide these by a five-day working week, and the mathematics show that I've spent the equivalent of about a dozen 'office weeks' on trains.

This does not, of course, include all the travel time to and from the destinations, delays, waiting at platforms, missing trains and so on. So, one way or another, I have spent quite a bit of time in and around stations.

I had not expected this when I set off to Crewe to meet my companions for the day at the end of platform five. But this is what can happen when you begin to take an interest in trains – they can begin, as I'm sure many a model-train lover knows, to eat up quite a lot of time.

I have been a very long way, and I have also seen how trains so often represent more than 'transport', just about everywhere I've gone: Crewe (which would not exist as it does now without trains); Kosovo (where the services to Serbia are still cut); China (with the sensitivity surrounding the line to Tibet); India (where Gandhi saw trains as imperialistic); Sri Lanka (with its reopened link to the Tamil north); Iran (where train tourism is part of opening up to the West); Russia (with its historical link between Nicholas II's extravagant railway-spending and the 1917 revolution); Australia (where the transcontinental line helped bring the huge nation together); America (where the Vanderbilts and the Hills contributed to catapulting the country into becoming the world's powerhouse); Bordeaux (hoping for a twenty-first-century railway revival). Across the globe, railways have acted as a key to unlocking stories about a place, not just as a means to see the scenery and sample the food in the buffet car.

So where do I stand on it all after taking the plunge into the world of trains?

I'll be straight up here and say: I love it. And this is not just because of the tales you pick up along the way.

Without intending to sound pretentiously 'deep and meaningful' or, indeed, depressing – and I apologise in advance here in case what I'm about to say drifts in both those directions – the planet is, as we all know, awash with problems, from global warming and fundamentalism to refugees, overcrowding, inequality, terrorism, wars, sabre-rattling, famines, floods, earthquakes, deadly epidemics, worldwide computer viruses, human-rights abuses, dictatorships and the mistreatment of women in many cultures. Stick this lovely lot in a pot with rising living costs and the growing pervasiveness of the internet, making switching off from work more difficult than ever, and what do you have? Rather a large amount of stress and worry.

With trains, you do not have stress and worry (when all is going smoothly, that is).

My motivation for writing *Ticket to Ride* grew out of wanting to understand the gentle pursuit of train interest. At one end of the spectrum: who are those people at the end of the platform with their cameras and notebooks? When I was at Crewe and during my time in Kosovo and Macedonia, I began to get an insight into this unusual-but-intriguing world. At the other end of the spectrum: why are so many people glued to their televisions watching programmes by the Michael Portillos, the Chris Tarrants and the Michael Palins? Even Joanna Lumley and film crew recently headed off on the Trans-Siberian, while prime-time shows about Indian trains seem to have an almost insatiable audience.

As well as this interest in 'rail enthusiasm' – spotting the trainspotters, if you like – there is also the simple question of why, in this age of fast, comfortable and cheap aeroplane travel, trains are doing so well just about everywhere. Travel companies, including Great Rail Journeys, Railbookers, www.Voyages-SNCF.com and Planet Rail, are packing in passengers very nicely indeed by all accounts; and that's just in the UK and Europe. Meanwhile, the spread of high-speed tracks across Europe and countries such as China and India shows that planes are not the be-all and end-all of long-distance travel that they might once have seemed.

Why do railways seem to have such staying power? What *is* it about trains?

On the Kent and East Sussex Railway, I get a few final clues to the answer.

In the buffet car, the passengers on the 10:40 to Bodiam know what they like about trains and they want to tell me.

'It's the smoke, the trundle, the countryside – and today we've got the sunshine,' says Geoff, in his sixties, from Bradford. He's sitting near me and wearing prescription tinted glasses, grey trousers and a blue jacket.

'I'm not heavy into trains,' he says as we pass rolling fields with sheep. Geoff has a notebook for 'train jottings' on his table and a camera round his neck. 'Oh no, I'm not so *heavy*,' he says. 'I do like the motion, though. The countryside, the movement.'

His friend Alan, also in his sixties from Bradford, is in almost identical clothing. He seems to be more *heavy* into trains, and other forms of transport, than Geoff. 'Steam trains and vintage buses – those are my things,' he says in a business-like tone.

He pauses and the train's whistle blows. We are somewhere near Northiam station. Startled wood pigeons flap out of solitary oaks.

Wispy willows stand sentry by picturesque little streams. 'It's the whole job lot really,' Alan says, looking out at the willows. 'This line represents a reflection of another time.'

Alan pauses once again to check that I'm getting his message, which I am: he likes old trains *a lot*. 'I'm not being rude,' he says, 'but many newspapers give the impression that there is something strange about trainspotters – about taking numbers. But if you have the interest as a child – well, it stays with you. I always take a note of a number.'

Geoff cuts in, mentioning the name of a national newspaper that 'made a comment that trainspotters are virtually morons... But we're completely harmless really.'

I look at them sitting there with their notebooks and cameras on a quiet Saturday afternoon. And yes, it's that word – that Charlie mentioned so long ago now in Kosovo – that gets it. Here we are on a slow train on the Kent–East Sussex border travelling ten miles one way and ten miles back because we just like the feel of the ride. There's no shopping, beyond a cup of tea and a scone from Debbie. There are no flashing screens with news updates on the latest disaster in the Middle East. There is no Wi-Fi, no internet hook-up. There's just a slow train on a sunny day, heading west.

No hurry. No fuss.

Harmless.

Alan, Geoff and I chat for a bit about this and that. I've come across their sort now, from Beijing to Pristina, Western Australia to the foothills of the Himalayas; even a few in Iran. No hidden agendas. No axes to grind (well, not usually). Simply the pleasure taken in the ride: of seeing things through a window on a train.

We sit in silence as the Kent countryside morphs into the fields of East Sussex, and I recall a word that I heard for the first time the other day. 'Ferroequinology' comes from the Latin *ferrum* (iron) and *equus* (horse), and it refers to the science of iron horses. A ferroequinologist, it follows, is someone who studies trains. Well, the ferroequinologists and I on the Kent and East Sussex Railway are having a grand old time. Lunch can wait. For that matter, everything else can wait.

We're on an old steam train *and the world is just fine*.

At Bodiam, the train draws to a halt. From the carriages, there are glorious views across a field to the battlements and turrets of the fourteenth-century Bodiam Castle, once home to Sir Edward Dalyngrigge, no less, and now run by the National Trust.

I do not get out, but I do ask a question of Kevin, the train's 'casual catering assistant'. Kevin has been regaling me with tales about his grandfather, who was once a platelayer on the Stockton and Darlington Railway, and has also been putting me straight about why trains are so wonderful: 'Life in the fast lane, Tom. Life is so fast in the fast lane, Tom. Get on a nice little train going along at twenty-five miles per hour. There's only a few people ambling about in the country: a few on the A-roads. Then you've got the wildlife: the kestrels, the owls, the sheep, cows and foxes.'

Kevin does me a favour. He has a word with the driver on my behalf – which is how I find myself in the cab of the locomotive on the return journey to Tenterden. I'm up by the furnace. And so to end my 49 unusual train journeys around the world, I can feel the heat of the orange embers, reflecting flickeringly on the shiny brass handles of the controls of the *Holman F. Stephens*. I am sharing the cab with Ian, the driver; George, the fireman; and Ben, a trainee driver.

It's too noisy to talk properly, though I learn they are all volunteers; that the coal comes from Russia and Poland; and that it's important to train up people like Ben or else there will be no drivers in the future and heritage lines such as the Kent and East Sussex Railway could die out. Most of the volunteers are of a certain age and can remember steam trains from their youth, whereas the new generation has not had that introduction. It's the same story told to me by Mike Lenz back at the Crewe Heritage Centre so many moons ago: no training, no trains.

The furnace pulsates with heat. The train traverses a level crossing. The chugging of the engine sounds wonderful up close: echoing, scraping, crackling, rasping, grunting. Steam hisses from the chimney. Ben shovels coal and sparks fly.

The Kent countryside slips by. I lean next to the gap by the loco door. Do I really understand the love of trains yet? *Maybe*, I'm thinking, *maybe*. We pass another level crossing, then a little winding stream. The whistle blows. A plume of steam shoots up. I ask myself the question again. Do I really understand?

Well, yes actually.

I think I do now.

AFTERWORD

SINCE my journeys for *Ticket to Ride*, much has already happened along the train lines that I travelled for this book. In the summer of 2015 in Macedonia and Kosovo, tens of thousands of refugees from Syria and Africa made their way along the tracks I visited, although they were going in the opposite direction. Footage of desperate figures crammed into carriages, some attempting to squeeze through windows, made tragic viewing. Since the peak of this rush, numbers of refugees have fallen, though this route into Europe is still being used.

A few weeks later, there was a crash on the Kalka–Shimla line in India, just ten minutes out of Kalka station, in which two Britons died and 13 were injured. They were part of a group of 37 Britons being led by the Indian train historian Raaja Bhasin, who told *The Indian Express*: 'I had just taken a seat minutes before the accident. It was God's grace that I was seated at that moment otherwise I wouldn't have been alive and talking to you.' The cause of the accident is unclear but the line is running once again.

In Iran, mass tourism by train has opened up in the wake of the decision made by Britain's Foreign and Commonwealth Office to relax its travel advisory and say that tourist visits to most parts of the country are 'safe'. How long this will last is unclear, but travelling about by train in Iran is now easier than ever. This said, torture of prisoners, unfair trials, discrimination against women and ethnic and religious minorities, as well as clampdowns on freedom of expression and the harassment of journalists – as chronicled by Amnesty International – continue. As I write, the *Washington Post* reporter Jason Rezaian remains in prison, where the paper says that 'he has been subjected to further interrogations, psychological abuse, and physical mistreatment. He is deprived of normal human interactions, forced to wear a hood when he is escorted around prison by guards or interrogators, and is closely monitored at all times'.

In France, at around the same time as the horrific Islamic State attacks in which 130 people were murdered in Paris in November 2015, a high-speed train derailed on a test run between Paris and Strasbourg, killing 11 people. There had been 49 technicians on the train at the time of the crash, which was blamed on 'excessive speed'.

Further afield, since my long-ago train ride from Beijing to Pyongyang, North Korea has a new ruler. Kim Jong-un has taken over as supreme leader from his father Kim Jong Il. Presumably his portrait now adorns the carriages of the pristine Pyongyang underground too. Meanwhile in China, the 'rail enthusiast' who attempted to con me out of a few yuan and who complained about the country's one-child policy must be a little happier now that the authorities have relented and, in an historic change of policy that made front pages across the globe, allowed couples to have two children.

I conducted two train-related interviews that did not make it into the book that I would like to mention briefly here. The first was with Sir Harold Atcherley, author of a vivid memoir about being a Japanese prisoner of war and working on the Burma–Siam Railway, also known as the Death Railway. His courage and humour while living under frightful conditions are captured in his diary *Prisoner of Japan*, which I highly recommend. Of his group of 1,600 prisoners to go to Sonkurai camp on the present-day Myanmar–Thailand border, just 182 survived the war. Many railways have bloody stories, but perhaps none more so than the Death Railway. A transcript of this interview can be found on my website – www.tomchesshyre.co.uk – along with pictures taken during some of the rides described in *Ticket to Ride*.

The second interview was with Dr Amanda Bennett, an autism specialist at the Children's Hospital of Philadelphia, with whom I discussed the connection between autism and an extreme interest in trains. She believes that there is 'no real evidence' of a link, although the desire among children to categorise objects, such as trains, suggests a pattern of behaviour in keeping with autism. Dr Bennett has written an interesting blog on the subject for Autism Speaks (www.autismspeaks.org), entitled *What Is It About Autism and Trains?* Equally interesting is the academic Ian Carter's book, *British Railway Enthusiasm*, in which Carter debunks Fleet Street's many attempts to overemphasise any rail-enthusiasm–autism connection, which he describes as a 'social myth created by generations of lazy journalists'.

I did not tackle the subject of the eco credentials of trains versus planes and cars as it has been much written about elsewhere – plus I took quite a few planes during *Ticket to Ride*. Eurostar once estimated that each passenger on a train journey from London to Paris emits 6.6 kg of carbon dioxide, while each plane passenger on this route is responsible for 103 kg. This does not take into account the greater effect on the environment of gases from planes. Some scientists believe emissions pumped directly into the upper atmosphere are 2.7 times more damaging than those released at ground level. So it would seem, even if these figures are slightly out, that trains are 'greener' than planes.

Finally, in many of the countries I visited, train services will undoubtedly have altered since I was there. What I describe here are snapshots, as I have said. It's worth checking regularly updated websites, such as The Man in Seat 61 (www.seat61.com), to find out the latest.

Names of those encountered on trains were in many instances altered; most of the journeys were taken in 2014–15.

ACKNOWLEDGEMENTS

DOZENS OF PEOPLE helped to make this book possible, many of whom are mentioned in the text. Setting up so many journeys was logistically tricky, requiring plenty of sometimes haywire last-minute travel plans as well as commissions from newspapers to make journeys feasible. I'm especially grateful to: Jane Knight, travel editor of *The Times*; and Lesley Thomas, *Weekend* editor of *The Times*; as well as to Frank Barrett, travel editor of *The Mail on Sunday*; and Wendy Driver, deputy travel editor of *The Mail on Sunday*. I would also like to thank Kate Quill, Lysbeth Fox, Vicky Norman, Luisa Uruena, Jamie Fox, John Kiddle and Danny Kelly for their words of encouragement, as well as my sister Kate Chesshyre, my brother Edward Chesshyre and my aunt Meg Chesshyre for their good common-sense advice, and to my mother Christine Doyle and father Robert Chesshyre for listening to me ramble on about train journeys.

Claire Plimmer, editorial director at Summersdale, 'got' the idea of this slightly offbeat book immediately, for which I am extremely grateful. I also owe thanks to Madeleine Stevens, formerly of Summersdale, for her careful copy-editing under a tight deadline; Chris Turton, associate managing editor at Summersdale; Debbie Chapman, editor at Summersdale, for her expert overseeing of overall production; and Jennifer Barclay for her sharp and perceptive chapter-editing. Thanks also to Stephen McClarence for his advice, Dean Chant for publicity, Joanne Phillips for the index, to Marianne Thompson for the inspired cover and inside cover design, and to Hamish Braid for maps and typesetting.

For assistance with trips, thanks to: Alan Heywood of Ffestiniog Travel; Katie Cosstick of Cox & Kings; Amrit Singh and Hari Daggubaty of TransIndus; Nomi Kakoty of Oberoi Hotels; Amit Kaul, manager of the Oberoi Cecil Hotel in Shimla; Jemma Purvis of Kuoni Travel; Charlie Dyer of Angel Publicity and Uga Escapes; Carole Pugh of Four Corners PR and Regent Holidays; Frank Tigani of Starwood Hotels; Maria Hanninen in Helsinki; Paul Charles of Perowne Charles Communications and Visit Finland; Jovanka Ristich of iPR and Great Southern Rail; Peter and Valmai Selman, for their generous support and good cooking in Western Australia; Polly Beech and Sarah Barnett from Brand USA; Mark McCulloch of Hills Balfour and NYC & Company; Cheryl Offerman from Minneapolis.org; Amanda Monroe of www.Voyages-SNCF.com; Gwenaelle Towse-Vallet of Office de Tourism de Bordeaux; Anna Nash (then of *Orient Express*); John Telfer of Explore; Michael Pullman (then of Cox & Kings); Sue Heady of Heady Communications; Sheila Manzano of Three Little Birds and Great Rail Journeys; Sir Harold Atcherley; Dr Amanda Bennett of the Children's Hospital of Philadelphia; and Richard Hammond of Green Traveller.

TRAINS TAKEN

1) Mortlake to Euston via Vauxhall – South West Trains to Vauxhall, 18 minutes, 9 miles; and the Tube to Euston – 10 minutes, 3 miles

2) Euston to Crewe – Virgin Trains, 1 hour 38 minutes, 169 miles

3) Crewe to Euston – Virgin Trains, 1 hour 38 minutes, 169 miles

4) Euston to Mortlake via Vauxhall – the Tube to Vauxhall, 10 minutes, 3 miles; and South West Trains to Mortlake – 18 minutes, 9 miles

5) Pristina to Peja – Trainkos, 2 hours 2 minutes, 52 miles

6) Peja to Pristina – Trainkos, 2 hours 2 minutes, 52 miles

7) Pristina to Skopje – Trainkos, 3 hours 42 minutes, 87 miles

8) Beijing to Xi'an – China Railway, 5 hours 46 minutes, 690 miles

9) Xi'an to Wuhan – China Railway, 3 hours 58 minutes, 508 miles

10) Wuhan to Nanjing – China Railway, 3 hours 50 minutes, 339 miles

11) Nanjing to Shanghai – China Railway, 1 hour 39 minutes, 193 miles

12) Pudong to Shanghai Pudong Airport – Shanghai Maglev Transportation Development Company, 7 minutes, 19 miles

13) Shanghai Pudong Airport to Pudong – Shanghai Maglev Transportation Development Company, 7 minutes, 19 miles

14) Shanghai to Beijing – China Railway, 5 hours 9 minutes, 819 miles

15) New Delhi to Kalka – Indian Railways, 4 hours 5 minutes, 190 miles

16) Kalka to Shimla – Indian Railways, 5 hours 10 minutes, 60 miles

17) Pathankot Cantt to New Delhi – Indian Railways, 7 hours 37 minutes, 298 miles

18) Colombo to Jaffna – Sri Lanka Railways, 6 hours 10 minutes, 250 miles

19) Sirkeci to Uskudar – Turkish State Railways 4 minutes, 8.5 miles

20) Istanbul to Tehran, via Boğazköprü, Golbasi, Van, Zanjan, Yazd, Isfahan and Shiraz – Turkish State Railways and Islamic Republic of Iran Railways, 102 hours, 2,700 miles

21) Helsinki to Moscow – VR Group, Russian Railways and China Railway, 10 hours 28 minutes, 693 miles

22) Komsomolskaya to Lubyanka – Moscow Metro, 4 minutes, 1.25 miles

23) Okhotny Ryad to Komsomolskaya – Moscow Metro, 5 minutes, 1.5 miles

24) Moscow to Beijing – Russian Railways, 150 hours, 5,623 miles

25) Perth to Sydney – Great Southern Rail, 65 hours, 2,720 miles

26) JFK Airport to Manhattan – AirTrain JFK and New York State Metro Transit, 40 minutes, 15 miles

27) Grand Central Terminal to Borough Hall – New York State Metro Transit, 17 minutes, 5 miles

28) Borough Hall to Grand Central Terminal – New York State Metro Transit, 17 minutes, 5 miles

29) New York to Chicago – Amtrak, 20 hours, 959 miles

30) St Paul to Seattle – Amtrak, 32 hours 25 minutes, 1,650 miles

31) St Pancras to Gare du Nord – Eurostar, 2 hours 15 minutes, 300 miles

32) Gare du Nord to Gare Montparnasse – Paris Métro, 18 minutes, 3.5 miles

33) Gare Montparnasse to Bordeaux – TGV, 3 hours 19 minutes, 360 miles

34) Bordeaux to Gare Montparnasse – TGV, 3 hours 19 minutes, 360 miles

35) Gare Montparnasse to Gare du Nord – Paris Métro, 18 minutes, 3.5 miles

36) Gare du Nord to St Pancras – Eurostar, 2 hours 15 minutes, 300 miles

37) Beijing to Pyongyang – State Railways, 26 hours, 560 miles

38) Renaissance to Glory – Pyongyang Metro, 10 minutes, 3 miles

39) Venice to Kraków – *Venice Simplon-Orient-Express*, 21 hours, 662 miles

40) Cusco to Machu Picchu – PeruRail and *Orient Express*, 4 hours, 41 miles

41) Gdańsk to Malbork – PKP Intercity, 34 minutes, 35 miles

42) Svetlogorsk II to Kaliningrad – Kaliningrad Railway, 1 hour, 28 miles

43) Klaipėda to Plungė – Lithuanian Railways, 51 minutes, 37 miles

44) Seville to Albacete, Tarragona, Barcelona, Zaragoza and Madrid – Renfe Operadora, 15 hours 40 minutes, 1,000 miles

45) Pontresina to Tirano – Rhaetian Railway, 1 hour 56 minutes, 27 miles

46) Inverness to Kyle of Lochalsh – ScotRail, 2 hours 37 minutes, 70 miles

47) Mallaig to Glasgow – ScotRail, 5 hours 20 minutes, 150 miles

48) Tenterden to Bodiam – Kent and East Sussex Railway, 50 minutes, 10.5 miles

49) Bodiam to Tenterden – Kent and East Sussex Railway, 50 minutes, 10.5 miles

Number of countries: 22

Total distance: 22,304 miles

Total time: 21 days, 1 hour 28 minutes

Please note: distances and times are approximate

BIBLIOGRAPHY

Allan, Ian *ABC of Southern Railway Locomotives* (1942, Ian Allan)

Allen, Geoffrey Freeman *Railways of the Twentieth Century* (1983, Winchmore)

Atcherley, Harold *Prisoner of Japan: A Personal War Diary* (2012, Memoirs)

Awdry, Christopher *Encyclopaedia of British Railway Companies* (1990, Guild)

Battuta, Ibn and Dunn, Ross E. *The Adventures of Ibn Battuta: A Muslim Traveller of the Fourteenth Century* (2005, University of California Press)

Betjeman, John *Collected Poems* (2006, John Murray)

Bhasin, Raaja *The Toy Train* (2013, Minerva)

Boocock, Colin *DMU Compendium* (2011, Ian Allan)

Bradley, Simon *The Railways: Nation, Network and People* (2015, Profile)

Byron, Robert *The Road to Oxiana* (1937, Macmillan)

Carter, Ian *British Railway Enthusiasm* (2008, Manchester University Press)

Fitzgerald, F. Scott *The Great Gatsby* (1926)

Gimlette, John *Elephant Complex* (2015, Quercus)

Greene, Graham *Travels With My Aunt* (1969, Bodley Head)

Gunesekera, Romesh *Noontide Toll* (2014, Granta)

Hamilton, Ray *Trains: A Miscellany* (2015, Summersdale)

Hidy, Ralph W. et al. *The Great Northern Railway: A History* (1988, University of Minnesota Press)

BIBLIOGRAPHY

Holland, Julian *Great Railway Journeys of the World* (2014, Times Books)

Holland, Julian *History of Britain's Railways* (2015, Times Books)

Kipling, Rudyard *The Man Who Would Be King and Other Stories* (1994, Wordsworth)

Koblas, John J. *A Guide to F. Scott Fitzgerald's St Paul* (2004, Minnesota Historical Society Press)

Martin, Andrew *Belles & Whistles: Journeys through Time on Britain's Trains* (2014, Profile)

McDonald, Angus *India's Disappearing Railways: A Photographic Journey* (2014, Goodman Fiell)

Newby, Eric *The Big Red Train Ride* (1978, St Martin's Press)

O'Brien, Sean and Paterson, Don (editors) *Train Songs: Poetry of the Railway* (2013, Faber & Faber)

Paterson, Banjo *Poems of the Bush* (1987, Lansdowne)

Portillo, Michael (introduction) *Great Continental Railway Journeys* (2015, Simon & Schuster)

Rajesh, Monisha *Around India in 80 Trains* (2012, Nicholas Brealey)

Roberts, Sam *Grand Central: How a Train Station Transformed America* (2013, Grand Central)

Ross, David *The Illustrated History of British Steam Railways* (2002, Parragon)

Saxton, Peter *Making Tracks: A Whistle-stop Tour of Railway History* (2015, Michael O'Mara)

Solzhenitsyn, Aleksandr *One Day in the Life of Ivan Denisovich* (1963, Praeger)

Stretton, John *30 Years of Trainspotting* (1990, Unicorn)

Subramanian, Samanth *This Divided Island: Stories from the Sri Lankan War* (2014, Atlantic Books)

Theroux, Paul *Riding the Iron Rooster: By Train through China* (1989, Penguin)

Theroux, Paul *The Great Railway Bazaar: By Train through Asia* (1975, Houghton Mifflin)

Theroux, Paul *The Old Patagonian Express: By Train through the Americas* (1979, Hamish Hamilton)

Thomas, Bryan *Trans-Siberian Handbook* (2011, Trailblazer Publications)

Tolstoy, Leo *War and Peace* (1868–1869)

Twain, Mark *Following the Equator* (1897)

Warrander, Gail and Knaus, Verena *Kosovo* (2010, Bradt)

Whittaker, Nicholas *Platform Souls: The Trainspotter as Twentieth-Century Hero* (1995, Victor Gollancz)

Wiesenthal, M. *The Belle Epoque of the Orient Express* (1979, Geocolor)

Wolmar, Christian *Blood, Iron & Gold: How the Railways Transformed the World* (2009, Atlantic Books)

Wolmar, Christian *Fire & Steam: A New History of the Railways in Britain* (2007, Atlantic Books)

Wolmar, Christian *To the Edge of the World: The Story of the Trans-Siberian Railway* (2013, Atlantic Books)

Zoellner, Tom *Train: Riding the Rails That Created the Modern World* (2014, Penguin)

INDEX

INDEX

Have you enjoyed this book?
If so, why not write a review on your favourite website?

If you're interested in finding out more about our books,
find us on Facebook at **Summersdale Publishers** and
follow us on Twitter at **@Summersdale**.

Thanks very much for buying this Summersdale book.

www.summersdale.com